American Kairos

AMERICAN KAIROS

Washington National Cathedral and
the New Civil Religion

Richard Benjamin Crosby

Johns Hopkins University Press
Baltimore

© 2023 Johns Hopkins University Press
All rights reserved. Published 2023
Printed in the United States of America on acid-free paper
2   4   6   8   9   7   5   3   1

Johns Hopkins University Press
2715 North Charles Street
Baltimore, Maryland 21218
www.press.jhu.edu

Cataloging-in-Publication Data is available from the Library of Congress.

A catalog record for this book is available from the British Library.

ISBN: 978-1-4214-4642-4 (hardcover)
ISBN: 978-1-4214-4643-1 (ebook)

Special discounts are available for bulk purchases of this book. For more information, please contact Special Sales at specialsales@jh.edu.

For Becca

The gold of her promise
Has never been mined

Her borders of justice
not clearly defined
. . . .

Discover this country
dead centuries cry
. . . .

                    Maya Angelou, "America"

CONTENTS

A Haunted House

"Every attempt to publish a book is an attempt to ward off death." So spoke Thomas Mole during a lecture at Brigham Young University late in the summer of 2018. Mole, a professor at the University of Edinburgh, was speaking by invitation to his fellow humanists about "the secret life of books." He argued that a book is the author's own fight for life, their own push to influence the world "across space" and "through time."[1] No doubt this same anxiety informs my interest in publishing *this* book, but I am also interested in warding off another death.

Prophecies of America's death have been around for centuries, but the current rate at which they are being published strikes me as unusual. More and more we see litanies of American failure and doom, from blundered military adventures to natural disasters that went unmanaged to financial crises that were papered over to the lurid politics of the Trump era; and all of it is frosted by a dystopian rhetoric—"angry, wounded, and without hope."[2] I have also read studies that accept the reality of America's faltering prestige but that strike a more hopeful tone. Jill Lepore cites a moment during the Lincoln administration when US attorney general Edward Bates declared that he could not find "a clear and satisfactory definition of the phrase 'citizen of the United States,'" even though the term is used no fewer than ten times in the Constitution.[3] The question of the meaning of American citizenship seems to animate current debates with the same mix of exasperation and hope. Everyone seems to wonder whether we can still find and live that meaning before the opportunity slips away.

The titular concept of this book is *kairos*, a Greek word that translates as "the opportune time." It is the kind of opportunity that arises at a critical point in history. If it can be apprehended, the trajectory of history can be changed. Whole new worlds become possible. But if it passes, it is unlikely to return. Kairos—with the capital K—was the youngest son of Zeus. He was known for flying about the cosmos, carried by wings on his heels, donning a forelock of hair, which is what one would grab if one were to catch him. He was also known to balance a pair of scales in his hands, symbolizing the importance of due measure. Kairos, both the god and the concept, strikes me as the appropriate symbol for the point at which the United States now finds itself. We all seem to recognize the urgency of our moment, but we are all jabbing out into space for that elusive opportunity to correct things.

Some citizens believe that we have fallen away from a sacred past and that the best solution to our ills is to return to the past, to anchor ourselves to a pretended history. That is not my view. I will argue for a return to the past, but only to find where we went wrong. Of course, there are many places where the nation went right, and many where it went wrong. This book is about one place in particular, a place that we only ever imagined and then abandoned so quietly as to forget it was ever an idea at all.

My attempt to ward off death in the writing of this book is like my attempt to ward off ghosts on a rainy night in the fall of 2008. I had traveled from Seattle to Washington, DC, to begin research for my dissertation. Washington National Cathedral had graciously offered to house me in its defunct College of Preachers, an institution that, in its prime, had hosted clergy, theologians, political leaders, scholars, and other members of the public whose interests aligned with the cathedral's mission. The Great Recession of 2008 had squeezed the life out of the College. It could barely keep the lights on, and the cathedral was in the process of shutting it down completely. Mercifully, the cathedral archivist had arranged for me to stay there, with the proviso that I would pay a small fee, the building would not be staffed, and I would be on my own for food, supplies, and so on.

On the night I got there, the place was empty. I had to type in a five-digit code above the iron handles of a medieval-looking door to gain access. I remember fumbling in my phone for the code as the skies grew darker and the rain fell faster. I breathed a sigh of relief when the code worked and the door opened. But once inside, I was no more at ease than before. I found myself in a large, unlit foyer with arched ceilings and an iron chandelier. To my left there was a dining hall. Portraits lined its sidewalls and an imposing fireplace spanned much of its back wall. To my right was a winding stairway. A note on a stand nearby told me where I could find my bedroom, which was up the stairs to the third floor and down a long, dim hallway. The doors to the dozens of other guest rooms were wide open, which gave the emptiness of the

Kairos, God of Opportunity, youngest son of Zeus. Roman copy from a Greek original. Museo Civico d'Arte Antica, Turin. Album / Alamy Stock Photo

building a kind of undulating effect, as if it could go on forever. My room had no lock, so it required no key; it also had no phone, TV, or bathroom. There was a bed, a closet, and a sink. A full, communal bathroom was at the opposite end of the hallway. To call it a "college" seemed fitting, since it had the feel of an old dormitory. And yet it was an unfamiliar space in an unfamiliar city, so I do not mind admitting I was a little spooked. I unpacked my stuff, shut the door, and, with some private embarrassment, braced a small wooden chair against the door handle, as if by doing so I could keep out the ghosts that were sure to siege me in my sleep.

It turns out I slept well and enjoyed the next several days in the archives, the first of several happy visits. That first night was by far the most memorable, though, if only because it was my first, but perhaps also because it has always struck me as suggestive of a broader anxiety. The main argument of this book is that the American Civil Religion, the implicit system of values, ideals, rituals, traditions, and symbols that lend shape and meaning to our citizenship, has never been properly imagined, and that, as a consequence, the nation's past is haunted by ghosts that presently grow louder and more violent. They clamor at our door, sweeping one another aside, shrieking in the shadows. They feel entitled to the nation's soul because the nation never created a soul that was whole and could defend itself in the first place. They claim our aging house divided for themselves, while we live tenuously inside it.

My argument begins with the story of Pierre L'Enfant, the artist and engineer enlisted by George Washington and Thomas Jefferson to design the nation's capital city. L'Enfant was the first to imagine Washington, DC's radiating boulevards, its presidential palace, its Congress House, its great Mall; but he also proposed a national church—not a state church or a sectarian institution devoted to any particular God, but a kind of temple to the republic in which our national ideals and heroes would be enshrined; a place where we could find refuge in moments of national crisis, a place to recover our soul as a people—in short, a haunt of our own. The failure of L'Enfant's church is in microcosm the failure of our civil religion. I outline the history of this failure in the chapters that follow, and I would be most comfortable to leave the matter at that and to let someone else do the crucial and thankless work of finding a solution. But there is something morbid about reveling in problems. In the end, I propose that we consider building L'Enfant's church. Doing so will not cure all our ills, but perhaps it will help us to imagine collectively what an American Civil Religion ought to be, or maybe it will just keep the ghouls at bay for a night.

I do not know what exactly this church ought to look like or do. The conclusion presents some ideas, though such a project strikes even me as quixotic. I feel certain, however, that to imagine such a church for the future of the United States, we must think in terms wholly original. As a scholar of rhetoric, I refer often to the classical Greeks, but I would not propose an homage to an ancient Greco-Roman ideal any more than I would suggest we defer to a medieval Christian creed. What is so dizzying about America's potential, as the Portuguese scholar and diplomat Bruno Macaes points out, is that it is untethered to any particular past. We have European roots, but long before or long since those roots were put down, others have borne into the soil: African, Jewish, Latin American, Mexican, Asian, to say nothing of the seemingly endless faith groups that have sprouted on our soil, or the groups whose class, gender, and sexual orientations were once suffocated but have since begun to blossom; or the indigenous roots that grew deep here long before European conquests. This multiple heritage has become our legacy and calling. But while I would have us imagine something wholly new, I would also dismiss any notion that we *reject* our past. As I will argue, it is precisely because we have forgotten our past that we now struggle to invent an expansive future.

Who is meant to define and build this temple, and how? The easy answer is always that famous god-term "The People," as if we, the people, are a singular entity, capable of making changes as a unit. The fact remains that we need institutions to work for us. For all its partisan tantrums, Congress *will* not do it. For all its bureaucracy, the executive branch *cannot* do it. For all its pettifogging mandates, the US Supreme Court does not inspire much optimism either. Perhaps this is the very reason L'Enfant imagined a great civil religious institution at the center of the republic. Perhaps all along this was the role of his church, to anchor our ideals in space and time, to be the sacred heart of our shared civic life.

ACKNOWLEDGMENTS

In his treatise *On Rhetoric*, Aristotle examines the concept of personal character, or what the Greeks called *ethos*. Aristotle believed that ethos comprises three key features: *phronesis*, or practical wisdom; *arete*, or excellence; and *eunoia*, or goodwill. In other words, a person with strong ethos is smart, skilled, and friendly. The people to whom I owe thanks are too many to remember, but they embody Aristotle's notion of ethos with unforgettable clarity. If we accept the truism that writing a book, or, for that matter, living a life, is like a journey, these are the people I have trusted along the way.

The practical wisdom of my colleagues in academia has shaped this book in ways largely unseen by them. At the University of Washington, these people included Leah Ceccarelli, my former advisor, who remains a mentor to this day and one of the highest embodiments of phronesis I have encountered in my career; Matt McGarrity, James Jasinski, and David Domke, whose teaching and research I regard as exemplary; and John Gastil, a veritable Poor Richard of practical wisdom for academics. Also included in this category are Paul Stob of Vanderbilt University and Dave Tell of the University of Kansas, whose work I admire and whose opinions I trust implicitly. I must add with enthusiasm Kenneth Butterfield, my diligent research assistant at Brigham Young University, whose digging into the history of Pierre L'Enfant helped to lay the groundwork for chapter 1 and for many of the book's arguments.

BYU's Faculty Publishing Service provided undergraduate and graduate interns whose assistance struck me as the work of seasoned professionals. Particular thanks to Jennifer Saldana for her calm, cool competence in helping to move this manuscript across the finish line. Ezra Rodriguez and Juliana McCarthy with Johns Hopkins University Press (JHUP) and copyeditor Steven Baker merit the same thanks for the same reasons. They have been a source of grounding in what would otherwise have been an overwhelming process. Laura Davulis, also of JHUP, saw something in this book worth investing in. Special thanks to her.

In the category of *arete*, or virtue, I think of my friends at Washington National Cathedral. Archivist Diane Ney, photo curator Elody Crimi, and former historiographer Richard Hewlett sit atop this list. Anyone who reads this book will know that I am both a critic and an admirer of the cathedral. What virtues that building embodies are represented wholly in the people with whom I have worked and interacted there.

In the category of *eunoia*, or goodwill, are friends and family. Many of these people are peer scholars or writers who have offered empathy and commiseration when the journey seemed endless: Micah Player, Jamie Moshin, Tony Moss, Jeff Dotson, Brian Jackson, Craig Rood, and Jon Balzotti. Some people in this category are not peers but elders. Ed Cutler of Brigham Young University and Jean Goodwin of North Carolina State University come to mind. So does Martin Medhurst, who completed the ultimate journey last year and who shared his goodwill with me freely, though he barely knew me. Family looms largest in the category of eunoia. Izzy, Theo, Adeline, and Alec have—often unknowingly—faced my morosity over this project with patience and love. I also think of my parents, Louise and Richard, whose love and encouragement are bottomless and whose endurance of the most painful stretches of life's path has set a new standard of grace and dignity for me; and of Carol and Stanford, who have made me and this book a sincere interest in their lives. But above all, I think of Rebecca, the dedicatee of this book; the most reliable source of ethos I know; the cadence of wisdom, excellence, and goodwill to which I can only ever hope to keep pace.

American Kairos

Introduction

When George Washington and Thomas Jefferson commissioned him to design the layout for America's "federal city," Pierre Charles L'Enfant teemed with visions. He saw a capital filled with monumental architecture, wide avenues, canals with cascading falls, open public spaces, and vibrant squares for celebration and learning. Although he was asked to provide only a general plot for federal buildings, the French-born American who had served as an engineer in the Revolutionary War saw a much bigger opportunity. He wanted to brand the new republic as a place of "grand," "sumptuous," and "*majestique*" landmarks.[1] Like his father, a French painter whose heroic panoramas graced the walls at Versailles, L'Enfant understood the close relationship between visual culture and national identity.

Although many of L'Enfant's proposals were not adopted and he would leave the job under a cloud of contention in 1792, barely a year after he was appointed, his influence on the city is indelible. Many of Washington, DC's most iconic landmarks, including the Capitol Building and the White House, were part of the original L'Enfant plan. Among the ideas that were never realized was L'Enfant's "great church for national purposes," which was to be a perpetual reminder of the role faith should play in the life of a powerful nation.[2] He proposed the church be built on a plot of land just a few blocks equidistant between the "Congress Building" to the east and the "Presidential Palace" to the west.[3] The church would be a spiritual junction between the houses of government, "one of three salient points" to which the eye is drawn on the district map.[4] No such church was ever built there. In editions of the city plan revised after L'Enfant was replaced by Andrew Ellicott, the plots for the houses of government remained, but the idea for a church simply vanished. For years to come, as the nation's capital expanded and planners tugged and warred over how to design the city, that plot remained just another muddy lot in a town of sprawling expectations. Eventually, the US Patent Office was built there, and soon enough, the church idea withered away altogether—until, that is, about a century later.[5]

In 1890, bishops of the Episcopal Church began planning a headquarters for their newly organized Washington, DC, Diocese. The edifice they envisioned would serve several purposes. First, it would provide much needed space for the growing population of Episcopalians in Washington, DC. Second, it would act as a kind of mother church for the communion's "loose confederation of dioceses," and Episcopal congregations everywhere would look to it as a symbol of their faith's national prominence.[6] Third, by establishing a building of such grandeur in the nation's capital, the organizers would make clear that the Episcopal Church was prepared to participate in the life of the nation. In the same year, William Reed Huntington, a revered Episcopal priest and intellectual, got wind of the cathedral idea and wrote to the organizers that this cathedral should send "a special message for our countrymen" and that patriotism as well as faith ought to move church leaders to see the project through.[7]

The idea came at just the right time. Toward the end of the nineteenth century, the Episcopal Church was beset with infighting. Some factions believed the church ought to be more evangelical; some felt it should be more high, or low, or broad in its liturgy; some promoted changes to the Book of Common Prayer; and some resisted change altogether.[8] In the 1880s, during the church's triennial General Conventions, leaders struggled to address the tensions. Their concerns were exacerbated by the success of competing faiths that seemed better coordinated in their growth and that were rapidly consolidating their influence in the nation's capital. Episcopalism, defined briefly, is the American member church of the global Anglican Communion, which is headquartered in London, England. Anglicanism's chief rival has historically been Roman Catholicism, which in the late 1800s was growing at a remarkable rate in the United States and had established a university and a massive cathedral of its own in Washington, DC.[9] The American Anglicans—meaning, the Episcopalians—could hardly stand by and watch as "popery" spread its tentacles across their beloved republic.

From the General Conventions emerged a reason for optimism. It came in the form of a document known as the Chicago Quadrilateral. Produced in 1886, just four years before the cathedral project was born, the document affirms four key precepts: the Holy Scriptures, the Nicene Creed, the sacraments of baptism and the Eucharist, and the historical episcopate adapted to local needs.[10] The precepts seem ordinary enough, but the church leaders who wrote them had two aspirations in mind. One was to impose greater doctrinal conformity among Anglicans themselves, a measure designed to address the immediate needs of the faith's factional strife. To enjoy communion with the national Episcopal organization, congregations would be expected to adopt the four precepts. The other aspiration was both more public and more ambitious. It was to create a blueprint that would unify Anglican, Roman, and Eastern Orthodox churches—essentially to return Christianity to its preschism roots. The House of Bishops declared, "Our earnest desire that the Savior's prayer, 'That we all may be one,' may, in its deepest and truest sense, be speedily fulfilled."[11] The quixotic second aspiration became the face of the Quadrilateral, because it positioned the church to lead the world into a new era of global unity. Episcopalians could pursue an ecumenist vision while transcending their own internal bickering.

The precepts of the Quadrilateral had been circulating for decades among Anglican leaders. In 1870, William Reed Huntington, the same American Episcopal priest who would write in support of the cathedral twenty years later, published *The Church-Idea: An Essay towards Unity*, in which he argued for a version of the same four precepts. Indeed, he is considered the unofficial author of the Quadrilateral. Like the document itself, Huntington's call for unity was grounded in "a consciousness that a spirit of change is in the air," that "the threads of social order have seldom been more seriously entangled," and, finally, that the agitations felt by Romans, Anglicans, and Evangelicals alike were evidence of a divine longing for a new "Catholicity" among Christians of all stripes.[12] For some time, then, Anglican leaders had observed a growing tension within not only their own communion but also Christianity broadly, and they saw an opportunity to help lead believers into a new reach of Christian history. While other faiths seemed to focus solely on growing themselves, the Anglican Communion, and the Episcopal Church specifically, pursued a vision for all of Christendom.

While it bore no official connection to the General Conventions of the 1880s, let alone the 1886 Quadrilateral, Washington National Cathedral was inspired by the same anxieties and visions. Proposed in 1890 and chartered in 1893, the cathedral project was driven by two key aspirations. The first, an internal-facing aspiration, was to establish a landmark sanctuary at the heart of the nation's capital. This sanctuary would serve as a mother church for the Episcopal Church's disparate congregations. It would be a symbol of prominence and a source of pride around which Episcopalians could unite themselves; it would also be an important administrative center. In this context, a "national church" simply meant a more cohesive and centralized network of Episcopal congregations. Almost all along, however, the cathedral's founders had something even bigger in mind, a yet inchoate dream that ran parallel to the Quadrilateral's second aspiration, a dream that would eventually claim, however imperfectly, the legacy left by Pierre L'Enfant a century earlier.

Henry Yates Satterlee's Westminster Abbey

Henry Yates Satterlee, the enterprising priest who became Washington National Cathedral's first bishop, must be at the center of any history of the cathedral. Satterlee was born into a world of material comforts and patriotic zeal. Both of his parents descended from high-society New York families, and they imbued Henry with a sense of purpose. By the time he graduated college, he knew he wanted to become a clergyman in the Episcopal Church. As a strong supporter of the Quadrilateral, he believed there was a special role for the Anglican Communion to play in uniting the nation's and the world's Christians, though as I show in chapter 3, he was less sanguine about including Roman Catholics in this unity of faith. Upon taking its helm in 1896, he framed the cathedral project as being central to that role. As William Reed Huntington was to the Quadrilateral, so Satterlee, Huntington's friend and confidante, was to the cathedral. His unofficial authorship of that building marks everything it became or sought to become, from its mission to its liturgy to its very architecture and decor.

The details of Satterlee's long and defining tenure over the cathedral are discussed in chapter 2, but the boldness of his vision merits recognition up front. Upon being elected after a falling-out between the project's original leaders, Satterlee began to craft the cathedral's identity as something far more than a centralized sanctuary for members of his own communion. Before he arrived on the scene, the purpose of the cathedral was limited to the internal-facing aspiration described above. It was to be a point of prominence and unity for the nation's Episcopalians. Although people like Huntington and the cathedral's original leaders had spoken vaguely of a much broader national and international mission, it was Satterlee who took up the idea and gave it shape. Perhaps, he mused, the cathedral could play a key role in unifying all of the nation's Protestant denominations "under the aegis of the Anglican Church."[13] He even privately admitted to the hope of building an American "Westminster Abbey," a house of worship with origins in a single faith but with formal responsibilities to the entire nation.[14] Early in his tenure as bishop, Satterlee almost always expressed these views privately, as in letters to trusted colleagues and friends. One of his great rhetorical talents was his ability to work behind the scenes, patiently piecing together grand visions without implicating his own agenda in the process. The task of building the nation's church would be monumental in its physical and financial scope, but it would also be a formidable public relations undertaking. Communication would be just as critical as funding and engineering.

One example of Satterlee's rhetorical sensibility is evident in his approach to the question of church and state. He was aware of how dearly citizens of the United States held the Constitution's Establishment Clause. But, whereas the state could not sponsor a church, he saw no reason a church could not be the official sponsor of the state, especially given that the state in question had recently stridden onto the global stage as a newly anointed "Great Power" and that a nation filled with such vigor and potential should have the proper moral guidance.[15] That is why, when he became the cathedral's leader, Satterlee promoted three key missions: the cathedral would be "a house of prayer for all people," "the chief mission church of the diocese," and "a great church for national purposes."[16] Phrases such as *all people* and *national purposes* seem to be taken directly from L'Enfant's master plan proposed a century earlier. To Satterlee and his successors, a "national church" truly meant the nation's church, and more. By 1906, a decade after assuming the bishopric, Satterlee would publicly claim that the cathedral could unify Christendom itself and claim for the Anglican Communion "spiritual leadership of the world."[17]

Satterlee's vision may seem unrealistic to today's reader, but it has shown remarkable traction. By May 1936, nearly three decades after Satterlee's death, the Cathedral Council felt perfectly comfortable authoring a report affirming that "it is our hope that Washington Cathedral may ultimately come to mean to the United States what Canterbury has meant to England, and Santa Sophia to the old Eastern Empire, a center for a nation's religious faith and aspirations, helping to lead it in each generation to a deeper consecration."[18] The incipient external-facing aspiration that grew out of the Chicago Quadrilateral had taken root, and it began to blossom in the form of Satterlee's cathedral. Arriving at such open declarations well into the twentieth century, however, was a matter of incremental maneuvers over time, and Satterlee, drawing on L'Enfant, was the one who laid the rhetorical foundations.

Satterlee's Unperfected Legacy

Satterlee's vision would never be fully realized. Washington National Cathedral has not unified Christendom, and the Anglican Communion has not assumed spiritual leadership of the world. But the Cathedral Church of Saint Peter and Saint Paul—also variously named the Cathedral at Washington, Washington Cathedral, Washington National Cathedral, or *the* National Cathedral—is one of the great, unknown rhetorical triumphs in the history of American religion.[19] Without government mandate or public vote, it has claimed its role as America's de facto house of worship, a civil-religious temple wherein Americans conduct some of their highest, holiest rituals, including presidential funerals and National Day of Prayer services.[20] At the building's September 29, 1990, dedication, after eighty-three years of construction, no one objected when then–US president George H. W. Bush declared, "Here we have built our church—not just a church, a house of prayer for a nation built on the rock of religious faith . . . [a] symbol of our nation's spiritual life."[21] It was a warm, sun-soaked midday when he made that declaration, and one could scarcely imagine a more clarion affirmation of the concept announced by L'Enfant 199 years earlier and echoed by Satterlee a century after that. With those words, Bush affirmed a relationship between faith and nationhood in which the role of the cathedral was made explicit. His language had an apostolic ring, as though he were not proposing an idea but pronouncing a sacred truth. Here, built from three hundred million pounds of Indiana limestone, was the nation's place of worship, its very own Bethel.[22]

It would be easy to write off George H. W. Bush's pronouncement as the hyperbole of ceremony if it were not for the building's history both before and after Bush occupied its pulpit. As this book makes clear, the claim that this church is the heir to L'Enfant is deeply complicated, even problematic, but it has become truer over time. And whether the claim is premised on truth is beside the question of whether such a claim has rhetorical force. One need only consider the most recent events in the cathedral's life to recognize the kind of American *dignitas* L'Enfant once foresaw. The memorial services of Senator John McCain and of President George H. W. Bush himself were nothing if not the full-throated worship of the country's most treasured myths. In both services, speakers and mourners blurred the lines between politics and religion so artfully as to confer upon these deceased the ethos of saints.

Here are the words of Meghan McCain, spoken from the cathedral pulpit on the occasion of her father's memorial service in 2018:

> My father, the true son of his father and grandfather, was born into the character of American greatness, was convinced of the need to defend it with ferocity and faith. John McCain was born in a distant and now vanquished outpost of American power, and he understood America as a sacred trust. He understood our republic demands responsibilities. . . . He grasped that our purpose and meaning was rooted in a missionary responsibility, stretching back centuries.[23]

Like Pericles of Athens, McCain ties the greatness of the departed to the greatness of the nation, and vice versa. She links her father to a long history spanning multiple generations of heroic character, faith, responsibility, and zeal. Her task is not simply to celebrate her father; it is also to inspire her listeners to recommit to America's founding ideals. Was not this ritual the very vision L'Enfant introduced in his plan for the capital? His church was to be a place to celebrate the ideals of the republic and to mourn and memorialize its heroes. It was to be a place to which all Americans could look to be inspired by the myths and dogmas of the nation itself.

Consider likewise the way George H. W. Bush was memorialized at the cathedral that same year. As the *New York Times* reported it, "This was the service Mr. Bush wanted, an Episcopal send-off with all of the majesty of the capital's cavernous cathedral."[24] Bush played a key role in his own funeral planning, intuiting the link between what the nation would observe in mourning and what the nation would comprehend about its mission in the world. Here is an excerpt from Jon Meacham's famous eulogy of the former president:

> George Herbert Walker Bush was America's last great soldier-statesman, a twentieth-century founding father. He governed with virtues that most closely resemble those of Washington and of Adams, of TR and of FDR, of Truman and of Eisenhower, of men who believed in causes larger than themselves. . . . And because life gave him so much, he gave back again and again and again. He stood in the breach in the Cold War against totalitarianism. He stood in the breach in Washington against unthinking partisanship. He stood in the breach against tyranny and discrimination. And on his watch, a wall fell in Berlin, a dictator's aggression did not stand, and doors across America opened to those with disabilities.[25]

Meacham situates Bush within a familiar narrative. Dating at least as far back as the ancient Greeks, a nation's heroes were to be valorized for both their deeds and their ancestry. One's forbears were an indicator of one's own virtue. Interestingly, it was also the Greeks who revised this tradition from a pedigree of blood to one of citizenship. When democracy was established in Athens, every freeborn Athenian man became heir to what the Greeks called *arete*, a term denoting the noble qualities that make a Greek excellent.[26] No longer the primogeniture of the aristocracy, *arete* became the birthright of every properly educated citizen. As the great German historian Werner Jaeger says of the classical Greeks, "It would have been unthinkable that education should be founded on anything but membership of the political community."[27] The mark of arete, in this view, was a matter of how well one embodied the ideals of the community.

Just so in the American case. The ancestry Meacham assigns to Bush is that of the presidential office, not a bloodline. The great leaders of the republic established a lineage of virtue, sacrifice, and bravery that Bush boldly claimed and magnified throughout his life. His presidential mission had the force of a religious calling, like a high priest ordained to lead God's people. The anaphoric clauses, "He stood in the breach. . . . He stood in the breach. . . . He stood in the breach," read like a political liturgy. Their cadence divides the world into good and evil. Totalitarianism, partisanship, tyranny, and discrimination represent a kind of hell that will overwhelm the world but for the determination of a great leader of an inspired nation. "On his watch," Meacham concludes, walls fell and doors opened. It is not difficult to hear the Old Testament undertones here. Whether tumbling the walls of Jericho or parting the Red Sea, the patriarchs of history remove boundaries by virtue of their steadfast commitment to higher principles and their resolve in facing down evil. They are not administrators. Thus mythologized, they become the prophets and pastors of great nations.[28]

How did this happen? How did a diocesan cathedral go from an abandoned idea in the 1790s to an ambitious sectarian project in the 1890s to a national civil-religious reality in the 1990s, a reality that continues to echo from the lips of presidents and their eulogists? Washington National Cathedral may not be the seat of a new global Christianity, but it has certainly established itself as a national sanctuary. From William McKinley and Theodore Roosevelt at the turn of the twentieth century to George W. Bush and Barack Obama at the turn of the twenty-first century, American leaders have stood in the cathedral's Canterbury pulpit to promote an accord between spiritual faith and national character.[29] There is nothing either new or legally dubious about a public discussion of faith, even by national leaders. What is unusual is that a single denomination—a single house of worship—should presume centrality to the life of a nation so intrinsically nervous about church-state relations. The puzzle of the cathedral's success animates this book, because it suggests a rhetorical agenda that has gone long overlooked. In this volume, I tell the story of Washington National Cathedral's 130-year claim that Pierre L'Enfant's orphaned idea of a national church has found a home on St. Alban's Hill in Washington, DC, in a building owned and operated by the Protestant Episcopal Church.

My study departs rather significantly from other histories of the cathedral. As I read them, these histories can be divided into three categories. In the first category, one finds histories produced by the cathedral itself or its acolytes. These studies speak from the same place of faith and mission that brought the cathedral into being so many decades ago. They include guidebooks, brochures, and faith-promoting annals such as Richard T. Feller and Marshall W. Fishwick's *For Thy Great Glory*, Marjorie Hunt's *Stone Carvers*, Robert E. Kendig's *Bible in Stone*, Elody R. Crimi and Diane Ney's *Jewels of Light*, and the institutionally authored *Living Stones* and *A New Century, a New Calling*. I have found these histories to be beautifully composed and helpful to my own research, but I do not share their intentions. Whereas these works use the cathedral as a lens into the mysteries of faith and worship, I use it as a lens into the history of America's messy relationship between faith and politics. Specifically, I use the cathedral as a lens into the life of what Robert Bellah famously calls the American Civil Religion, a concept I define in detail below.[30]

In the second category, one finds scholarly studies of the cathedral. These include graduate school theses and dissertations but not yet full monographs published by academic presses. For instance, in the cathedral archives, one finds copies of Paul M. Gunther's "Does the United States Have a National Cathedral?" a historical study of the cathedral as a means to examine questions about church-state laws and practices in the United States; Christopher Rowe's theoretically rich "World without End," which engages the cathedral's architectural history in light of the philosophy of one of its principal architects, Philip Hubert Frohman; Theresa Morales's "The Last Stone Is Just the Beginning," a rhetorical history of the cathedral that may have the most overlap with my own interest in the edifice. Morales wrote her dissertation, coincidentally, at the same time I was writing my own a couple of thousand miles away in 2009. She and I even ran into each other in the archives one gray November day. Morales's work identifies the way the cathedral rhetorically creates two ethoses, one based in its sectarian identity and one based in its national identity. In this way, Morales examines the uniqueness of the cathedral's "rhetorical voice." What these strictly academic studies reveal is that the building allows us to explore otherwise oblique concepts, the sort of concepts academics are interested in: ethos, kairos, time and space, church and state. My own study is similar in that I am interested in theoretical concepts, especially kairos, but my intention is not to use the cathedral as a means to illuminate such concepts so much as to do the reverse. I draw on the concept of kairos, for instance, to pursue my interest in better understanding the cathedral as it relates to the nation's civil-religious history.

In the third category, one finds the more traditional histories, written by highly qualified authors who have some angle on the cathedral's history that needs telling. For instance, Frederick Quinn's 2014 history fills a gap in the literature on the cathedral. Quinn recognizes that the complexity of the cathedral's history had not been shared before. Key figures such as Henry Yates Satterlee were still being observed in their clerical distance. So he set out to create something "beyond standard alumni magazine biographical fare."[31] Whereas Quinn was among the first scholars to publish a full monograph that makes use of the cathedral archives, Richard Hewlett is the scholar who practically built the archives. Hewlett, who died in 2015 at the age of ninety-two, spent most of his career as a historian employed by the Atomic Energy Commission, but in his "retirement" he became the historiographer for the Washington, DC, Episcopal Diocese, a position he used to organize the cathedral archives. The archives themselves are his great achievement, but he was also a highly competent writer. In 2007, for the cathedral's centennial celebration, he wrote *The Foundation Stone*, which, despite its celebratory occasion, remains a reliable and straightforward history of the cathedral's early years. He also wrote an earlier history of the cathedral titled *Washington Cathedral and Its National Purpose: The Emergence of an Ideal*. Hewlett was no critic, but neither was he given to encomiums. Both of his histories, like Quinn's, are thoroughly researched, and both are essential to a full grasp of the cathedral's history and mission. However, both are published by sectarian presses, and both speak primarily from a place of faith and hope, not only in the Christian gospel but also in the role the cathedral might play in that gospel. Finally, both are exactly what they purport to be: histories of the building. My history of the building is merely a means to a larger controversy about how Americans define and live their civil religion.

Defining American Civil Religion

The founding of any political community must address the question of how it will ensure the loyalty and cooperation of its citizens. Because laws are based on behavioral markers, they are good tools for enforcing obedience, but they do little to inspire devotion. If leaders want citizens who are willing to make sacrifices in the name of national duty, then religion, or something like religion, must play a role. Plato's *Laws* in the West and Confucius's *Analects* in the East are merely two examples of how the ancient world grappled with this very question. In both cases, the philosophers consider how elements of religion, politics, and education might be integrated to promote the interests of the state. As Ronald Beiner puts it, many thinkers have confronted the political challenge of religion by expressing "not a little sympathy for some manner of theocracy."[32] In other words, political leaders and social philosophers have long recognized that it might be better for the state to enlist rather than to purge the gods.

One reason for this embrace between religion and the state has to do with human nature. People are inspired by a belief that their participation in the community has some higher purpose, such as fulfilling a covenant with the gods or playing a role in the arc of human history—something more than slavish obedience to laws for the sake of order. When members of any social order, such as a tribe or nation, are invested with this kind of animating spirit, their conformability to the order's interests is more likely to come from a place of conviction, even passion. Good citizenship becomes a sacral act. In turn, the state takes on a "sacred authority."[33] Perhaps this is why Yuval Noah Harari argues that all social orders, especially large and complex ones, are made more fragile without religious elements.[34]

While the principle of civil religion has been around for thousands of years, the concept of civil religion was not named until the eighteenth century when French philosopher Jean-Jacques Rousseau argued that there are certain religious convictions that transcend any single sect or denomination and that might serve key purposes in managing civic life. According to Rousseau, these convictions include belief in a deity, belief in an afterlife that grants rewards and punishments, and general tolerance for sectarian differences.[35] Governments have the right and opportunity to impose these beliefs in order to promote civic order and virtue. One need not agree with Rousseau's tenets to appreciate the larger principle to which he points. The sacralization of citizenship is the raison d'être of civil religion.

Given these premises, I define *civil religion* as the appropriation of religious things, such as myths, rituals, and sacred symbols, by a given political community in order to invest that community's members with a sense of civic devotion. This definition calls for some key distinctions. First, as Peter Gardella argues, this level of devotion pushes beyond mere patriotism. An effective civil religion moves members of the community to a willingness to die or kill for that community.[36] I might add that such members are willing to die or kill not only to preserve the physical community but also to preserve the abstract values and myths upon which that community is based. Patriotism entails certain convictions and feelings about one's country. True civilreligious faith, however, means that citizens may regard their nation as having a destiny in the divine order of things.

Second, civil religions also come in many different shapes and sizes. John A. Coleman describes three types. There is secular nationalism, which removes most or all religious competition in the interests of making the state itself the most transcendent force in the lives of the citizens. In this case, the civil religion is the only religion. Think, for instance, of the Soviet Union. Then, there are those civil religions that Coleman calls "undifferentiated," meaning that they draw on the supernatural and spiritual tenets of an existing religion but are tied inextricably to the state. Think, for instance, of state-sponsored churches such as the Church of England, especially in the sixteenth through nineteenth centuries. There are other civil religions, which Coleman calls "differentiated," that exist more or less autonomously from the given state or church hegemony. This autonomy allows for multiple interpretations of the nation's ultimate meaning and destiny in the world. As Coleman puts it, this third form of civil religion has "a content, not so specific as to alienate or contradict Protestant, Catholic, or Jew, yet specific enough so that the nation (not the national government as such) became endowed with churchly attributes."[37] In describing the American Civil Religion in these terms, Coleman celebrates its "peculiar genius." He regards the American Civil Religion's differentiated nature as an advantage because it allows diverse religious traditions to regard the state as the agent of their own theological vision.

Third, civil religious zeal does not require a belief in a divine being. One of the most widespread misunderstandings about religion is that it must affirm a deity. A number of Eastern religions, including Buddhism, Confucianism, and Taoism, demonstrate highly sophisticated religious beliefs and behaviors, yet they are vague about the character or even the existence of a god or gods. Instead, these religions rely on carefully crafted values, symbols, and rituals that bond people to a sense of higher purpose. In its most compelling iterations, civil religion operates the same way. Without necessarily specifying a god or some other object of worship, it promotes suprarational devotion to the community and its values.

Fourth, civil religion is rhetorical. A community must be persuaded to buy in to an abstract vision of itself as participating in some higher ideal, some cause that merits devotion, not just passionless obedience. The United States provides an example. Robert Bellah argues that the founding documents of the United States avoided biblical imagery; instead, they spoke "in the accent of mankind in general." Even when biblical imagery was invoked, it "was sufficiently pruned of anything specifically Protestant, so that both Catholics and Jews could easily echo it."[38] A diverse community, like that of the United States during a time of enlightenment and revolution, calls for a civil religion that embraces ambiguity, so that citizens may thread their own faith into the national patchwork. Civil religion must therefore be sensitive to audiences, and it must be able to adjust its appeal based on the historical moment.

For this reason, Jason Edwards and Joseph Valenzano III edited an entire volume devoted to the rhetoric of civil religion in the United States. They point out that civil religious principles have been employed for a variety of rhetorical purposes, including the evangelization of American values. They also reveal that the differentiated nature of the American Civil Religion has led to a profusion of different approaches and modes, many of which openly compete for supremacy in the American imaginary. These modes include the priestly and the prophetic, the traditional and expansive, the fundamentalist and the liberationist. All of these dichotomies correspond roughly to either a conservative or a liberal worldview, which is why the rhetorical perspective is so important. We can often recognize the political interests behind a civil religion when we understand the rhetorical mode in which it is deployed. I study these civil religious rhetorics through the prism of Washington National Cathedral because it is a microcosm for the American Civil Religion itself. Over the decades, these competing rhetorics have sought to inhabit the singular space of the cathedral, resulting in an unsettling tension. If I am right that the cathedral is a microcosm for the American Civil Religion, what the cathedral uniquely reveals is that this tension (1) is endemic to our civil religion and (2) must be rooted out and replaced.

American Civil Religion: A Short, Messy History

Visiting the United States in the 1830s, French scholar and aristocrat Alexis de Tocqueville noted that "from the earliest settlement of the emigrants politics and religion contracted an alliance which has never been dissolved."[39] This contract was neither an accident nor some idle fancy; it was "indispensable to the maintenance of republican institutions." Tocqueville further observed that "religious zeal is perpetually stimulated in the United States by the duties of patriotism."[40] Writing barely half a century after the nation's founding, Tocqueville observed an interplay between faith and citizenship that would become an essential element of the American Civil Religion. Religious faith was empowered by the political culture, and the political culture was empowered by religious faith.

Roughly a century later, another visiting European intellectual—in this case, British writer G. K. Chesterton—perceived a communion between religion and citizenship in America. In his 1922 book, *What I Observed in America*, Chesterton characterized the United States as "a nation with the soul of a church." He referred not to America's diversity of sects and denominations but instead to the nation's sense of political mission. He called the nation's founding documents a "creed," and he regarded the country's political principles as being "set forth with dogmatic and even theological lucidity."[41] A few decades after Chesterton, Jewish American theologian Will Herberg further developed these ideas. In his 1955 book, *Protestant, Catholic, Jew: An Essay in American Religious Sociology*, Herberg recognized a common American faith, what he called a "democratic faith," that "constitutes the 'common religion' of American society."[42] In Herberg's view, standard American values and practices, from religious freedom to capitalism to representative government, are a means to a "new order of things," a "way of life" premised on the notion that certain political freedoms constitute sacred human rights that, when put into practice, show veneration for something holy. These values, or some variation on them, have since been enshrined as America's "five founding ideals," which are typically listed as democracy, rights, liberty, opportunity, and equality. These ideals constitute the pillars of what James Truslow Adams coined in 1931 the "American Dream."[43] From the very outset, then, America's political principles have been leavened with a sense of sacred vision.

Following on these thinkers, Robert Bellah gave a name to this communion between religion and citizenship in the United States. He called it the

American Civil Religion, which he defined as "a genuine apprehension of universal and transcendent religious reality as seen in or, one could almost say, as revealed through the experience of the American people."[44] In other words, the American Civil Religion is a civil religion designed by and for Americans. Gardella goes so far as to say that the American Civil Religion "may claim to be the strongest and most elaborate civil religion of the world."[45] America's citizens have no common ethnic origin. They speak a borrowed tongue. They inhabit a conquered and colonized continent. Perhaps more than the citizens of any other major nation on earth, they have relied on shared political myths and symbols to craft a core identity. Like Bellah, Gardella argues that the United States did not merely invoke a few generic beliefs; it embraced many of the trappings of a full-blown religion, with its own myths, martyrs, relics, scriptures, holidays, and so forth.[46]

This definition seems straightforward enough, but it raises the question of who Americans are. What defines and unites Americans as a political community? Are there not many different American experiences? Numerous possibilities follow, many of which seem to exist in contradiction to one another. Do Americans define themselves like the Puritans of old, according to a shared sectarian identity, one that promotes community and care? Or do Americans define themselves according to an unfettered self-drive, a sacralized pursuit for individual prosperity? If they claim both approaches, how do they reconcile the two? A civil religion of the sort Bellah describes is liable to have its own orthodoxies, factions, subcultures, zealots, and apostates. Given enough time, it will also likely have its own epochs and perhaps even schisms. It is this potential for conflict embedded within the American Civil Religion that so often goes underexamined.

Time and again, Americans have tried to cast the nation's founding myths according to their own brand of sectarian, ethnic, or ideological dogma. Such efforts reveal an American Civil Religion that is passionately contested, a cultural space that has long been occupied, challenged, defended, reshaped, and mutilated by different interest groups. The history of the American Civil Religion is largely the story of this ongoing contest: many souls trying to inhabit and command a single body politic. What makes Washington National Cathedral such an illuminating artifact for study is the way it has embodied these tensions over the course of its lifespan. The present study is simultaneously the history of a building and the history of a profoundly complex idea.

When we read the observations of thinkers like Tocqueville, Chesterton, Herberg, or even Bellah in his original essay on the subject, we might get the impression that the American Civil Religion is a fixed and bounded concept, that it is a unitary "way" rather than a profusion of competing "ways" of life. As I hope I have already shown, it takes little effort to complicate this sense of cohesion. Many thinkers do not well account for the implications of what Coleman calls a "differentiated" civil religion when the ideologies that lay claim to a nation's civil-religious functions find themselves at loggerheads. In such cases, the civil religion may no longer serve as a haven for diverse religiosities. In place of an umbrella, one might just as easily find a bludgeon.

A legally permitted American who walks peacefully onto a university campus with a semiautomatic assault rifle strapped to his back is likely to be under the impression that he is not just protecting himself and others from potential harm, or merely exercising a legal right in a so-called open-carry state. He may also believe that he is participating in a sacred civil religious rite to demonstrate his devoutness to the nation's doctrines. Likewise, a protestor marching with a cardboard sign probably sees herself as doing something bigger than calling for, say, a ban on handguns or assault weapons. She likely also sees herself as participating in a kind of ceremony that situates her and the civic space she inhabits within a sacred tradition. These two hypothetical individuals are being moved by the same civil-religious consciousness, but that consciousness may be pushing them in different directions, directions that may even drive them to turn their faith against each other. The fact that these two individuals may inhabit the same public sanctuaries and invoke the same legal sacraments speaks to the permeability that is at the heart of the American Civil Religion.

One of the main purposes of this book is to look beneath the surface of our founding ideals to learn that they are far more unifying in the abstract than in historical practice. Gardella argues that American Civil Religion has undergone seven phases in a more or less neat sequence, from colonial to revolutionary to national to sacrificial and all the way to the present, multicultural era.[47] Despite its many crucial insights, Gardella's argument suggests that Americans have moved collectively on; yet we see that each of these phases lives in the hearts of rival American identities to this day. It would not take long to find whole swaths of the American population that do not believe we ever really moved on from, say, the sacrificial phase, when Americans warred over slavery, or the imperial phase, when Americans embarked on global conquests.

We cannot dismiss the Puritan theocrats of our history any more than we can the slave-trading plutocrats or the Deist revolutionaries. They are cut from the same patchwork cloth. We can find examples of their shaky fusion in institutions like slavery, which was often justified on the backs of republican rights, material prosperity, and Christian theology. But, although these strains cannot be disentangled from one another, certain groups have played more defining roles than others at key points in history. The Christian nationalism of the seventeenth-century Puritans was the basis of a civil religion that framed American colonists as a people called by God to establish a new Israel. The Great Awakening and the Enlightenment of the eighteenth century destroyed that frame, and in its place appeared a neoclassical republicanism that formed the basis of revolution and a new political imperium in North America.[48] In subsequent decades, this frame was reshaped by a radicalism that was equal parts primitivist Christianity and democratic liberalism. This *Second* Great Awakening, in the nineteenth century, set the stage for abolition, civil war, and a new purchase on the proverbial American Dream.[49]

With each historical shift, the old civil religious order faded, but it did not disappear. Its ghost lived on in the bones of the new frame. Puritanism, revolution, neoclassicism, imperialism—each was haunted by its predecessors. The result was a collection of unsettling and sometimes beautiful grotesques. Southern Christians, for instance, venerated the pagan Greco-Roman world for its normalization of slavery. Many southerners viewed as more than coincidence the notion that it was the "southern slave states of Greece and Rome [that] had given to the world all the civilization, arts, literature, laws, and government which antiquity offered."[50] Slavery was thus justified not only on the basis of a biblical, Old Testament social order that sanctioned the practice, and not only on the basis of republican self-government or the economic interests of the southern farmer, but also on the grounds that the classical regimes had relied on slavery for their attainments. In the decades leading up to and immediately following the Civil War, southern plantation mansions and public buildings seized on the Greek Revival style as a way of announcing this cultural lineage.[51] My point is that we can find, even in single institutions, evidence that Americans do not exactly move on from their prior civil religious commitments. They absorb them, even if doing so means they have to mangle them. Some of these combinations can be found in the very same person. George Whitefield, perhaps the most influential preacher in American history, defended slavery in the economic interest of his Christian orphanage, a rational leap that combined chattel slavery, free-market capitalism, and altruistic charity.

The combination worked the other way, too. Frederick Douglass drew his philosophy of justice from the Old Testament prophets but learned how to give speeches from *The Columbian Orator*, a manual on the art of eloquence modeled after the classical *progymnasmata*.[52] His renowned speaking style made it seem as though Jeremiah and Cicero had merged into one person. "The rich inheritance of justice, liberty, prosperity and independence," he declaimed in his famous Fourth of July address, "bequeathed by your fathers, is shared by you, not by me. The sunlight that brought life and healing to you, has brought stripes and death to me. This Fourth [of] July is yours, not mine. You may rejoice, I must mourn. To drag a man in fetters into the grand illuminated temple of liberty, and call upon him to join you in joyous anthems, were inhuman mockery and sacrilegious irony. Do you mean, citizens, to mock me, by asking me to speak to-day?"[53] Even a cursory analysis of the speech reveals a command of the classical figures, including a masterful use of metaphor, antithesis, and eroteme. One imagines such an address would be at home in the Roman senate, yet Douglass's call to national repentance is directed at the Rochester Ladies Anti-Slavery Society.

Rhetorician James Darsey's work provides some insight here. He observes throughout American history the presence of two rhetorical traditions, the Hellenic and the Hebraic. The Hellenic tradition, which derives from the classical Greco-Roman world, can be found in America's institutional discourses: the debates that take place in congressional, judicial, and executive chambers; the panegyrics broadcast on national holidays; the forensic reasoning of court decisions; and so on. The Hebraic tradition, which derives from the Judeo-Christian world, can be found in America's radical discourses: the protests that take place in city streets; the placards and symbols that marchers carry in demonstrations; the civil sermons that sound like biblical prophecy calling the country to repentance.[54] Darsey's theory implies not only two separate civil rhetorics but also, as I read it, two competing civil-religious traditions, which typically occupy separate civic spaces but can, from time to time, merge into each other.

What I am suggesting is that perhaps the American Civil Religion we have invested so much hope in was never a very stable thing in the first place. Perhaps all along it has been a chimera, composed of competing philosophical strains, always in tension and transition, never comfortable in its own skin. The Frederick Douglass example is powerful because it shows that when these strains intersect, they betray a pressure. It may be contained for a time, but it always threatens to explode and set its surroundings on fire. As Matthew

Arnold puts it in his *Culture and Anarchy*, the sweetness, order, and light of the Hellenic ideal is offset by the "fire and strength" of Hebraic zeal.[55] We can certainly celebrate this strange compound, but we should not overlook its explosiveness.

By the middle of the nineteenth century, the civil-religious combinations had become too volatile to contain, and the nation erupted in civil war. Out of that conflagration arose a president who looked every part the ancient patriarch. Abraham Lincoln's Cooper Union Address, Gettysburg Address, and Second Inaugural Address have become the founding civil-religious texts of the postbellum United States. Lincoln knew that subduing the enemy was not enough to heal the nation's underlying illness. So, in the name of union and reform, he proclaimed a "new birth." His call amounted to a new testament of the American Civil Religion, a fulfillment of the old law in favor of a higher law that was, he argued, always encoded in the founding documents. "But enough!" he declared at Cooper Union in 1860, prior to his election and the war. "Let all who believe that 'our fathers, who framed the Government under which we live, understood this question just as well, and even better, than we do now,' speak as they spoke, and act as they acted upon it. This is all Republicans ask—all Republicans desire—in relation to slavery. As those fathers marked it, so let it be again marked, as an evil not to be extended."[56] Not yet president, or even the Republican nominee, Lincoln channeled his hope into the nation's legal foundations. A few years later, in his Gettysburg Address of 1863 and in his Second Inaugural Address of 1865, Lincoln spoke with a different voice, as though he could now see the nation in cosmic terms. "Four score and seven years ago," he said at Gettysburg, "our fathers brought forth on this continent, a new nation, conceived in Liberty, and dedicated to the proposition that all men are created equal." That nation now faced a great test of its faith that, if passed, would lead to "a new birth of freedom," after which "government of the people, by the people, for the people, shall not perish from the earth."[57] What had been a test of our legal system had become a test of our soul. After enduring hundreds of thousands of war casualties, Lincoln himself became the culminating blood sacrifice for this new birth. He sealed his testament with his own life, and, after the brief, disappointing tenure of Andrew Johnson, the nation marched into the future under the leadership of one of Lincoln's sincerest devotees, Ulysses S. Grant.

Grant's fidelity to Lincoln's vision is famous. Reflecting in 1875 on his relationship with the fallen president, Grant wrote as if he were describing an American Christ figure: "To know him personally was to love and respect him for his great qualities of heart and head, and for his patience and patriotism. With all his disappointments from failures on the part of those to whom he had entrusted command, and treachery on the part of those who had gained his confidence but to betray it, I never heard him utter a complaint nor cast a sensure [*sic*] for bad conduct or bad faith. It was his nature to find excuses for his adversaries. In his death the Nation lost its greatest hero."[58] Like the chief apostle to the martyr, Grant revered Lincoln, celebrating his heroism and charity in the face of the apostates who betrayed him. More important, Grant zealously supported measures designed to promote racial equality and to ensure that Lincoln's vision for the Union reborn would live on. He was instrumental in supporting and enforcing the Civil Rights Act of 1866, the Reconstruction Acts of 1867 and 1868, the Naturalization Act of 1870, the Fifteenth Amendment (1870), and a series of subsequent "enforcement acts."[59]

For a while the higher law appeared to be working. Between Lincoln and Grant and the end of the Civil War, Americans were coming to terms with a new identity. Black Americans, including those in the South, were finding their way into state legislatures, juries, and even Congress. With the ratification of the Fifteenth Amendment, new generations of Black Americans seemed positioned to participate fully in American life. In addition, the military investments made over the course of the war led to new infrastructure in factory work, mass transportation, and economic planning. Combined with a new military prowess, these developments made the United States an up-and-coming monolith. By the turn of the century, US military and diplomatic initiatives claimed territory from the Atlantic to the Pacific to the Gulf of Mexico, a swath of the globe that included some of the most arable plains, massive mountain ranges, lush forests, and accessible seaports in the world. A new, vigorous empire was billowing across the West, flush with resources, intrepid leaders, and high ideals. A coherent civil religious order seemed within reach.

But the nation's success masked a spiritual turmoil. As early as the 1870s, southern resentment over Reconstruction began to breed Jim Crow laws. Local governments in the former Confederate states were chipping away at the Union reforms by imposing racial segregation in matters of education, transportation, recreation, and economic development. Meanwhile, the ongoing colonization of the continent was erasing whole indigenous cultures and populations; and industrialization, for all its charming efficiencies, was spawning dehumanizing work conditions and inequalities. None of this quite mattered, though. The economic opportunities seemed to prove the American Dream to be real, and millions of immigrants poured into the country from faraway shores. As a result, new debates over cultural citizenship emerged, and gatekeeping became an avid American practice.

Calling it one of "the ironies of American history," Reinhold Niebuhr noted that the American tendency to moral conceit, which began with the Puritans but extended well into the twentieth century, reinscribed the nation's racial conceits.[60] Northerners and southerners who were still struggling to reconcile their own differences over slavery could at least unite around a shared sense of American supremacy over Italians, Asians, Irish, Jews, Mormons, and others. So, while racism festered, nativism surged. Just as the nation's revolutionary birth was hamstrung by slavery, so the rebirth of the Union was blighted by segregation, xenophobia, and genocide in the name of empire. The American Civil Religion, whatever there had been of it, remained astray.

Kairos and the Cathedral

The history I have outlined here is not meant to demonstrate particular depth or comprehensiveness, only to reveal the contours of a rot that lies at the root of the American Civil Religion. In the following chapters, I intend to show that the United States was never comfortable with its spiritual identity and that this pattern of founding and failure can be traced in the history of the nation's capital city, its aborted national church, the cathedral that rose in its place, and the various ways these locations have been rhetorically framed. The gaps created by the nation's civil religious failures have become filled over time by interest groups making arguments for their own civil religious visions. These arguments continue to belie any claims to a coherent spiritual identity for the nation. Henry Yates Satterlee and other early cathedral leaders were well meaning, but they were not virginal saints struggling to preserve some national creed. When they determined to make the cathedral national in scope, they entered into a civil-religious vacuum with an agenda as to what the nation ought to look like. Despite their progressive ideals, these leaders drew upon rhetorics of nativism and imperialism to secure financial and political backing for their vision. They presumed a Christian hegemony that was not warranted by the nation's founding documents. On the other hand, the cathedral of Bishop Satterlee at the turn of the twentieth century is a very different institution from the cathedral of Francis B. Sayre, who half a century later made the cathedral a lodestar for the nation's civil rights movement; or the cathedral of Mariann Edgar Budde, who another half-century later issued a rebuke of resurgent American xenophobia.

From the same pulpit where Martin Luther King Jr. once called for an end to America's war-first preoccupations, George W. Bush revealed the so-called Bush Doctrine, which amounted to a call for unlimited, preemptive warfare.[61] For better or worse, Washington National Cathedral betrays a vexed longing for some supplement to civic life, a supplement that has the visceral power of shared symbols and spaces, something religious. But as much as this longing has brought Americans together in times of crisis or celebration, it has also driven them to label one another heretics of their nation's sacred ideals. When George H. W. Bush declared, "Here we have built our church," the "we" was disquieting, for we have never seemed to know or be comfortable with who "we" are.

Ultimately, this is the story Washington National Cathedral allows one to tell. At the heart of the American Civil Religion is not a stable doctrine or a set of orthodoxies but rather an agitation over the meaning and function of American identity. This agitation is enshrined in the public addresses that have been delivered from the cathedral's pulpit, as well as in the pastiche of the cathedral itself. It is a confusing space, and I have come to believe that this confusion says less about the cathedral than it does about the country's own dissonance. Inside the cathedral, one is as likely to see a statue of George Washington as to see a statue of Saint Paul. One is as likely to come across a memorialized stone from the moon or the GITMO detention camp as one is to come across a stone from a field in Bethlehem or a ruin in Canterbury. One can find sacred images of the White House threaded into images of the Israelite exodus, or statues of American luminaries next to those of Christian saints. It is a beautiful and bewildering balance. It merits admiration if only for its boldness, but it never feels resolved, as if it is always questioning the purpose to which it is dedicated. The book concludes by asking, *What then?* I suggest two possibilities: a civil-religious schism, which I define as a breakdown of American civic life along ideological lines; or a civil-religious kairos, which I define as a point of contact between unlike political souls.

I explore the concept of kairos in further detail in the second part of the book, but the term merits discussion here. I embrace the concept of kairos because it is central to conversations in both religion and rhetoric. In its simplest sense, kairos denotes "the opportune moment." The term comes from Greek mythology, where Kairos is said to be the youngest son of Zeus and the god of opportunity. He is often depicted with wings on his heels and shoulders, flying about the cosmos. He has a forelock of hair on his head, which, if grasped in time, symbolizes the apprehension of opportunity and the possibility for change. This approach to defining kairos has produced many related terms, from *occasion* to *due measure* to *fitness* and *proportion*.[62] These concepts place kairos in opposition to chronos, which is *quantitative* time, or as one scholar puts it, "ordinary if relentless time."[63] Chronos, where we get the adjective "chronic," denotes the drone of accumulated moments, minute upon minute, day upon day, seeping through the centuries. Change certainly takes place in chronic time, but it happens almost imperceptibly. One hardly knows it is taking place at all. Kairos is *qualitative* time. It represents those rare moments of sudden transformation when one is altered as if by a burst of inspiration. Kairos is like a breakage that sets chronic time on a new trajectory. For this reason, kairos has been called "rhetoric's time."[64]

The concept of kairos became even more rich and complex once theologians got a hold of it. In Christian theology, kairos is God's time, or sacred time; and chronos becomes earthly or profane time. This difference is underscored by the notion that there is something revelatory about kairos. Dale Sullivan goes so far as to call it a "divine madness," because that moment of inspiration can be so powerful as to transform the soul itself.[65] When sacred time confronts profane time, it is as if God has entered the world to reveal new realities, truths, and imperatives for belief and action. Drawing on the work of Mircea Eliade, I have argued elsewhere that this is the purpose of churches, temples, cathedrals, and other sacred spaces. They are constructed to sustain that opening into transformative time. Kairos, then, is not just a moment; it is what Scott Consigny calls "an opening into what is truly real, an aperture through which we may find our truest selves."[66] Theologian James L. Kinneavy argues that kairos is essentially the *space* in which rhetoric takes hold.[67] When a pilgrim inhabits a sacred site, they are not merely contemplating the miraculous events that took place there but are also participating in the events themselves. They coexist in an eternal present with the heroes and angels of the mythic past.

I have chosen kairos as the guiding concept for this book because an effective civil religion must, like any effective religion, create kairotic spaces through which citizens can be cultivated into something more than just mundane constituents of the state. In kairos, they take on commitments beyond themselves. All of which is to say, when Pierre L'Enfant envisioned a "great church for national purposes," what he really envisioned was an American kairos, a sacred space wherein citizens could be moved by their experience of the country's heroes, deeds, and ideals, a space wherein citizenship becomes a holy practice. Satterlee, too, envisioned such a space. To this day, officials and students of Washington National Cathedral call it a kairotic space. Cathedral archivist Diane Ney writes that "eternity lies at the heart of a cathedral . . . : a sense of kairos, of non-linear time that allows reaching across the centuries to bring all into communion in prayerful awe of the forgiving and eternal love of God for his creatures."[68] Although I argue that Washington National Cathedral is *not* the church L'Enfant intended and may not be the church the nation needs, its kairotic commitments mean something. As Americans struggle to find their moral footings, to build a strong and lasting national faith, this church reminds us that the window of opportunity has not yet closed.

Parts and Chapters

This book is divided into two parts. The first part explores the historical and theoretical foundations of the cathedral. It answers the question of where the cathedral idea came from and how it was realized. Chapter 1, "Pierre L'Enfant's Great Church for National Purposes," explores the idea of a national church in the early American republic. The story of Washington National Cathedral must begin with a look at an understudied civil-religious debate that began a century before the building's foundation stone was laid. This chapter considers where L'Enfant's idea came from, why it was not realized, and what became of it in the intervening hundred years prior to Bishop Satterlee.

Chapter 2, "Henry Yates Satterlee's Westminster Abbey," and chapter 3, "The National Church in an Age of Nativism," open the archives on the cathedral's origins and, in particular, its first bishop, Henry Yates Satterlee. Bishop Satterlee's sense of grandeur and urgency during the building of Washington National Cathedral was motivated in part by a high level of anxiety about Roman Catholic expansion in the nation's capital and the potential impact such an expansion might have on the nation's religious and political identity. The building of America's "house of prayer," it turns out, may well be read as a gambit in the competition for denominational control of civil-religious life in the United States. Archival research into the building's history, design, and operation reveals much about the nature of American civil-religious culture and its attendant debates, tensions, ambiguities, and pieties during the early twentieth century. Still, remarkably, this building and its intrepid first bishop have remained largely unknown to scholars of American history. Taken together, these first three chapters set the stage for the kairotic whiplash that has marked the American Civil Religion from the beginning. One can build a sacred space, but what happens when there are disagreements? A civil religion becomes lost in the wilderness.

Chapter 4, "Francis B. Sayre the Prophet and Mariann Edgar Budde the Pastor," marks the cathedral's shift to the political left. Satterlee's vision of an American Westminster Abbey sponsored by a distinctly Christian, Anglican worldview never fully materialized. In fact, Satterlee's original vision speaks to an aging civil-religious model in which the nation's soul is an object of sectarian conquest. It was under Dean Francis Sayre's leadership during the 1950s and '60s that a new orientation began to take root. Sayre embraced the cultural changes of his time, becoming a vocal opponent of right-wing conservatism and an equally vocal proponent of civil rights. Budde, the bishop of the Washington, DC, diocese at the time of this writing, has continued the tradition established by Sayre by pleading with the nation to return to a former sense of dignity in light of resurgent xenophobia. However, this chapter also reveals a sharp contrast between the styles of these two leaders and asks the question of whether this contrast promotes or undermines the coherence of the cathedral's mission. What I hope to reveal by this point in the book is that there can be no shared civil religion unless there is a shared kairos—that is, a shared space and time, a point of contact between unlike souls. This point of contact is, I argue, what L'Enfant had in mind all along. He imagined a space that would enfold the sectarianism of the nation's religious and political tribalisms.

In the second part of the book, we move out of the archives and into the cathedral's more public space. Here I use rhetorical analysis to engage with some of the cathedral's signature speeches and symbolic artifacts, including talks and sermons, windows and statuary, and the very design and ambience of the space. Rhetorical analysis is the process of approaching a persuasive artifact in the spirit of understanding its influence on a target audience or audiences. It considers the artifact in terms of the historical context from which it emerges, the goals and constraints of the person or institution that authors it, the needs and values of the audience that is meant to respond to it, the exigencies it is designed to solve, the opportunities it is designed to leverage, and the success or failure it ultimately achieves. My rhetorical analysis is concept driven, meaning I consider these rhetorical artifacts in terms of the way they draw upon kairos to promote a civil-religious agenda. In this part of the book, I further develop my argument that a coherent civil religion calls for a shared kairos. What my analyses reveal is a series of divergent kairoi—competing interpretations of sacred time that point us back to the fractured premises that have impeded our civil religion from the outset.

Chapter 5, "Philip Hubert Frohman's Fourth Dimension: A Close Reading of Washington National Cathedral," establishes the cathedral's physical structure as a rhetorical artifact worthy of analysis. It would be shortsighted to regard the building as a collection of individual rhetorical messages. The building was always designed to act as a unitary composition with an agenda or set of agendas. Like all Gothic cathedrals, it approaches the Christian narrative as a sequence of events culminating in the death and resurrection of Christ, but it also threads into this narrative a series of key events in American history, which seems to conflate the political and religious elements of the building in strategic, if sometimes confusing, ways. The only way to capture this conflation is to experience the space for oneself, to walk and absorb the building as a text. If kairos is meant to provide entry into a new, transcendent reality, in which we become our true selves and, as Consigny argues, "experience life in its truest intensity and 'reality,' becoming one with the irrational flux of Becoming," then my experience would suggest this cathedral is not it. To the contrary, rather than enfolding the nation's competing identities into a kind of harmony, the space can feel fraught with competing truths, each muscling or sidling its way into view. In place of a coherent civil-religious vision, in other words, I observe what civil religious scholar Robert Wuthnow calls "a confusion of tongues."[69]

Chapter 6, "Martin Luther King Jr.'s Sacred Time," and chapter 7, "The Bush Presidents' Rock of Religious Faith," compare the visions of three of the cathedral's best-known speakers. By performing close analyses of King's sermon, Bush Sr.'s dedicatory remarks in 1990, and Bush Jr.'s National Day of Prayer Address following 9/11, I demonstrate the American Civil Religion's protean nature, which reveals the ongoing contest over what the American Civil Religion means, what it is capable and incapable of doing, and how it can be used and misused. The confusion of my own experience in the cathedral, as articulated in chapter 5, will be born out in a more formal analysis of these prominent speeches from figures we may regard as clerics of the competing versions of American Civil Religion.

Chapter 8, "Civil Seership: The Revelatory Project of Cameron Partridge and Gene Robinson; or, The Revelation of Matthew Shepard," brings us back to the present day. This chapter observes the contours of a new effort to settle the American Civil Religion. Fueled by the success of the LGBTQ+ movement, the cathedral's leaders are attempting to create a kairotic space and moment in which different bodies, identities, spiritualities, and politics are met. I liken the concept of kairos to John Durham Peters's notion of the "caress," a point of sacred contact, which, I argue, creates the possibility for a resilient civil religion. In this chapter, I consider the interment of Matthew Shepard, who was brutally murdered in 1998, and a sermon delivered during that same year by transgender priest Cameron Partridge. These two events are especially illustrative of the civil-religious tensions and possibilities I aim to articulate throughout the book.

The conclusion, "American Kairos," reviews the book's central arguments and presents a metaphor that may help us understand the critical role the cathedral has played in the nation's history. I suspect we will never be able to accept Washington National Cathedral as the nation's spiritual home, even though it has aspired—nobly, for the better part of its history—to that role, but we can regard the cathedral as a kind of spiritual orphanage. For most of its history, the cathedral has striven to provide refuge for the nation's wandering soul. It has loved and nurtured us the best it could, but most of us flounder with its creeds and rites, and we feel foreign to its customs and history. Grateful but graceless, we sit at the cathedral table dressed in someone else's clothes. I conclude that it is time for the nation to build a spiritual home. I am under no illusion that civil religions are simple things to create and maintain. On the contrary, they are notoriously theoretical and contested. This fact does not mean that they cannot be key to a nation's spiritual identity. For this reason, David C. Innes calls civil religion a "political technology."[70] Civil religion has been key to the flourishing of nations from antiquity to the present day, across the divides between East and West.[71] To abandon the dream of a coherent civil religion seems, therefore, cynical, especially for a nation whose only claim to peopleness has always been based in its shared civic ideals.

I will not be Pollyannaish. The book's conclusion is followed by a short epilogue in which I consider the cathedral's Robert E. Lee and Stonewall Jackson bay and windows and their contested removal in 2017. What the controversy surrounding the windows' removal reveals, more starkly than the subjects in any of the other chapters, is a sense of how fraught the dream of the American Civil Religion has been since its inception. Here I consider the fatalist possibility that this dream might never be redeemed and that, instead, it may be on a collision course with its own troubled history.

PART ONE

UNFINISHED HISTORIES

CHAPTER ONE

Pierre L'Enfant's Great Church
for National Purposes

Other than the leading role he played in planning Washington, DC, Pierre Charles L'Enfant remains mostly unknown to the general public. Still less has been revealed about his role in shaping the American Civil Religion, a notion that lies at the heart of Washington, DC's conception and design. If civil religion is, as Rousseau argued, a means of cementing the loyalties of the people to the interests of the state, and if the American Civil Religion is, as Bellah argued, a set of fundamental beliefs about the sanctity and mission of the United States, then Washington, DC, is, in a civil-religious sense, a holy city. Its marble monuments, built like temples over the landscape of a vast garden, commemorate the prophets, saints, and martyrs of the republic. Its squares and open spaces behave like sanctuaries for the nation's sacraments—prayers, protests, commemorations, mournings, holidays. In its halls the nation's relics are preserved and reverently displayed; its founding myths are repeated with liturgical precision by tour guides, docents, and other officiants.

That Washington, DC, is such a city is no accident. It is largely the vision of L'Enfant that made it so, yet L'Enfant's grand notions did not come from nowhere. They were cultivated in the civil religion–rich soil of his home country. This chapter explores the way Pierre L'Enfant's upbringing in Paris shaped his civil-religious vision and the way that vision shaped the American capital and the nation more broadly. This process of shaping was not nearly as straightforward as L'Enfant had hoped or expected it would be. He and his greatest ally, George Washington, promoted an awe-inspiring design for the capital, one that would befit the nation's loftiest ambitions. This approach came into direct conflict with another strain of American Civil Religion, this one promoted by Thomas Jefferson and his Anti-Federalist allies, who envisioned a capital that reflected the nation's political restraint. One of the casualties of this collision was the notion of a church for national purposes. The idea of this church, including its mysterious appearance and disappearance from the plan for Washington, DC, lies at the heart of the debate over what sort of civil religion the United States would plant at the center of its fast-expanding empire.

An Education in Civil Religion

Though not a noble himself, Pierre Charles L'Enfant was descended from courtiers, and his family enjoyed connections in the royal circles of Paris (fig. 1.1). His mother was the daughter of a queen's officer; his father was a royal artist. For some years, the senior L'Enfant was the director of the Gobelins Manufactory, the famous center of French tapestry making in the heart of Paris. The Gobelins served the imperial interests of France, weaving images of French royals into scenes of military or diplomatic action or into solemn portraits that would decorate the salons of palaces and state museums. Young Pierre not only would have been exposed to these works but also would likely have attended the technical school for the manufactory workers' children, where his early talents with a pencil would have gained some notice.

In addition to being director of the tapestry manufactory, the senior L'Enfant had connections with several other French institutions, connections he leveraged in order to educate his son on the story of French empire. He was an academician at the Royal Academy of Painting and Sculpture, where the junior L'Enfant got much of his formal training. He was also a successful artist for the court at Versailles, where he spent much of his time as a painter of heroic battle scenes and landscapes and where he assisted in the design of the Hotel de la Guerre. To this day, the senior L'Enfant's paintings of a series of famous French sieges adorn the walls of the Royal Palace. For eight formative years, he guided his son among the plazas, fountains, gardens, and radiant avenues of the French capital.[1] It was as if the spirit of the Gobelins tapestries had come to life and formed a city. Versailles was a paradise for patriotic aesthetes like the L'Enfants. Not even a century old, its influence had spread across Europe, inspiring the design or redesign of London, Rome, and St. Petersburg.

Versailles was in essence a civil-religious temple complex. Strategically set apart from the metropolis of Paris, it was designed from the ground up to embody the sacred ideals, ornate rituals, and heroic history of French royalty. The brainchild of the Sun King, Louis XIV, and his chief designer, André Le Nôtre, Versailles was constructed beginning in the 1660s, transforming the

MAJOR PETER CHARLES L'ENFANT
Redrawn from wood cut

Fig. 1.1. Undated image, derived from woodcut of Pierre Charles L'Enfant, labeled with his Anglicized name, Peter. Library of Congress Prints and Photographs Division, Washington, DC

small hamlet into the nerve center of French political life. Everywhere one turned in Versailles there was another impeccably conceived square, terrace, or monument, or a lush wood or a canal and garden fed by Le Nôtre's innovative system of hydraulics. Its principal buildings included the royal apartments, a series of lavish halls, and the Royal Theater. Towering over them all was the Royal Chapel (fig. 1.2), the final building completed by Louis XIV after a series of what he considered to be less-than-perfect attempts to create

Profil de la Chapelle Royale de Versailles.

LES PLANS, COUPES, PROFILS ET
ELEVATIONS.
De la Chapelle du Chasteau Royal de
VERSAILLES,
Levez & Gravez Par PIERRE LE PAUTRE Architecte
& Graveur du Roy.
*Se vendent a Paris chez le Sr DE MORTAIN Marchand d'Estampes
sur le Pont Notre Dame aux Belles Estampes*
AVEC PRIVILEGE DU ROY

Fig. 1.2. A seventeenth-century drawing of the planned Royal Chapel at Versailles. Author's collection

the court's sacred centerpiece. In its fifth and final version, the Royal Chapel was a Baroque masterpiece and a focal point for the ancien régime.

The city and its cost were breathtaking. Estimates are uncertain as to the final price tag, but they range all the way up to $300 billion in today's currency.[2] The stifling taxes levied on the public and the debts incurred by the government were shrugged off. The Sun King and his collaborator were building a city not to organize a bureaucracy but to inspire a people. To his credit, Louis XIV did not use the capital for his own comforts only. He imposed upon himself a protocol of ceremonies, including daily rituals for waking and going to bed, planned walks—more like small parades—on the grounds with his entourage, regular meetings with strict agendas, and weekly attendance at mass. He performed these tasks in front of audiences of courtiers and other observers because he believed that by ritualizing and publicizing even his most quotidian activities, he would embody the solemnity of the nation. This demonstration of his convictions led to his nickname, the Sun King. A pious monarch must always behave as the sun, "this centre, visible from all points of the circumference."[3] Such a symbol, Louis believed, was "the most vital and the most beautiful image of a great monarch."[4] It ought to be observed upon rising and setting, and its steady presence ought to be felt throughout the day, for by its light the nation may truly see what it is meant to become. Young Pierre, still a student and fledgling painter, could hardly have imagined creating anything on such a scale, yet he absorbed the spirit of the place like an ardent disciple, and he drew on that spirit two decades later.

A Revolutionary Career

To understand L'Enfant's commitment to the American cause and to appreciate French support for the Revolution, one must also understand the French aristocratic culture of the time. In the eighteenth century, the French love for war was nothing less than Homeric. As Scott W. Berg puts it, "No young Frenchman during the mid-eighteenth century would have had a moment's trouble recognizing it: stronger than family, friendship, or sexual desire, gloire was the grail of a wholehearted quest for personal and national distinction, ideally realized through an achievement on the battlefield."[5] This thirst for glory intensified among the young, prestige-hungry nobles in the summer of 1776 when copies of American revolutionary texts, including the Declaration of Independence and the writings of Benjamin Franklin, began to circulate in Paris. For these young men, the news from America seemed less like reportage than a call to adventure and an opportunity for vengeance. By joining the American cause, they could win glory for themselves and redemption for their country, which had been humiliated by the British in North America and elsewhere throughout the eighteenth century.

When he learned that Pierre Augustin Caron de Beaumarchais, the eccentric French polymath, was working with the Americans to recruit French servicemen, young L'Enfant was among the first to enlist. L'Enfant was tall, about six feet, with a dignified bearing, but he had no military experience to speak of, no contacts in America, no promise of rank, and connections only barely sufficient to get himself on a boat. Although his talents as an artist were considerable, a career in that field seemed less and less likely, given the competition in Paris. He would find his purpose with a bayonet if not with a pencil. Beaumarchais managed to find a spot for L'Enfant as an engineer under the standout brigade chief Phillipe-Charles-Jean-Baptiste Tronson Du-Coudray, who resented L'Enfant's lack of experience but took him on begrudgingly, noting that L'Enfant "has indeed some talent for drawing figures, . . . but nothing of use for an engineer."[6] L'Enfant's troubles with DuCoudray continued all of the way over to America, until the cocky brigade chief–turned–major general died when his horse got spooked and fell off of a pontoon bridge, pinning the rider beneath the water.

Following DuCoudray's death, L'Enfant found his way to Valley Forge during the winter of 1777–78. There he became known for the one skill Du-Coudray had noticed in him: his ability with a pencil. Soldiers began to seek out the Frenchman—*what was his name, Longfont? Langfang?*—for the portraits he was producing of his fellow servicemen. When the Marquis de Lafayette, a major general in the Continental Army, requested that L'Enfant walk the mile through camp to the stone cottage of General Washington and produce a sketch of the future president, L'Enfant's heart must have leapt. He knew that Lafayette and Washington were intimately close and that Lafayette had not thought lightly about making the request. Lafayette, barely more than a teenager despite his high rank, saw in Washington a fatherly icon. Washington saw in Lafayette the son he never had. The only record we have of the portrait L'Enfant produced of Washington that season comes from an exchange between Lafayette and Washington the following summer. "Give me joy, my dear general," wrote Lafayette. "I schall have your picture, and Mister hancock has promis'd a Copy of that he has in boston—he gave one to the Count d'estaing, and I never Saw a man so glad of possessing his sweet heart's picture."[7] In response to Lafayette, Washington blushed: "When you requested me to set for Monsr Lanfang I thought it was only to obtain the

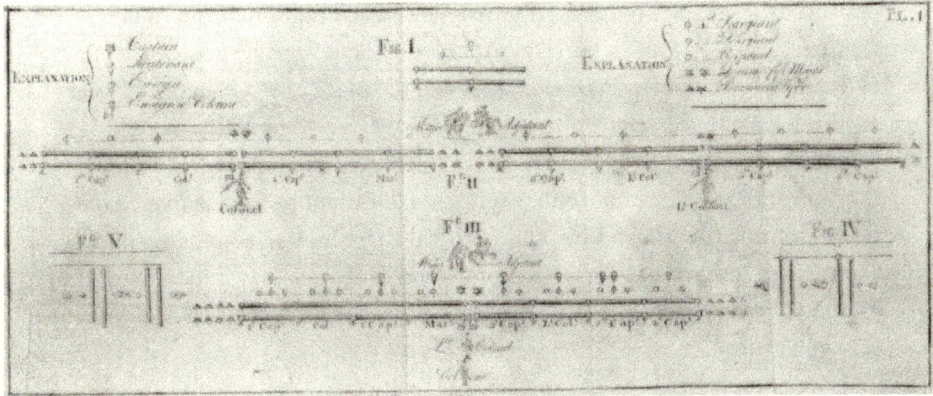

Fig. 1.3. A technical drawing by Pierre L'Enfant, used in the military manual *Regulations for the Order and Discipline of the Troops of the United States,* commonly known as the *Blue Book.* Library of Congress, Books / Printed Material

outlines and a few shades of my features, to have some Prints struck from." Washington was referring to the sketch made by L'Enfant the preceding winter at Valley Forge. The sketch that L'Enfant produced did not survive, but the foundation of a historic partnership was begun.

From that point forward, L'Enfant began to build his reputation as the "Artist of the American Revolution."[8] While still at Valley Forge, he was asked to illustrate Baron von Steuben's famous *Blue Book,* the American army's first comprehensive training manual. Washington praised the manual for its remarkable clarity, citing its rejection of "everything superfluous."[9] Unlike the portrait of Washington, the manual still exists, and it shows L'Enfant's precision as a designer. The illustrations are ordered by clean lines and shapes, a sensitive balance of positive and negative space, and a sparing use of text (fig. 1.3).[10] It was clear to anyone who viewed the illustrations that L'Enfant's talents went beyond portraiture. He had the spatial and strategic sensibilities of a planner.

Following the war, L'Enfant spent years cultivating a working relationship with the president. In April 1782, he organized an elaborate gala at which American leaders celebrated the birth of a French prince. To the acclaim of attendees, L'Enfant designed a pavilion for the occasion and decorated it with French and American national symbols. Washington was so impressed that he invited L'Enfant to design the insignia for the Society of Cincinnati, for which assignment L'Enfant traveled to France to oversee the engravings and organize a French branch of the society. Again, his work was enthusiastically praised. In 1784, he organized a procession in celebration of the Articles of Confederation. In 1788, when New York's City Hall was to be converted into Federal Hall, seat of the First Congress and the place of Washington's swearing in, L'Enfant was chosen to create and oversee the building's redesign. The hall soon became one of the most celebrated pieces of architecture in the United States.[11] For more than a decade, L'Enfant proved himself a master of architecture, branding, and political theater. As Caemmerer puts it, "Whenever something in any way connected with art was wanted during the War or for years after the War, [L'Enfant] was appealed to."[12] President Washington was smitten.

The City Plan

By the time the opportunity arrived to design the federal city, L'Enfant had earned a reputation for the grandeur and beauty of his work. He was also by then a decorated veteran, having endured a musket ball to the leg during the siege of Savannah and spent a year or so as a prisoner of war. While the Pierre L'Enfant of Valley Forge had been obliged to be methodical and supplicating, the *Peter* L'Enfant of 1791—he had Anglicized his name as a show of loyalty— was a war hero with an unparalleled résumé. When he heard that the government had at last settled on building a new capital from scratch, he wrote to Washington in a barely contained frenzy: "The late determination of Congress to lay the Fundation of a City, which is to become the Capital of this vast Empire, offers so great an occasion of acquiring reputation, to whoever may be appointed to conduct the execution of the business, that your Excellency will not be surprised that my Embition and the desire I have of becoming a usefull Citizen should lead me to wish a share in the Undertaking."[13]

Early in 1791, L'Enfant was officially selected for the job, whereupon he lost all sense of restraint, if he ever had any. Questions of cost and scale were for him vulgar annoyances. "Regular plan[s]" he scorned as "tiresome and insipid" and "wanting a sense of the real Grand & trewly beautifull."[14] There could be no more glorious a commission than to design one of the world's great capitals. What he had seen and learned under the tutelage of his father in Paris and Versailles became a blueprint for something of even greater significance. For L'Enfant, at the heart of the American experiment should lie an opulent city, and at the heart of that city was to be a church, a temple of the republic.

Thomas Jefferson, still agitated by debts L'Enfant had incurred during previous projects, saw a problem.[15] It was well known that L'Enfant could get out of hand on matters of budget. More concerning was the fact that he was, from an iconographic point of view, a product of the Bourbon court and a creature of Parisian excess. To Jefferson, a minimalist and strict constitutionalist, these traditions represented everything the United States should not be. Many of Jefferson's Republican colleagues shared his antipathy.[16] Washington, however, made a habit of defending L'Enfant, granting that, despite the artist's "untoward disposition," "perverseness," and profligate ways, "he was better qualified than any one who had come within my knowledge in this country."[17] Washington was also a Federalist sympathizer, and he understood the potential of an awe-inspiring capital city to unite a scattered and vulnerable people.[18] The minimalist approach could work, he reasoned, only if there were a strong, centripetal force at the base of the government. For him, that force was a thriving, metropolitan capital.

L'Enfant knew that Washington was on his side, and he used this alliance to his advantage, especially in his dealings with Jefferson, with whom tensions surfaced almost immediately. When L'Enfant was given the job as designer, Jefferson instructed him merely to make a sketch of the selected lands for the purpose of plotting out some public buildings: "The special object of asking your aid is to have a drawing of the particular grounds most likely to be approved for the site of the Federal town and buildings. You will therefore be pleased to begin on the Eastern branch and proceed from thence upwards, laying down the hills, valleys, morasses and waters between that and the Potomac . . . and connecting the whole with certain fixed points on the map Mr. Ellicot is preparing. Some idea of the height of the lands above the base on which they stand would be desirable."[19] Washington was more ambiguous in his view of L'Enfant's role. L'Enfant was under the impression that Washington had given him carte blanche in terms of the planning, since, after all, Washington never attempted to contract the vision L'Enfant communicated in his letters and notes. Similarly, Jefferson was under the impression that Washington did not object to his (Jefferson's) practical concerns about money and scale, since Washington never openly pushed against them. In his diary, Washington seems to favor the more constrained view of L'Enfant's task. Following his trip to DC in June 1791, he writes: "I went out with Majr. L'Enfant and Mr. Ellicot to take a more perfect view of the ground, in order to decide finally on the spots on which to place the public buildings and to direct how a line which was to leave out a Spring . . . belonging to Majr. Stoddart should be run." There is no record of conversation about designing monumental buildings and other grand edifices.[20]

It is clear that Jefferson regarded L'Enfant's expected contribution mainly in technical terms. To Jefferson, L'Enfant was little more than a landscape sketch artist and draftsman of grids whose work on von Steuben's *Blue Book* had shown his utility. Jefferson's tone also presages an ever-widening gap between his own interpretation of the project and that of L'Enfant. As Kirk Savage puts the issue: "Was the United States to be a classical republic of farmers—modest, frugal, self-restrained, and self-contained—or an empire with visions of eternal growth and progress?"[21] The design of the capital city would provide the definitive answer to this question, and everyone seemed to know the stakes.

L'Enfant interpreted the job in the most grandiose terms, and he wasted no time before packing his things and leaving New York for George Town. He traveled several days by coach, until the coach broke down and he was obliged to complete the journey on horseback and then on foot, hiking much of the way through rain and fog on his injured leg. He reported at the home of the mayor of George Town late on the evening of March 9, 1791, soaked and exhausted but anxious to begin his work.[22] As Le Nôtre saw the virgin landscape at Versailles, so L'Enfant perceived the countryside on the banks of the Potomac. "Nature has done much for it," he remarked, "and with the aid of art it will become the wonder of the world."[23] L'Enfant believed that he and Washington would create a city to rival all other world capitals, including his beloved Versailles.

He made his intentions clear in August 1791 when he wrote to Washington that he "wished to promot in the delineation of a plan wholy new, and which combined on a grand scale will require Exertions above what is the idea of many. . . . I remain assured you will conceive it essential to pursu with dignity the operation of an undertaking of a magnitude so worthy of the . . . grand Empire in the compleat achievement of the which the Honor of this is become so eminently concern and over whose progress the ayes of every other nation envying the opportunity deny'd them will stand juge."[24] Once he had revealed the project's magnitude, his letters became more descriptive. They teemed with visions of "aggrandizement & embeleshment," "wealth," and "majistik aspect" and buildings "unparalleled in point of beauties." He foresaw intersections of diagonal, vertical, and horizontal boulevards; grand vistas punctuated by monuments; and sprawling pools with intricate fountains.[25] He recognized that, as much or even more than a denomination or sect, a nation's iconography could instill in the hearts of its citizens a sacred fire and that doing so was at least partly a matter of arranging symbols.

In spite of Jefferson's instructions for a simple survey and some landscape sketches, L'Enfant refused to take the hint. Instead, he behaved almost as if Jefferson had never sent the message. With a not-so-subtle name drop of the president, he petitioned Jefferson for more materials to pursue his vision, including

> what Ever map may fall within your reach—of any of the different grand city now Existing such as for example, as London, madry [Madrid], paris, Amsterdam, naples, venice, genoa, florence, together with particular . . . as you may know to be the most compleat in thier Improvement for notwithstanding I would reprobate the Idea of Imitating and that contrary of Having this Intention it is my wish and shall be my Endeavour to delinate on a new and original way the plan the contrivance of which the President has left to me without any restriction so Ever.[26]

Ever the diplomat, Jefferson obliged L'Enfant by providing a number of city maps that he had collected during his years in Europe, but he did not miss the opportunity to reaffirm his view of the president's mind as well his own preference for simplicity and restraint. On April 10, 1791, in the letter with which he enclosed the maps, he wrote: "I make no doubt that, in explaining himself to you on the subject, he has interwoven with his own ideas, such of mine as he approved: for fear of repeating therefore what he did not approve . . . , I avoid interfering with what he may have expressed to you."[27] Then, with no record of any response from L'Enfant, he added in August of that year: "I would suggest to you the idea of [laying out the plan] on a square sheet to hang upwards, thus the outlines being N.W. N.E. S.E. S.W. the meridians will be vertical as they ought to be; the streets of the city will be horizontal and vertical, & near the center, . . . here will be no waste in the square sheet of paper."[28] Jefferson's politeness here is belied by the indirect reminder that he, too, has influence with the president and that L'Enfant's job is one of drafting, not philosophizing or nation building. Far from the overwrought monuments and radiating avenues of Europe, the American capital would be best served by a grid of blocks. Moreover, the city's size ought to be scalable to a "square sheet." No doubt Jefferson had got wind of L'Enfant's notion of a city of six thousand square acres; Jefferson believed fifty should do.[29]

The private letters between Jefferson and L'Enfant point to a much more public tension. The nation's early leaders were aware that the United States was at a crossroad and that the manner in which they navigated that crossroad would set the course for how American citizens viewed themselves as a people for generations to come. What did it mean to be an American? What identities and responsibilities did it entail? How would this identity bear up against the threats of a volatile world? L'Enfant came from a civil-religious tradition that would never think of limiting the majesty of national image. A nation's highest ideals must be enshrined in spectacles of stone and marble and in the landscape of the dominion itself. In this version of civil religion, a nation reveres its heroes as demigods and its civic spaces as quasi-temples.

Jefferson was of a different civil-religious order. While he was famously practical on matters of financing and scale, his overriding concern was the effect such questions had on American citizenship. Jefferson admitted that European centers had much to recommend them, including their elegant buildings, but he believed that an extravagant capital ran counter to everything a democratic republic ought to hold sacred: limited government, distributed powers, the sovereignty of the states and their people. Great public leaders and spaces were, in his view, to be recognized but not sacralized. The two sides fell along partisan lines—the Federalists in favor of L'Enfant's view, the Republicans in favor of Jefferson's. Each side had its supporters—members of Congress, cabinet officials, commissioners—but most decision makers shared one view in common: the president's opinion mattered a great deal.

Washington was a pragmatist. In his view, the loose ties that bound the states together would come undone if there were no governing force sufficient to hold them. Local interests would dominate policy decisions; states would end up competing against one another with little regard for broader interests; new confederacies might grow up and engage each other in war. Worst of all, the nation's geopolitical rivals could pounce at any sign of weakness. The nation needed a "strong centripetal force at the center of the country."[30] Where L'Enfant and Jefferson were purists of their respective philosophies, Washington simply saw a problem that needed solving. The capital city on a grand scale would allow the country to push beyond mere polity and build something that could civilize and unify the states and their citizens.[31] His support of the L'Enfant plan grew out of this pragmatism, and it became even more pronounced when he saw L'Enfant's preliminary drawings and witnessed the reaction of the commissioners and local land speculators who, capturing the breadth of L'Enfant's plan, doubled down on their investments in the city.[32] Washington realized that the more expansive and beguiling the vision, the more likely the money was to flow.

It was true, as Jefferson had indicated to L'Enfant, that Washington approved of the grid plan, but it was also true that Washington approved of

L'Enfant's massive scale and style for the city. L'Enfant's plan made use of Jefferson's beloved grid, but the grid was subdued within an ornate mesh of diagonals and intersections. Nicholas Mann argues that, when viewed at a proper elevation, the plan reveals the golden ratio in a series of interlocking circles and cascading star shapes. To Mann, these patterns point to an ancient cosmology linking heaven to earth and, in this case, spirit to republic.[33] Whether or not this level of detail was L'Enfant's intention, people who viewed the plan were mesmerized. For L'Enfant, the federal city ought, like Versailles, to be a unified, sacred work of art meant to inspire citizens to faith and piety.

The monumental centers created by this layout expanded outward in a motif of imperialism. The network would, L'Enfant wrote, "admit of statues, columns, obelisks, or any other ornament . . . [commemorating] those whose usefulness hath rendered them worthy of general imitation, to invite the youth of succeeding generations to tread in the paths of those sages or heroes whom their country has thought proper to celebrate."[34] Set strategically on rises in the landscape, the monuments would declaim the nation's ideals and teach visitors, particularly the young, what models to imitate. For the city "must leave to posterity a grand idea of the patriotic intertest which promoted it."[35] The plan would also reserve major intersection points whereupon the states could enshrine their own heroes or other objects of veneration. This measure would allow each state to thread itself into the nation's civil-religious cosmos. Because of the way L'Enfant's plan opened each square onto another avenue that led to yet another square, the state-sponsored intersections would serve not as demarcations but as nodes radiating outward from the federal center. In this way, the states would be symbolically linked to one another and fixed to the federal center, just as the Founders had hoped the location of the federal district would tie North to South.[36]

The city core, which would provide the basis from which this network fanned out, was defined by four prominent points: two of these points would form the basis for the nation's legal administration; the other two would serve as spiritual anchors. The first two were the Congress House and the Presidential Palace. Both structures were designed and built in the grand, neoclassical tradition. The second two structures were the great national church and the monument to the nation's first president. According to L'Enfant's layout, the monument to Washington was to be the axial center of the whole city: point A on his map. He envisioned a heroic equestrian statue of Washington, lofted high on a pedestal within view of all principal points. Like the Sun King, the likeness of Washington would be the light to which all things pointed and from which all things emanated. As Savage describes it, the image of Washington "would be a moral compass for the nation's leaders. Like an ancient cult figure, it would guarantee that astronomical, mathematical, and political orders were all in alignment."[37] From this cardinal point stretched a vertical axis leading to the Presidential Palace and a horizontal axis leading to the Congress House. These two buildings were then linked by a diagonal boulevard—now Pennsylvania Avenue—that formed the hypotenuse of a right triangle.

The fourth prominent point at the heart of L'Enfant's map was the "Great Church for National Purposes." If one were to bisect the right triangle, drawing a diagonal line from the monument to Washington straight into the top-right quadrant of a square, one would land at L'Enfant's location for the church. Barely six blocks equidistant from the Presidential Palace and the Congress House, the church would keep a watchful eye on the executive and legislative branches (fig. 1.4). The importance of its placement was also signified by the fact that, in contrast to most intersections in the city, the church created a closed vista for the viewer, suggesting its exceptional role in the city's design, at once in touch with and removed from the business of government.[38] These four points, the Presidential Palace, the monument to Washington, the Congress House, and the national church, constituted the nation's most hallowed precincts, and L'Enfant would insist that they were designed without the hinderance of "petty saving."[39]

Once these four points were established, L'Enfant added vivid descriptions of the cityscape. The streets and squares connecting the palace and the Congress House "will be beautifull above what may be Imagined . . . from the grand walk from the water cascade under the federal House to the president park and dependency extending to the ban[k] of the Potomac, and also the severals squar . . . offering a variety of situations unparalleled in point of beauties—suitable to every purpose, and in every point convenient." These "several squares" would host judicial courts, a national bank, a national theater, and a market and exchange—all of which combined would give the city a "degree of splendour and greatness unprecedented."[40] L'Enfant also set aside plots for a national university and other academies and societies "whose object is national."[41] Like leaves in a garland, these additional buildings would fill out the cityscape around the four principal landmarks. The plan's copiousness was breathtaking, and it was a rebuke of the likes of Jefferson and his minimalist tastes.

The Church Plan

There was never any question that of the four principal structures the two most urgently needed were the Presidential Palace and the Congress House. The president and Congress needed places where they could do the day-to-day work of governing. Once plans for these buildings were firmly in place, however, it was the national church that seemed to get most of L'Enfant's attention, and the political climate of the time suggests some reasons why. Decades since the First Great Awakening and decades before the Second, most Enlightenment Americans had little patience for a Christian state along the lines of England or France. Here of course is where L'Enfant differed from Le Nôtre and the old French court. A century earlier, the Sun King had built a grand church at the center of his city, and it was only natural that he, a Roman Catholic, should do so. France in the 1600s was a proudly Catholic state and would remain so for many more decades. The United States of 1791, on the other hand, branded itself an "empire of liberty" and promoted its freedom of religion—a thriving slave trade and vestigial state-affiliated churches notwithstanding. By the time L'Enfant was designing the federal district, France was in the midst of its own revolution, and it too had become suspicious of state religions. The French government had already canceled the taxing power of the church and stripped the clergy of any special rights. It had also begun confiscating church property, and in the very month that L'Enfant was busy with the first drawings of the capital, the pope denounced France's new constitution.[42]

One of the most telling developments of France's abandonment of state Catholicism was its repurposing of the Pantheon, which had been designed as a Roman Catholic cathedral dedicated to Saint Genevieve. The cathedral's construction was not finished at the time the French Revolution broke out, and as the Roman Catholic Church became the target of much national contempt, the project seemed more and more like a cultural albatross. The Marquis de Vilette suggested the edifice be finished and repurposed as a shrine to the nation itself. On April 4, 1791, not four weeks after L'Enfant had arrived at George Town on the other side of the Atlantic, the French Assembly declared that "this religious church become a temple of the nation, that the tomb of a great man become the altar of liberty." In almost the same breath, it decreed that the text adorning the church's pediment should be changed to read: "A grateful nation honors its great men." Later that year, many of the church's most explicitly Christian elements were altered or destroyed and

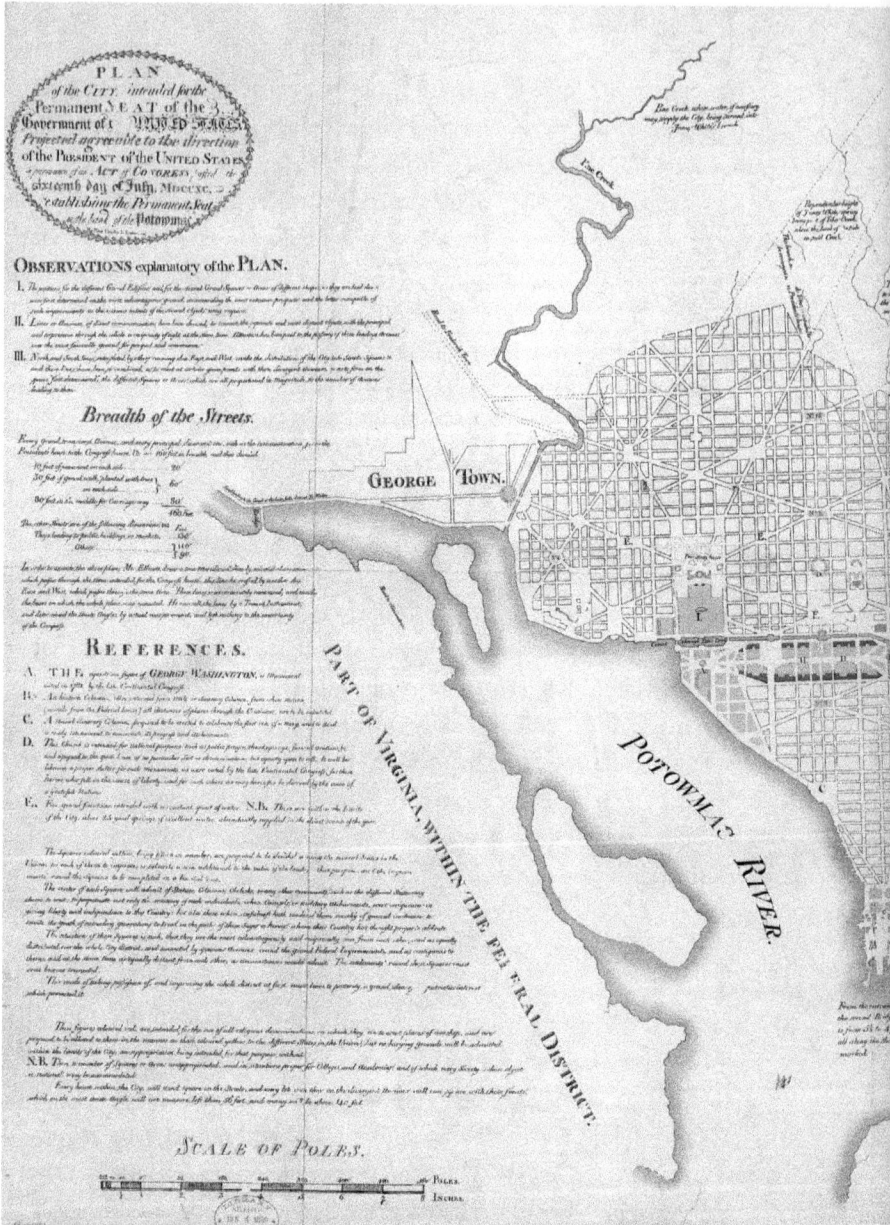

Fig. 1.4. L'Enfant's 1791 plan for the capital city, with his notes. US Coast and Geodetic Survey; Library of Congress

EASTERN BRANCH.

PART OF . . ARYLAND, WITHIN THE FEDERAL DISTRICT.

Lat. Congress House, 38. 53. N.
Long. 0. 0.

References.

E.
G.
H.
I.
K.
L.
M.

N.1.

Fig. 1.5. The peristyle and pediment of the entrance to the Pantheon of France. This bas-relief sculpture replaced the original, which contained religious themes. Here, the central figure, The Nation, distributes crowns to distinguished leaders, scholars, and warriors. Translated, the inscription reads "To great men, from a grateful nation." Jerome Labouyre / Alamy Stock Photo

replaced by more patriotic images.[43] Two bas reliefs over the main entry proclaimed the building's new purposes: "public education" and "patriotic devotion." Ultimately, the building's principal frieze would depict neither Christian prophets and apostles nor martyrs and saints, nor the creative cloudburst in Soufflot's 1777 plan for the church, but personifications of the Nation and Liberty, flanked by statesmen, scholars, and soldiers from France's very own history (fig. 1.5).[44]

There appears to be no obvious link between France's Pantheon and L'Enfant's church for national purposes—nothing in the way of correspondence or private notes—but it would be foolish to think L'Enfant was not monitoring the developments in Paris. His descriptions of the great American church parallel the sentiments of the French revolutionaries. In his notes on the plan, he included the following description: "This Church is intended for national purposes, such as public prayer, thanksgiving, funeral orations etc. and assigned to the special use of no particular Sect or denomination, but equally open to all. It will be likewise a proper shelter such monuments as were voted by the last Continental Congress for those heroes who fell in the cause of liberty, and for such others as may hereafter be decreed by the voice of a grateful Nation."[45] In his original handwritten notes, L'Enfant wrote that the church would not be assigned "to the particular use" of any sect, but he crossed the phrasing out and wrote instead that the church would not be assigned "the special use" of any sect. The change may have been a matter of style, but it underscores the principle L'Enfant wanted to communicate about the relationship between the nation's sects and the nation itself. All sects could practice freely the *particulars* of their faith, but no sect would be granted "special" status in the nation's eyes, and this "church" would make clear as much.[46]

The emphasis on fallen heroes and the phrase "grateful Nation" seem near duplications of the new direction of the French Pantheon. What is also striking about L'Enfant's description is what it does not include. There is no promotion of Christ or the rituals of any tradition beyond the celebration of national affairs. This absence is of course consistent with the Deism of the eighteenth century, especially among so many of the Founders, who supported a religiousness based on social utility, reason, and cosmopolitanism and who believed in an inspired system of order and harmony that, incidentally, became a force in revolutionary France.[47] The few prescriptions L'Enfant did make for the church point definitively away from the worship of a sectarian god and gesture instead to something more like an American version of the French Pantheon, a place where all gods have a place and where the deeds and heroes of the nation are venerated.

The parallels between the American national church and the Pantheon of Paris are strong enough that some scholars take the link for granted, though with varying degrees of certainty. Sarah Kite describes L'Enfant's church as a "pantheon to the illustrious dead," though, despite her choice of words, she draws no explicit link to the church in Paris.[48] Savage describes L'Enfant's church as "clearly modeled on the Pantheon in Paris."[49] Cyril M. Harris describes it as a "secular national temple" that was "possibly influenced by the Pantheon of Paris."[50] Harris goes on to point out a telling discrepancy between L'Enfant's initial drawings, which did not include a church, and his later, more public drawings, which did include the church along with several explanatory notes for its purpose. Harris speculates that the president must have proposed the idea to L'Enfant after seeing the initial plans.[51] I suggest an alternative theory, which is based on the timing of L'Enfant's revised plan. In the late eighteenth century it typically took six to twelve weeks for news to travel across the Atlantic. L'Enfant showed his original drawings to Washington in June 1791, about six weeks after the Pantheon of Paris had been approved for repurposing, suggesting a possible, though unlikely, timeline for the Pantheon to have influenced his design. L'Enfant's revision came on August 19, a full fourteen weeks following the events in Paris, well after news of the Pantheon would have reached the States. It seems far more likely that at this point L'Enfant was influenced by the sea change in his home city. He wanted to build Versailles, but it had never made sense to recommend a Christian church on the order of the Sun King's; however, France now provided the perfect model. The Pantheon was a sanctuary for an enlightened, democratic age.

Assuming L'Enfant had read descriptions or seen renderings of the Parisian Pantheon, he would have agreed not only with its spirit and purpose but also with its architectural style. The Pantheon is a high-style classical affair, not unlike the ancient Pantheon of Rome, with a portico of Corinthian columns topped with a pediment. The building is dominated by a central tower and dome, comparable in size to St. Peter's in Rome and St. Paul's in London. The exterior was not brick; rather, it was built with a white stone that echoed the civic and religious buildings of the classical world. Similarly, L'Enfant and Washington had insisted that the fronts of the capital's public buildings be turned out in stone rather than brick, so as "to awe with respect" all visitors and to project a noble spirit befitting the future of the nation, when the "wealth, population & importance of [the city] shall stand on much higher ground."[52] Their capital city was to be timeless, and the timeless style was classical. More to the point, the classical style connoted the kind of democratic, republican identity the young nation was trying to project.

Although L'Enfant never made any drawings of the proposed church, the markings on his famous map show an expansive oval shape, an ellipse rivaling in size the footprint for the Congress House. Unlike the cross-shaped floorplan of a medieval cathedral, with a transept and orthogonal wings, here was something like a laurel wreath, as if it were meant for the enlightened head of republican empire. L'Enfant and Washington were distancing the capital city from Christian motifs. It would serve not only as a place of national mourning, thanksgiving, and celebration but also as a center for civil-religious education where the nation's highest ideals would be promoted and its greatest heroes reverenced. Just as the capital city would be tied to no particular state, so the national church would be tied to no particular faith. After the plan was delivered, L'Enfant highlighted this parallel in an explanatory letter to Washington. He suggested "an appropriation of the several squar as [are] proposed in the plan to be alloted to each of the Individual states as also the making of a free donation to Every particular religious society of a ground for House of worship a mode from which Infinit advantages most result."[53] In other words, the nation's churches would be to the national church as the nation's states would be to the national government: both coordinate and subordinate. As L'Enfant said, the national church would be "equally open to all," but its heart must beat to the drum of the republic.

Dismissal and Death

In the months between August 1791, when L'Enfant presented his revised plan, and the end of the year, L'Enfant's head grew as large as his vision. His colleagues had always known him to be inflexible in his dealings with others, but they, Washington especially, had considered this inconvenience to be part of the price for his art. L'Enfant's behavior, however, fast reached a level of insubordination that could not be shrugged off. He repeatedly ignored the directives of the district commissioners who had been assigned to oversee the planning and to whom L'Enfant was to conduct himself in strict deference, for the commissioners, Washington made clear to L'Enfant in a letter, stood "between you and the President of the United States."[54] Washington's admonition here was in reaction to one particularly gross display of lawlessness on L'Enfant's part. L'Enfant had ordered and overseen the demolition of a private home that had been built prior to L'Enfant's plan; the home had breached by a few feet one of his precious boulevards. The incensed owner of the house, a Mr. Carroll of Duddington, who happened to be one of the wealthiest residents of the city, complained to the commissioners, who immediately reported the incident to Washington and Jefferson. L'Enfant managed to be surprised at the frustrations his actions had caused.[55]

L'Enfant made little attempt to mend his relationship with the commissioners, and they in turn were inflexible. While L'Enfant was away in Philadelphia on business, he sent a series of directives to his loyal overseer in the federal city, a man by the name of Roberdeau. Roberdeau made L'Enfant's will known to the commissioners, requesting a hefty supply of workers, wheelbarrows, and other materials, only, in the end, to be rebuffed. Roberdeau responded to the rebuff with impassioned and public insults. He was later arrested and his letters to L'Enfant were intercepted or delayed.[56] The breach was insurmountable. L'Enfant was repeatedly admonished, first diplomatically, then forcefully by both Jefferson and the president for his noncompliance with the will of the commissioners.[57] In one provocative exchange with Jefferson, L'Enfant declared that "I have no longer to act in subjection to their [the commissioners'] will and caprice," adding that if doing so were a condition of his employment, he "would not up on any consideration submit myself to it." Even Washington was alarmed by L'Enfant's defiance and asked for Jefferson's advice. Jefferson made it clear that diplomatic correction was useless. Direct threats were needed. Washington consented. "I wished you to be employed in the arrangements of the Federal City," Washington wrote, his patience worn thin. "I still wish it: but only on condition that you can conduct yourself in subordination."[58] But L'Enfant had become incapable of seeing matters in any way other than his own. He had long taken his friendship with Washington as political insurance, as if he and the president were in league in the same way Le Nôtre had been allied to the Sun King at Versailles. Now it appeared that his friend and the object of his highest adoration was turning.

In one of his final letters to L'Enfant, Washington warned: "Your precipitate conduct will, it is to be apprehended, give serious alarm, and produce disagreeable consequences."[59] The disagreeable consequences came in the form of a letter from Secretary Jefferson dated February 27, 1792: "I am instructed by the president to inform you that notwithstanding the desire he has entertained to preserve your agency in the business the condition up on which it is to be done is inadmissible, & your services must be at an end."[60] Jefferson was glad to be rid of L'Enfant. "I am persuaded," he wrote to George Walker just days later, "the enterprise will advance more surely under a more temperate direction," signaling his hope not only that the interpersonal tensions would be mitigated but also that the excesses of the plan itself might now be reconsidered.[61] In the war between two civil-religious visions, Jefferson had just won a significant battle.

The concept of a national church would disappear as mysteriously as it had emerged. By the time L'Enfant was removed from his role as planner, the church idea was simply gone. We know only that in the drawings prepared by Andrew Ellicott, L'Enfant's replacement, the square city block that had been reserved for the great church was left blank without explanation. In place of the laurel-like oval, there was a generic rectangle, suggesting that the square still awaited some large monument. But what? Not until the mid-1800s when the federal government undertook an ambitious building program would the barren Eighth Street square finally sprout its shrine: the US Patent Office. The choice seems, as Adam Goodheart puts it, "like a typically Washingtonian triumph of bureaucracy over poetry." Goodheart reasons that the Patent Office did become a sort of Pantheon in the sense that it displayed the artifacts of American genius, items that proved the virtues of the nation's democratic values and forward-looking energy.[62] Surely there is something civil religious in that role, but such an interpretation comes off as contrived. An office building where L'Enfant had envisioned a grand church? The artist would have retched.

The church was not the only building that dropped out of the plan. Other notable buildings eventually disappeared as well: the bank, the theater, the exchange, the university, even the equestrian statue of Washington. Many of the squares and boulevards remained in place, leaving the map's sacred geometry but draining the city's civil-religious character. In the bottom-right corner, L'Enfant's name was replaced by Ellicott's. Where were the didactic monuments and temples to democracy? How could a city of empty lots, boardinghouses, slave depots, and fallow tobacco fields inspire citizens to something greater than themselves? The city was home to maybe 150 houses scattered irregularly across the landscape. Livestock roamed the streets. The Mall was a scrubland. Contemporary visitors dubbed it "wilderness city," the "city of magnificent distances," and "village monumental."[63] The only national role it seemed to serve was as a collision point for angry politicians and competing states, and the only commerce in which it excelled was the slave trade. Devoid of any vision or soul, the capital seemed chained to a financial and moral rot.

Washington's death in December 1799 accelerated the demise of the L'Enfant plan. Without L'Enfant's chief defender in the way, Jefferson and his allies began to cast their final blows. Even the idea of a monument to General Washington became a matter of heated debate. The Republicans viewed the idea of an awe-inspiring monument as political idolatry; the Federalists viewed it as a symbol of veneration for the republic. They believed that the grander the monument, the more forcefully it could inspire citizens to emulation. The puzzle, as Savage puts it, was "how to replace devotion to the monarch with devotion to the nation."[64] It was a fundamentally civil-religious question. Republicans and Federalists were not battling over what would be best for the nation materially; they were battling over what would be best for it spiritually. What implicit moral values would Americans be inclined to adopt based on the branding of this all-important city?

The only buildings that proceeded from L'Enfant's plan were the executive residence, which was being radically scaled back, and the Congress House. The residence was not occupiable until November 1800, and even then, it remained unfinished. It was burned to a ruin during the War of 1812, rebuilt, and finally reoccupied in 1817. The Capitol construction was marked by incompetence and venality from the outset. The foundation collapsed, a foreman stole thousands of dollars, revenue from land sales to fund the project dried up, and getting federal money to pay for the building was like wringing water from a rock. One usable wing was finished in 1800, but it would be three decades before the building had some semblance of completion, and three decades more before it became the domed masterpiece we recognize today.[65] In the meantime, Americans sprinted across the continent, grabbing land and resources, displacing Native populations, strong-arming foreign governments, and building the economic empire the Founders had foreseen. Left in the dust were questions of national conscience. Whatever spiritual identity the new republic was supposed to have cultivated was left languishing in the heat swamp on the Potomac.

During this period, elements of L'Enfant's plan found their way into the parts of Washington, DC, that were being built. Washington and Jefferson had made an open effort to assign the Capitol the role of a "national temple" modeled after the great temple of Jupiter on the Capitoline Hill in Rome—hence the building's designation as the *Capitol*.[66] Although Jefferson was a committed Republican, he was not opposed to a Roman aesthetic. He wanted only to ensure that public venerations remained focused on the republic and its core principles. Perhaps it was he who, having never warmed to the idea of a national church and wanting to extend an olive branch to Washington, recommended that the Capitol take on many of these sacred elements. The Thornton plan for the Capitol was an explicitly classical affair with a large central dome and rotunda, which echoed the Roman—and, by relation, the Parisian—Pantheon. The design won an open competition judged by the commissioners and the administration. It was put into motion in 1793, well after L'Enfant's dismissal and the alterations to his plan were complete. Jefferson had particular praise for Thornton's plan. It was "simple, noble, beautiful, excellently distributed."[67] For Jefferson, the design was the ideal expression of the meaning of the new republic. No doubt he was relieved to know that any sacred elements the Capitol embraced would be muted by the practical business of government going on inside. Having the Capitol serve both purposes was a mark of Jeffersonian efficiency.

As planning for the Capitol continued, however, the design took on more and more sacred elements, including the notion of a crypt to be located directly beneath the rotunda. Like a cathedral dedicated to a saint, the Capitol would house the relics of its patron and father of the country. Washington appears to have approved of this idea, believing that his remains could be used as a means of fixing the soul of the nation in a single, rooted place. Washington also likely recognized that his interment in such a place was at the heart of the lost national church idea he and L'Enfant had promoted.[68]

For Jefferson, this addition was a bridge too far. A crypt holding the president's relics at the center of the city smacked too much of dynasty and divine right. Of course, as a subordinate to the president, he had to go about his objections obliquely, just as he had done with L'Enfant. Over the course of months and years, Jefferson used third-party objections to the Capitol's engineering schematics to justify delays in completing the rotunda.[69] When Washington finally died in 1799, plans were set in motion to retrieve his remains for burial in the Capitol as planned, but by this time Republicans had found stronger footing in Congress and Jefferson was days away from being elected president. Further muddying the interment plan was a new proposal for a freestanding mausoleum to house the first president's remains.[70] Once Washington was dead and Jefferson was sworn in, Republicans pursued without subtlety their agenda of reduced government and decentralization. They openly objected to the crypt, believing that it would set a dangerous precedent. John Trumbull, a former military aid to Washington, lamented that the Capitol could become too much like London's Westminster Abbey, a place of relics rather than laws.[71] No crypt ever became part of the Capitol, and the mausoleum bill was soon lost in the Senate.[72] Washington was buried at his home in Mt. Vernon, where his remains are to this day.

L'Enfant's death echoed the demise of his church and his city. It came gradually, unceremoniously, and almost without notice. For decades after his dismissal, L'Enfant complained of poverty. He had never copyrighted his prints, so he enjoyed no royalties when his beautifully drawn plan was widely copied and circulated. Records show that he repeatedly petitioned the federal government for remunerations that rarely came, and when they did come, they were snatched away by creditors.[73] He was granted a few large contracts, including the plan for Patterson, New Jersey, and the design of the Philip Morris residence in Philadelphia, but none of these projects gave him a lasting income or prestige, and as often as not he was dismissed for the same reasons he had been sacked in Washington: inflexibility, spendthriftiness, arrogance.[74] He spent his final years on the outskirts of Washington, living as a guest on the farm of the William Dudley Digges family. He frequently explored the city. Still tall and noble in bearing, still arrayed in his overcoat and bell-crowned hat, he looked as important as ever walking along the expansive boulevards he had laid out himself, but he was always grieving his losses, always wincing at what should have been. He died on June 14, 1825, at the age of seventy, possessed of little more than some books, watches, and surveying materials, all of it worth less than fifty dollars. He was buried without a headstone at the foot of a tree on the property of his hosts.[75]

Resurrection and Return

After L'Enfant's death, the American Versailles continued to hobble along in the dust, and its identity crisis continued throughout the first half of the nineteenth century. The debate over the monument to General Washington, which continued for decades, became a kind of microcosm for the contest over the capital itself and, by extension, the nation. The nation's leaders knew they were being asked to fashion more than a memorial to a beloved general. They were building what Savage calls "a specially valued place." The city of Washington—at least, the idea of the city of Washington—was to function like "a pilgrimage site, where communities of believers actually come together in the act of occupying a holy site."[76] In other words, the stakes were too high to mess things up, and so the battle dragged on. It was during this time that L'Enfant's plan fell into its deepest obscurity. Even a half-century after L'Enfant's death, Washington, DC, was a mostly empty city of political gridlock, unkempt spaces, and "magnificent intentions."[77]

Things began to turn around in the second half of the nineteenth century with a resurgence of interest in monumental building. The City Beautiful movement was pushing hard for conscientious planning and beautification measures fit for a civilized people. Beginning around 1880, the spirit of improvement took on a more insistent tone. Articles started appearing in the national press criticizing the capital city. Some people even started to dust off L'Enfant's old plans. A club was formed in 1892 to resuscitate the planner's memory.[78] Around the same time, the federal government had more money to work with, and the empty streets and squares of the capital city began to fill in. It seemed as if L'Enfant's long-dormant vision was starting to emerge, however altered. There was also a push by the postwar government to flex its union muscles. By the turn of the century, Washington, DC, had become an object of investment and national pride, a city of statues, gardens, fountains, stately buildings, and grand boulevards. At the city's centennial celebration in 1900, members of the American Institute of Architects attempted a full-scale reclamation of L'Enfant and his plan. Further vindication came two years later when the Park Commission—also known as the McMillan Commission, after the Michigan senator who led it—announced its "universal approval" of the old L'Enfant plan and declared that historical departures from it were "to be regretted and, wherever possible, remedied."[79] A few years later, with some prodding from the French ambassador and, of all people, the district commissioners—heirs to the bureaucrats L'Enfant had found most contemptible—Congress joined in the adulation and agreed to transfer L'Enfant's remains from the Digges farm to Arlington National Cemetery, where they would be buried on a slope overlooking the city's monumental core.[80]

The celebrations that followed were L'Enfantian in scale. The designer's remains were transported by an official hearse wrapped in the common colors of the French and American flags. The transport was accompanied by French diplomats and military engineers. The remains lay in state in the Capitol Rotunda. On April 28, 1909, President William Howard Taft, Vice President James Sherman, and representatives of Congress and the Supreme Court, plus members of the Society of the Cincinnati and a number of other national organizations gathered to deliver orations in L'Enfant's honor and recommit to the alliance between his two home countries. Two years later, President Taft presided and spoke at another ceremony, this one commemorating a monument to L'Enfant that was installed above the planner's gravestone; the white marble monument was crafted to look like a large table with six posts, or legs, to support it; on the surface was engraved a portion of L'Enfant's original plan for the city (fig. 1.6). Hundreds of guests attended. A band played the national anthem as the American flag was raised.[81]

But, for all its pomp, the capital city's embrace of the L'Enfant plan was still a kind of simulacrum. It lacked the coordinated vision of the artist. From the 1880s through the McMillan Plan in 1902 and the many updates over the following couple of decades, the city certainly filled out. But there was no national church, no national university, no market and exchange. Impressively, the Mall emerged where L'Enfant had planned a grand walk, and its Victorian landscape was in the process of being redesigned to resemble the more formal gardens of Versailles, but other elements appeared in haphazard fashion. The Washington Monument, finally and tortuously completed in

Fig. 1.6. Tomb of Pierre L'Enfant, overlooking Washington, DC's monumental core. NCinDC; CC-BY-2.0, https://creativecommons.org/licenses/by-nd/2.0/legalcode

1888, was planted at an askew angle to the White House and Capitol building, a concession to engineering concerns. The Supreme Court appeared asymmetrically over the shoulder of the Capitol building. The monumental office buildings L'Enfant had envisioned lining the boulevards were given the go-ahead, but the McMillan Commission decreed that they were to be built in the manner of Westminster, in classical geometric layouts but with an overtly Gothic style. Perhaps this recommendation was a concession to the Gothic Revival in American architecture that was well under way. The list goes on.

The events leading up to the McMillan Plan made it clear that the government was only too happy to let the private sector implement its own interpretation of the federal district. The government would not fund a national university, but it would, in 1893, charter the Methodist Church's American University. It would not build a national church, but it would, also in 1893, grant a charter to the Episcopal Church to build its national cathedral. The McMillan Plan claimed L'Enfant as a source of inspiration, but its proposals were riven by compromises. Ironically, in the name of reclaiming L'Enfant, the federal government was outsourcing his vision, often by way of Christian interests. Perhaps this development was to be expected. By the turn of the twentieth century, the United States was experiencing a surge of Christian nationalism and nationalism's favorite accessory, nativism. Churches were claiming more and more ground, both literally and philosophically, in the nation's capital. Competition for influence was fierce, and gatekeeping in the name of American identity was the order of the day. These developments will be discussed in subsequent chapters. For now, it is enough to note that the civil-religious winds had shifted. L'Enfant's plan would have to bend or break.

CHAPTER TWO

Henry Yates Satterlee's
Westminster Abbey

On its "About the Cathedral" webpage, Washington National Cathedral announces the following: "Grounded in the reconciling love of Jesus Christ, Washington National Cathedral is a house of prayer for all people, conceived by our founders to be a great church for national purposes."[1] The statement amounts to a public declaration that the spirit of L'Enfant's national church has been incarnated at last. To any admirer of the capital's first planner, the language is recognizable because those phrases originated with L'Enfant's 1791 plan for the federal city.[2] The statement also raises questions. Take the reference to Jesus Christ. Did L'Enfant ever mean to make such an invocation with his church? Then there is the reference to "our founders." Does it refer to the nation's founders or to the cathedral's founders? Or are we to believe they are one and the same, even though the founding of the nation took place more than a century before the founding of the cathedral? In this simple announcement, one finds the whole puzzle of Washington National Cathedral: Is Washington National Cathedral L'Enfant's long-abandoned national church, or something else?

It was Henry Yates Satterlee, the cathedral's original bishop, who first publicly adopted L'Enfant's language.[3] It was also he who insisted that this notion of a national church be paired with a distinctly Christian worldview, and despite his sectarian commitments, it was also Satterlee who claimed the mantle of the Founders—the nation's founders. In his private journal, Satterlee invokes L'Enfant and George Washington: "Major L'Enfant, the architect employed under General Washington to lay out the plan of the Federal City, projected a State Church, to be built on the site of the present Patent Office, as a kind of American Westminster Abbey, yet to belong to no denomination. . . . The State Church was never built; yet here was the germ of the idea of a Christian cathedral."[4] Satterlee attempts to reconcile L'Enfant's vision with what seems to be his own. That L'Enfant's nondenominational, public temple should germinate a private, Christian cathedral seems a case of nature taking its course rather than a strategic appropriation on Satterlee's part. In a way, Satterlee was right. By the time he emerged as leader of the project, the country's Deist roots had decayed, and with them had wilted the Founders' grand classical visions. In their place was a growing Christian nationalism and a Gothic Revival, which Satterlee would leverage to will the church into existence.

This chapter begins the story of how Satterlee's cathedral laid claim to the legacy of L'Enfant and demonstrates how that claim, well-intentioned though it may have been, has done considerable damage to that legacy. The disconnect between L'Enfant's and Satterlee's vision has implications that ripple beyond the branding of a single church. These two visions represent very different trajectories for what we now call the American Civil Religion. Each of the two churches, one frozen in the imagination of the early republic, the other now concretized in limestone on Wisconsin Avenue, acts as a touchstone for a civil-religious philosophy that precludes the other. Satterlee's church not only departs in significant ways from L'Enfant's but also subverts L'Enfant's vision and, by extension, undermines the Founders' civil-religious sensibilities even as it purports to carry their banner.

Three Differences

There are three differences between Satterlee's church and L'Enfant's church worth highlighting right away. First, perhaps the clearest evidence of Satterlee's subversion is that, whereas L'Enfant refused to assign the church a sectarian identity, Satterlee saw an opportunity for the Episcopal Church to assume custody of the nation's spiritual life. Satterlee acknowledged that L'Enfant had no affiliation in mind, yet he presumed that L'Enfant's idea was "the germ" of a Christian sanctuary, and a decidedly Anglican one.[5] Today, the leaders of Washington National Cathedral present the cathedral to the public as a house of prayer for all people, and they take this identity seriously by pursuing an ecumenical and civic mission perhaps unrivaled by any other American church. However, most visitors to the cathedral may not know that this church is also a diocesan headquarters for the Episcopal Church, that its formal name is the Cathedral Church of Saint Peter and Saint Paul, that it holds regular worship services in the Anglican liturgical tradition, and that it has no official relationship with the federal government. My point is not to suggest that the cathedral's administration conceals the church's sectarian identity for some nefarious purpose, but to point out that in the interest of its more public mission, the cathedral's sectarian commitments often get overlooked.

In a 1903 address to the Episcopal Church's Eighth Annual Convention, Satterlee emphasized the cathedral's role in guiding the nation: "The same influences which are tending to make the United States the richest and most powerful of all nations may, and probably will, make it also the most secularized country of the world."[6] Where Satterlee differed from L'Enfant was in the matter of sectarianism. Satterlee believed that secularism would lead to a national moral rot "unless the Church of Christ ceaselessly and with strenuous efforts overcomes the evil with good."[7] L'Enfant believed that to allow any private church to fill the role of educating citizens in the national moral code would contradict the very ideals of the Founding Fathers. Satterlee believed that to allow any other private church to fill this role would be irresponsible. Only the "Church of Christ"—and by that he meant an Anglican-led Protestant front—could save the nation and the world from evil.

Second, L'Enfant never intended the national church to be so far removed from the city core. As his drawings make clear, he would have placed the church on the same plane as, and in immediate proximity to, the major government buildings, one joint among many that would frame the tissue of the city. The church was to be situated not dominantly but conjunctively. Satterlee's church, on the other hand, sits well apart from the district's political nerve center, atop a high bluff called Mt. St. Alban or St. Alban's Hill. There it presides over the capital like a divine magistrate. In 1990, when cathedral leaders marked the building's centennial, they celebrated the symbolism of this unique placement: "And it would be located at one of the highest points in the city, overlooking the halls of government, the monuments, the signs and symbols of a nation's life."[8] Even today, casual observers riding in taxis, rideshares, and busses; cycling along bike paths; or strolling along sidewalks are often surprised when they look to the northwest of the city's monumental core and notice the cathedral looming in the semidistance.

The third difference is that L'Enfant did not imagine a Gothic church. Although he never prescribed an architectural style for the building, his and Washington's overall plan for the city emphasized a neoclassical palate that would embody the values of republicanism, progress, reason, and sylvan beauty. The Gothic Revival had not yet begun to flourish in the United States, and many Americans still associated medievalism with the superstitions from

which their forebears fled. The affinities in both style and philosophy between American and contemporary French political culture, not to mention
the gaping rift between the revolutionary republics and the British monarchy, seem to foreclose any possibility that, back in 1791, Pierre L'Enfant would
have looked to England as a model. Almost surely, he had in mind the classi-
cally domed Pantheon of Paris, not the severely towered abbey of Westminster. A century later, when Satterlee took the helm of the cathedral project,
Gothic style was back in vogue, and for an anglophile like him, the English
Gothic was especially captivating. That such a medieval landmark would stand
out from its neoclassical environs was a point of pride for Satterlee.

Just as Washington National Cathedral's claim to L'Enfant can be traced
directly back to Satterlee, so can each of these three differences. The story of
how the cathedral came to be what it is today—an homage, an appropriation,
a subversion—cannot be separated from this man's own story. Like the French
artist whose vision he claimed, Satterlee was a man of rigid convictions and
aristocratic privilege, and he pursued his vision with a sense of sacred duty.
Also like L'Enfant, he took on the project at a time when the nation was full
of gilded self-confidence. Whereas L'Enfant had foreseen the United States as
a global empire, Satterlee had witnessed the country become a global power,
and his cathedral took on a sense of civil-religious conquest. Both planners
believed the United States needed a moral code to guide its growth, but they
were the products of very different civil religious philosophies.

A Brief History of Origins

Throughout the second half of the nineteenth century, the Protestant Episcopal Church suffered an identity crisis. Its dispersed parishes and dioceses
were beset with disagreements, infighting, anemic growth, and shrinking
influence. Leaders and members of the church could not agree on how high
or low the liturgy ought to be, whether the Book of Common Prayer needed
drastic reform, whether the church was sufficiently evangelical, what role
the church ought to play in public affairs, and numerous other issues.[9] In
reality, these tensions had shaped the Episcopal Church since the Revolution, when the church was forced to rethink its links to England. Without a
centralized authority to make such decisions, the church exhibited no clear
strategy, which led only to more hand-wringing.

These frustrations are captured in the 1887 lament of famed Episcopal
preacher Phillips Brooks, who feared the church was fast becoming "a small,
fantastic sect, aping foreign ways, and getting more and more out of sympa-

thy with the great life of the country."[10] The problem was exacerbated by the success of more populist movements, such as the Baptists and Methodists, as well as by the staggering growth of Anglicanism's chief rival, Roman Catholicism.[11] Caught between the wave of frontier evangelism and the monolith of "Papism," the Episcopal Church spent its General Conventions debating how to maintain relevance as an American faith. Its numbers were strong, even growing, in parts of the American Northeast and South, such as New York and Virginia, but beyond these strongholds, the denomination struggled to establish a presence.

Even as debates raged over big-picture issues, day-to-day frustrations continued to mount. One of the most stubborn controversies had to do with the pew rent system, a common practice in the nineteenth century in which churches rented pews to families of means. When, as a result, space for lower-income families became scarce, bishops were inclined to look for immediate and short-term solutions, which usually meant building larger or additional sanctuaries and missions. Such was the case in the fall of 1890 when rectors from two of Washington, DC's largest and most elite parishes became frustrated with the lack of space for Sunday services. The number of churchgoers was growing; between 1880 and 1910, the city's population more than doubled, from about 150,000 to well over 300,000.[12] In addition, when Congress was in session, the population of well-off Washingtonians in the city's urban center ballooned.

George Douglas, who led Saint John's Church, in Lafayette Square, and Randolph McKim, who led the Church of the Epiphany downtown, believed the best answer to this old problem was to build more space. They set their sights on the Dupont Circle area, where families with new, post–Civil War wealth were building luxury homes. The neighborhood was not far from the original plot L'Enfant had identified for a national church a century earlier, but this coincidence was likely lost on the rectors, whose hope was not so much to make room for the poor as it was to build a gleaming cathedral in the heart of the capital so as to attract the growing number of government aristocrats.[13] They knew that pooling resources from their two parishes alone would not be adequate to construct a new cathedral, so they considered a cathedral foundation, which would allow them to seek resources from outside their own parishes.[14]

The idea was ambitious by diocesan standards but sensible in that it addressed the pew rent problem. If more space were needed, then by all means it should be built—and why not make that space a jewel in the capital city's growing garland of monuments? With the City Beautiful movement in full swing and the nation's prosperity at a historic high, Washington, DC, was filling up fast with iconic structures. Organizations like the American Institute of Architects and the Park Commission were promoting more aggressive planning and building measures for the capital, including an effort to reanimate the L'Enfant plan from a century earlier.[15] These were heady days for the district. Monuments, educational institutions, upscale neighborhoods, parks, and museums were being planned or built with unprecedented optimism.

As Douglas and McKim continued discussing the cathedral idea, they allowed it to expand still further. The freedom to raise money beyond their parish boundaries meant they could imagine a sanctuary that was not just larger in space but also in mission. This cathedral could headquarter an entirely new diocese in the nation's capital. This was an idea that had been tossed around Episcopal conferences for decades, at least as far back as the early 1850s, but that never seemed viable, because the city was not large enough. Washington remained part of the Maryland diocese. Now, with its population swelling and its prominence at an all-time high, the federal district seemed a good spot for a new diocese, and more. This cathedral could stand as a symbol for the Communion itself and provide a unifying and consolidating influence after nearly a century of churchwide friction over matters of liturgy, policy, and even theology. In a letter to Douglas from William Reed Huntington, a major church influencer whom I discuss below, there seemed to be an understanding that this cathedral could both represent the whole Episcopalian Church and deliver "a special message for our countrymen."[16] In other words, maybe the cathedral could do more than address the quotidian problem of pew space. Perhaps it could be a revitalizing influence on the church and nation in some way.

The two rectors knew that announcing such a vision prematurely might elicit more criticism than support, but they remained upbeat. Douglas in particular seemed well prepared to take on a project of notoriety. Not yet forty years old, he sported a square jaw and thick mustache, a look softened somewhat by his spectacles and trim build (fig. 2.1). He was also a man of means. Having married into a wealthy Newport, Rhode Island, family, he moved comfortably in social circles. His rectorship of the Lafayette Square parish was also a source of prestige. One block from the White House, Saint John's is famously known as "the Church of the Presidents," as every president since James Madison has attended services there and several early presidents were communicants.[17] Records also indicate that as early as 1816, the church em-

Fig. 2.1. George William Douglas, leader of St. John's Church, Lafayette Square, Washington, DC, late nineteenth century. Washington National Cathedral Archives

ployed a committee to accommodate the sitting president. For more than two centuries, the church has reserved a pew exclusively for use by the nation's chief executive.[18]

Douglas was also a confident sermonizer. He spoke in an opulent style, and he was not shy about making patriotic encomiums. In one published Thanksgiving Day homily titled "Four Hundred Years of American History as Testimony to Christianity," he stated: "I believe that that which the history of these United States has proved and is proving to the minds of men who are really thoughtful and really conscientious is this above all else,—the absolute necessity of spiritual ideals and religious methods to meet the conditions of mankind as man."[19] Douglas concluded that the civic force of Christianity is the answer to the world's dangers, which include materialism and imperialism.

Fig. 2.2. Randolph Harrison McKim, leader of the Church of the Epiphany in downtown Washington, DC, late nineteenth century. Washington National Cathedral Archives

Between his high-profile connections and high-style oratory, Douglas was already a force in Episcopal circles, and he seemed the perfect candidate to lead the new cathedral.

Not quite a decade older than Douglas, McKim was far more seasoned both in experience and appearance. Having served in the Confederate Army as a soldier, field chaplain, lieutenant, and even aide-de-camp to Stonewall Jackson, he had the bearing of a mature military man: thick gray sideburns, a piercing stare (fig. 2.2). In 1910, he published *A Soldier's Recollections: Leaves from the Diary of a Young Confederate*, in which, among other apologias for the Confederacy, he defended the time on a clear April night in 1861 when he and six other students at the University of Virginia sneaked into the campus rotunda, forced their way to the roof, and set the flag of the South to waving.[20]

It was only days after this exploit that President Abraham Lincoln called for Virginia's complement of Union soldiers and the state responded by throwing in its lot with the South. As many as 155,000 Virginian men, McKim included, fought in the Confederate forces, while only 32,000 fought for the Union.[21] To his death, McKim believed he had been fighting despotism.[22] For all his grit, however, he was rather cultivated. He earned a doctorate from William and Mary College, had a command of several languages, and was a scholar who published on both biblical and American history.[23]

The two rectors made a formidable duo. While Douglas provided youth and a touch of glamor, McKim brought maturity and mettle. In 1890, they brought their idea to William Paret, the sixty-three-year-old bishop of Maryland, whose diocese included Washington, DC, and whose permission was essential to the project. Paret had the weary appearance of someone who had spent an entire career gatekeeping (fig. 2.3). He had tired, suspicious eyes and a mouth that seemed forever drawn into a skeptical frown. He was every bit the contrast to Douglas and McKim. Paret was known to be a staunch conservative both liturgically and administratively. He was also strict with the church purse and resistant to grandiose ideas. In his own *Reminiscences*, he highlights his aversion to costly "brick and mortar" solutions to problems of limited space, unless such solutions are "an absolute necessity."[24] He favored instead more creative and conservative use of existing facilities. He credits this tendency in getting him his appointment as rector of the Church of the Epiphany in Washington, the position that led to his promotion to bishop of Maryland eight years later.[25] More concerning still for Douglas and McKim, Paret opposed the relatively new tendency within the Episcopal Church to build large diocesan cathedrals, which he felt smacked too much of Oxford Movement Anglicanism and its gross affinities with "Romanish" ritual.

Douglas and McKim decided to limit their pitch. They sent a letter proposing the idea of a new diocese with a new cathedral, but with the nominal intention of better managing church growth in the region. They kept to themselves their vision of a great national center for the church, a place to which Episcopalians everywhere could look for unity, direction, and pride. The only clue that they had bigger ideas was their mention of forming a cathedral foundation, which would allow the project to solicit resources from outside the area more easily. Initially, Paret seemed enthusiastic. "Unless something shall greatly modify my judgment," he replied by letter, "I could be ready heartily to act with you." He added, however, that he could not support a project that

Fig. 2.3. William Paret, Bishop of Maryland, late nineteenth century. Washington National Cathedral Archives

might shrink or otherwise undermine his own Baltimore-based diocese. "Baltimore shall hold equal place with Washington as a Diocesan Center."[26] Douglas and McKim knew that this condition put their long-term goals at risk, but they were encouraged by Paret's tone.

As time wore on, Paret's parochialism and skepticism got the better of his support. He began to express reservations both about building a large cathedral and, more important, about dividing up the Maryland diocese to create a new diocese specific to Washington, DC, but he also knew there were serious considerations that needed to be made with respect to population growth in the region. Paret was torn. He could not bring himself to support an initiative that so clearly violated his philosophy on church governance, yet he could not deny the exigencies the rectors were trying to solve. With the booming population, the Episcopal Church needed to solve problems related to space, logistics, and governance. Douglas and McKim were trying to do just that, even though the scope and expense of their approach made him nervous. Paret decided to take a middling approach. Noting his concerns, he gave conditional permission to explore the idea.[27]

As word got out that church leaders were thinking about a diocese specific to Washington, DC, and a grand cathedral to match, momentum built quickly. Members of the local parishes began to offer property and funds. Episcopalians outside the diocese began to express enthusiasm. Douglas, feeling encouraged by the public support, arranged another meeting with Paret, this time to reveal the project's true long-term goals. No doubt concerned that Paret's reticence would get in the way of the project's progress, Douglas also revealed that he believed the cathedral chapter should be independent of the controlling diocese and its bishop. Paret balked, but over the following few months, public enthusiasm only increased. He received scores of letters pledging support for the project. Feeling himself not up to the task of reversing momentum, he soon approved the appointment of a committee to select a site.[28] From this point, the project moved into the full light of scrutiny. The logistics of acquiring a charter, addressing diocesan organizational challenges, finding money and space, establishing a foundation and committees, and drawing up architectural plans got under way.

Paret, however, was not done vacillating. There were instances when he appeared to be wholly invested in the project, providing prompt reviews and approvals for business, but such instances were offset by more changes of mind. In one meeting with several wealthy laymen who wanted to support the project, a meeting that should have been perfunctory and positive, Paret peppered the discussion with reservations instead of simply welcoming the proffered support.[29] In another instance, Paret's objection to the inclusion of non-Episcopalians in the cathedral body of incorporators nearly derailed the cathedral's hopes of a charter.[30] Perhaps the most galling reversal came after Douglas and the cathedral committee had managed to produce and submit a draft of a charter for Congress's approval. The achievement had been hard-won and Paret had granted his approval earlier, but it did not last. In the weeks that followed, Paret changed his mind, citing his concern that the charter granted too much power to incorporators and too little to the diocesan bishop. He threatened to rescind the charter application and rewrite it himself. With each debacle, Douglas had to salve the committee members and revive the bishop's assent.[31]

As time wore on, donors and organizers became more frustrated with Paret.

Major bequests were on the verge of being pulled. Committee members were threatening to resign. Mary Elizabeth Mann, one of the most prominent, dedicated, and informed members of the committee, as well as one of the original authors of the charter draft, penned a scathing rebuke to the bishop: "If you persist in your present course, of exercising singly the authority possessed by the Committee, only, you will prevent us from obtaining any charter at all from the Congress. And if you force the issue, there will remain no alternative but for me to lay your letters before the chairmen of the two committees."[32] At one point in the letter, Mann quotes a communication from Paret to her personally, in which the bishop asked her to cede her authority on the charter committee to him: " 'Can you not yield it to me and give your effective and valued help to my leading?' I say *no*," she replies emphatically, "for the good and sufficient reason, that, in my estimation, you do not possess one characteristic of a successful leader."[33] The relationship appeared unsalvageable, but Douglas again tried to repair things. He offered explanations to Mann and convinced Paret to keep quiet about the matter, and to avoid talking to Mann at all costs. Mann was calmed for a time, but she soon resigned her position in bitterness.

Douglas marshaled all of his energy and charisma to rally the remaining committee members, and together they pressured Paret not to make good on his threat. In a lengthy missive to Paret on October 14, 1892, Douglas reminded the bishop that the charter is *"permissory* not *mandatory*, and it need never be acted upon,"[34] He also appealed to Paret's reputation and sense of shame, reporting that "prominent clergymen" were privately attacking Paret's motives, insinuating that he was delaying the project under false pretenses just to protect his own diocese. "I dislike, unspeakably, to say this," Douglas assured Paret, "but you ought to know." Finally, Douglas begged. He addressed Paret as though he were trying to prevent a tyrant from committing an atrocity. "I beg you, and all of those who know the situation and are your friends would beg you, let it alone now. It is too late to do anything but harm." Douglas signed the letter with an urging that Paret should burn it after reading, and that enclosed there was another letter, presumably with a similar but more diplomatic message, signed by the committee members. In the end, Paret was convinced that to rescind the charter application would set the project back a year, whereas to amend it after its approval would cost little time and effort. By January 1893, the cathedral had a charter from Congress authorizing construction, but relationships were wounded.[35]

Douglas was exasperated. He began to take more frequent and lengthy trips away from Washington. Officially, the trips were to rest his ailing wife, but it seemed more than coincidental that the further out of control the project became, and the more he had to mollify Paret's anxieties, the more he tended to excuse himself. The final straw was when Paret changed his mind on an important matter relating to the cathedral's architectural style, a violation of one of the conditions of the project's most generous donor, Phoebe Hearst. Paret had not planned for the consequences that this latest reversal would entail, and yet again he found himself responsible for a threat to the project's progress. Yet again, he relied on Douglas to open the impasse, but by 1895, Douglas had had enough. He resigned and accepted a plush New England rectorship, which he resolved to keep despite pleas from committee members to change his mind.[36] In a muddled power move, Paret rejected Douglas's resignation but refused to speak to him on the matter. He also refused to assume the new bishopric himself, even though he was the most eligible candidate as an interim replacement. Five years after its inception, the dream of a new diocese and cathedral in Washington, DC, seemed doomed.

Enter Henry Yates Satterlee

Still in New York serving as rector of Calvary Church, Henry Yates Satterlee was absorbed with his own parish business when the cathedral project in Washington, DC, was quietly collapsing. He was not even present at the 1895 Minnesota conference where an election to replace Douglas as bishop of the new diocese was under way, the same election in which Satterlee was elected in absentia and unbeknownst to himself. Arthur Powell, rector at Grace Church in Baltimore, had been present at the conference and reported to Bishop Satterlee by letter on the election proceedings: "I would I could give you some idea of the remarkable way in which your election was brought about," he wrote. He described how the procedure seemed to resist resolution at every turn, how all present seemed to suffer from "great anxiety of heart," how the whole process seemed beset with "strife and bitterness." Each vote turned up mixed results, giving no one candidate a clear path to the bishopric. Satterlee's name was included in the mix, and more and more his profile seemed suited to the challenges ahead. Powell concluded: "When they returned, with marvelous unanimity, they selected you as their Bishop; and no sooner had they done that than a peace which passeth all understanding settled down upon the Convention."[37] To those present, Satterlee had been called by God. The plainness of a divine hand in the process seemed to ratify both his rise to the bishopric and the decision to organize the diocese and build the great church once and for all.

Upon hearing the report, Satterlee, too, seemed inspired. He had been an effective and popular rector, first in Wappinger's Falls, New York, then in New York City at the high-profile Calvary Church. He had previously passed up opportunities for promotion, including a bishopric, but this moment was somehow different.[38] He felt called to consent. When his election was made public, the *New York Times* reported that the new diocese in Washington would be led by someone in whom "the earnest Christian, well-equipped scholar and clergyman, and the man of business are seen in rare harmony and proportion."[39] The *Washington Examiner* recognized Satterlee's work as "the broadest and soundest kind. He unites conservative churchmanship with unflagging evangelistic and humanitarian zeal. He is an eloquent preacher, a most wise and kind pastor, and the efficient organizer and inspirer of a wide-reaching and many-sided work."[40] The articles make no mention of any extradiocesan or extradenominational ambitions he might be harboring. Satterlee's imagination, though, had been stirred (fig. 2.4).

Whereas Paret had embraced the idea of a new diocese for the nation's capital but resisted the idea of a grand cathedral, and whereas Douglas and McKim had actively sought a new diocese as a unifying center for the nation's Episcopalians while promoting the idea of a grand cathedral, Satterlee envisioned a civil-religious polestar, something cathedral leaders would continue to affirm more than a century later as "the spiritual home for a robust and young nation."[41] Under the direction of Bishop Satterlee, this church would not only serve the Washington diocese, or even the whole Episcopal Church, or even, for that matter, the global Anglican Communion. This church would serve the nation itself and thence influence the whole world. It would claim the legacy of L'Enfant.

Satterlee's Blue-Blooded Path

Henry Yates Satterlee's upbringing was a master class in the norms of American aristocratic life in the nineteenth century. His paternal grandfather, Edward Rathbone Satterlee, was a wealthy businessman and pillar of the Hudson River Valley community. Henry's father, Edward Rathbone's son, also named Edward, was a talented artist and collector. Henry's mother, Jane Anna Yates, was also descended from a prominent New York family. Together, Edward and Jane pursued a life of self-cultivation. They favored paint-

Fig. 2.4. Henry Yates Satterlee, first bishop of Washington, DC.
Washington National Cathedral Archives

ing, music, and study to the world of business, and they devoted themselves to their children. After a failed effort to establish himself as an artist in New York City, Edward brought the family back to upstate New York, where they took up residence in a stately Dutch mansion—the former home of several New York governors and, at the time, still the home of Anna's grandfather Yates. While there, Edward finally agreed to join his father's business.

Flush with wealth and now having the run of an expansive estate, the family built an idyllic life. The children were educated by tutors and were encouraged to spend their free time reading, exploring, and playing. Young Henry became fond of books, insects, experiments, even social events, such as his parents' balls.[42] Charles Henry Brent, author of a 1916 hagiography of Henry Yates Satterlee, describes Henry's childhood as having "a peculiar fragrance that is attached to congenial home life under the best conditions."[43]

Brent refers to Edward as "the companion and friend of his children. . . . His were times when high minded men felt the responsibility and joy of domestic ties."[44] Jane is given no less credit as a devoted parent, and it is clear that Henry received all the benefits of a cultured, sheltered, and resource-rich childhood.

In 1856, when Henry was thirteen, Edward decided to make a second go of life as an artist in New York City. He moved the family to a posh neighborhood near Madison Square Park. Henry was enrolled in the Columbia Grammar and Preparatory School, where he completed a course of study in classics under the direction of Charles Anthon, the famous translator and professor. Two years later, at the age of fifteen, Henry passed the entrance exams to Columbia College, but his university education would have to wait. Edward wanted to expose his son to the architectural and artistic wonders of Europe.

In 1858, Edward and Jane Satterlee set sail for Europe with their two oldest children. For nine months, they toured the continent and took a relatively brief excursion to the Holy Land. Edward had hoped it would entice Henry to consider a career in the art world.[45] He led his family from London to Paris to Vienna to Rome and practically everywhere in between, immersing them in the museums, galleries, palaces, and libraries of Europe's great cities. The family also took time to enjoy the company of other patrician American travelers, who would periodically get together for small parties.

To some extent, Edward's plan worked. Henry's latent interests in art, architecture, and culture began to blossom. He willingly absorbed the history and ideals of Christian Europe. He embraced the opportunity to study, he wrote florid descriptions of the Italian landscape, and he commented in detail on the paintings and drawings of the artists whose work he observed in the Berlin museums.[46] In a letter to his aunts back in New York, the precocious teenager describes his travels in Germany: "The Royal Chapel is in this Palace and it is magnificently fitted up. The floor is beautifully inlaid and the cross, back of the pulpit, composed entirely of precious stones, is said to have cost over five hundred thousand dollars."[47] He continues in this style, even joking at one point that upon visiting the King's Palace, "we were requested to put on list shoes that were half too large for us, I suspect the reason was for us to polish their bare floors, by sliding along, as that is the only possible way to keep the shoes on."[48] He wrote from memory of other rooms, accoutrements, and paintings, as well as interactions with docents, journeys on trains, and other details that would have been lost on the average teenager.

During one stint of several weeks in London, Henry immersed himself in the British Museum, reading book after book on English history. When the curator gently admonished him for taking on books that were too advanced, Henry was irked and redoubled his study for several more days.[49] This fifteen-year-old boy was not some sullen youth held hostage to the whims of his parents. He embraced the opportunity to learn, and he honed his ability to communicate insights. He also began to develop strident views on the role of architecture and urban planning in civilized cultures. When the family finally returned to New York in 1859, Henry was a full-blown Anglophile, and, at sixteen years old, he could not have been more prepared to pursue his postsecondary education.

In 1861, at the end of his sophomore year in college, Henry found himself at a crossroad. Like many of his university peers, he was inspired to join the Union army. For both Union and Confederate regiments, soldiers had to be at least eighteen years old to fight, a fact of no concern to Satterlee, who had turned eighteen that year; however, men between the ages of eighteen and twenty also needed parental permission.[50] Henry pled his case to his father, but Edward would provide consent only on the condition that Henry earn an appointment to West Point. In addition to the family's homes in New York City and the Hudson River Valley, Edward maintained a family estate on the river near West Point, where he kept much of his prized art collection.[51] A West Point appointment would not only grant Henry automatic distinction as an officer but also keep him close to home, at least for the time being.

Henry accepted the condition and set about preparing his application. At six feet, two inches tall and full-bodied, he was virile in appearance. Throughout his life, he was pictured with a resolute stare, set jaw, burly mustache, and a thickly coiffed head of hair. He was said to have a soldierly air about him.[52] All of these endowments, combined with his moral certitude and self-discipline, gave Satterlee the makings of a would-be military leader, but the letters of application he had prepared and hand-delivered to congressmen with such care received taciturn rejections. All spots at West Point were filled. Satterlee was a young man of talent, conviction, and connection, but it was not enough. He would have to find some other way to distinguish himself.[53]

By now it is likely clear that there are telling parallels between the upbringing of Pierre L'Enfant and that of Henry Yates Satterlee. Both boys were born into families with aristocratic connections. Each had an artistic father who harbored ambitions for his son's artistic interests. Each had a father who gave extended tours of national and religious landscapes and buildings, highlighting the way these spaces informed civic and moral culture. Both young men chose to defer careers in art for careers in battle, inspired as they were by the idea of personal and national glory. Of course, whereas L'Enfant managed to join the ranks of military heroes, Satterlee was denied and forced to find a different outlet for the same ambitions.

Here is where the men's paths diverge. Nearing graduation at the age of nineteen, Satterlee began to feel drawn to the ministry. His father wanted him to consider a career in the art world, and his options in the professions were unlimited. He had family members with connections in law, politics, and medicine, but the more Satterlee considered the ministry, the less it seemed like just another option and the more it seemed like a calling. In due time he was directed to Cleveland Coxe, the rector of Calvary Church, a Manhattan Episcopal congregation that was popular among New York's "old-monied elite" and that was conveniently located just a few blocks from the Satterlee home.[54] As a historian and theologian of some note in the New York diocese, Coxe took an immediate liking to Satterlee, and he helped navigate Satterlee once and for all into the Episcopal Church.

Coxe was also known for his anti-Catholic sentiments, which likely played some role later in Satterlee's own prejudices. No doubt Satterlee's Anglophilia also influenced his decision. As the American member church of Anglicanism's global dominion, the Episcopal Church reawakened interests that had roots in Satterlee's tour of Europe, where he had grown so fond of English culture. Like all patriots, though, he believed America could improve upon old traditions. "European cathedrals," he would write during the cathedral's early days, "are all fettered by Mediaeval traditions and customs, which really paralyze the real work of a Cathedral. In America, we are free, [and it is our task] to separate the wheat from the tares."[55] As Satterlee saw it, the beauty of Episcopalism was the way it could discern and apply a better way of religious life.

Nineteenth-century Episcopalism also reflected a certain cachet. The denomination was relatively small in size, and between the mid-eighteenth and mid-nineteenth century, it struggled to remain relevant among the country's frontier communities; but in the Northeast it was an enclave for society's elect. At the height of the Gilded Age, the Episcopal Church claimed a remarkable number of old-family aristocrats, not unlike the Satterlees, as well as tycoons of the nouveau riche, including the Vanderbilts and Morgans. It also named among its past and present members a startling number of politicians and other high government officials, including several former presidents. And with roots stretching all the way back to Jamestown, Episcopalism combined all of its wealth and influence with an antique American prestige. Satterlee, ever drawn to his "betters," felt right at home.

Satterlee's formal career is marked by a conservative approach to matters of doctrine and a progressive approach to social initiatives. He promoted protections for factory girls, night schooling for men and boys, and a library for the town.[56] In 1893, at the height of his Calvary ministry and, incidentally, the same year Washington National Cathedral was chartered by the Episcopal Church's Maryland leaders, the US economy was halted by an economic depression that would last several years. In New York City, where unemployment peaked at around 35 percent, twenty thousand people became homeless within the space of a few months.[57] Satterlee established a mission near Calvary's chapel for the less well-off members of his parish, many of whom could no longer worship in Calvary's chapel thanks to the pew rent system. He started a workingmen's club to foster good character and self-reliance among the neediest of his flock. He also enlisted some of his better-off parishioners to visit the area hospitals to minister to the sick; he assigned others to minister to the jailed or otherwise dispossessed, an effort that saw 83 prisoners released, 142 women freed from the courts, and 211 people assigned lawyers.[58]

And yet, still a patrician at heart, Satterlee was not comfortable with the "social gospel" label. He worried that it elevated scientific and secular concerns above the spiritual ideals that must always be the cornerstone of the church.[59] In addition, while his ministry goals were progressive, his principles and style remained traditional, even conservative. He imposed strict behavioral rules within the growing list of institutions connected to Calvary's ministry. On one occasion, he singled out from the pulpit a member of his parish who had been living "in immoral relations with his housekeeper." In another instance, when he felt he had been affronted in his home by a good friend, he did not hesitate to "sharply express his mind," an act he considered a duty.[60] While he aggressively borrowed and spent money in pursuit of his social initiatives, he also devoted precious resources to the redesign of Calvary's chapel and liturgy to better align the parish with high Anglicanism's ritual, authority, and tradition. He became known as a "practical idealist" and a "genuine force for civic righteousness."[61] Progressives could be inspired by his high ideals; conservatives could be consoled by his uncompromising Anglicanism. The formula worked. Whether at Zion or Calvary, his initiatives flourished, his flock multiplied, and his reputation grew.[62]

Satterlee Resurrects the Cathedral

Satterlee was consecrated bishop of Washington on March 25, 1896, at his beloved Calvary Church in New York. Before he arrived in Washington, DC, a month later, he could not have known just how tattered the cathedral project had become. The cathedral still lacked a well-articulated mission just as much as it lacked reliable funding, but how close the project had come to death was likely lost on Satterlee. Only after he got settled in Washington did he see how Paret's hapless equivocations, Douglas's final abandonment, and the donors' threats—to say nothing of other advisory committee members who had been flirting with quitting for some time—had given the project a pallor from which it might never recover.

In his "Private Record," Satterlee recalled those early days. In addition to the project's more public obstacles, he noted three events that opened his eyes to the extent of the challenges:

> I visited Bishop Paret, at Baltimore, and he told me that there had been some friction in the Board of Trustees. Dr. Douglas resigned his position, both as Dean and as trustee.
>
> The second event was a visit I received, in Calvary Rectory, from Mr. Flagg and Col. Britton, in which they brought plans with them. I was scrupulously noncommittal, of course.
>
> The third event was a visit that I paid to the Cathedral grounds about a month before I became Bishop. I was deeply distressed. I saw that of the eighteen acres not more than half could be utilized.[63]

The problems Satterlee faced could be described in almost any terms: structural, attitudinal, political, spiritual, and certainly financial. Ultimately, though, they boiled down to rhetorical challenges. The breakdowns that plagued the cathedral project almost always had to do with breakdowns in communication and with what Satterlee felt was the proper message the cathedral leaders were sending to the public. In other words, Satterlee viewed his challenges as matters of relationships and branding. These problems could be split into two subgroups: the private, or internal, and the public, or external. Internally, there was no system for regular deliberation among the decision makers. Meetings were haphazardly scheduled and infrequent. Distances between parties too often necessitated mail, which was slow. Donors and board members were not being attended to, and relationships were breaking down. Externally, the project lacked a coherent vision. Although Episcopalians had hoped the cathedral would mitigate the communion's struggles with mission and identity, the cathedral seemed only to mirror them. It could not settle on a brand.

Addressing the Internal Problems

If one single act can capture Satterlee's command of private planning issues, it is perhaps the way he swept aside New York architect Earnest Flagg's design for the cathedral. A celebrated American architect trained at the Ecole des Beaux Arts in Paris, Flagg was asked to prepare two proposals for the cathedral design, one in Renaissance style, the other in Gothic. Prior to Satterlee's election, the building committee and Bishop Paret had voted unanimously to approve Flagg's Renaissance drawings. Despite some resistance from Randolph McKim, who vehemently opposed the Renaissance style, a sense of inevitability had collected around Flagg's classic vision.[64] The design included a three-hundred-foot tall dome, cupola-topped towers, Greek crosses, and Corinthian columns. The entryway was to feature a soaring, rounded arch, a recessed portico, and, to cap it all off, a pediment complete with an ornate tympanum (fig. 2.5).[65] It was a full-throated Renaissance display, as if the Pantheon of Paris had been used as a starting point, then elevated to something even more sublime.

Affirming up front that he did not much care which of his designs the committee chose, Flagg nevertheless made clear which he thought was better. In a memorandum submitted with his drawings, he noted, "Men cast off gothic art just as they cast off gothic superstition. The Renaissance style is emblematic of modern times and liberal ideas."[66] In other words, he felt that the Renaissance style was more consistent with the spirit of the city and the origins and ideals of the nation. Who knows but that L'Enfant would have approved? Later, Flagg expressed to a *Washington Post* reporter other reasons for his preference: the Renaissance approach would allow for better sightlines, more space, more grandeur, and greater longevity by many years, thanks to advances in technology. "It seems to me foolish," he concluded, "to copy the Gothic style of the old cathedrals."[67]

To his voice and that of the committee was added that of the Park Commission, which was also clear in its preference for a classic style. Finally, the cathedral's most generous benefactor, Phoebe Hearst, was obliged to exert her considerable influence. When McKim, still dogging people to change their minds, wrote to Hearst to see if her financial support was contingent on her preference for the Renaissance style, she responded: "I do consider that

Fig. 2.5. Ernest Flagg's drawing of the Renaissance-style cathedral that was rejected after Satterlee's election as bishop. Washington National Cathedral Archives

the Trustees are under obligation to carry out the above mentioned plans and I wish it to be emphatically understood that if they break faith with me, I shall feel at liberty to withdraw my gift."[68] Consensus had emerged on all fronts. By the time Satterlee became bishop the following year, the matter seemed to be settled.

Yet the monolith that rises today from the top of Mt. St. Alban is a model of Gothic architecture with a distinctly English flavor. The building is a marvel by any standard, but there is nothing remotely Renaissance about it.[69] As for Flagg, his work is nowhere to be found on the cathedral close. Whence the total change? Like McKim, Satterlee had always been passionately in favor of a Gothic cathedral. Long before he was ever in charge of the cathedral project, he had fallen in love with English Gothic architecture, an affinity that became ingrained during his European tour as a youth. There is no doubt that Satterlee played a key role—likely the key role—in reimagining the cathedral in Gothic style, but he tried assiduously to conceal his part in the process. To him, Gothic was "God's style," and there could be no reason to think otherwise.[70] Whereas, at first, he managed to remain neutral on matters of style, his tendency to assert opinion as though it were a priori fact could be contained only so long.

One gets a hint of his plans in his "Private Record," quoted previously, where he uses the phrase "scrupulously noncommittal" to describe his reaction to the Renaissance plans. Hewlett observes with amazement that, in all the pages of Satterlee's "Private Record," which covers his tenure as bishop beginning in 1896, "there is not one mention of architectural style" until nearly a decade later. This lacuna is strange, given that architectural style was a subject that had consumed the board of trustees for so long and with such contention, to say nothing of the fact that it was a subject for which Satterlee himself had a strong passion since youth. When Satterlee did finally mention architectural style, he did so as if the matter were already settled in his favor. In January 1906, he acknowledged that at least two of his advisors "expressed with great emphasis their judgment that to accord with the Government buildings of Washington, the Cathedral ought to be built in the style of the classic Renaissance."[71] His next mention of architectural style did not come until six months later, when he simply reported that his advisory committee had agreed to correspond with architects in Europe and America who specialized exclusively in the Gothic style. Then, in December of the same year, he remarked, "I could scarcely have believed, six months ago, not only that the architects should have been the unanimous choice of the board, but that the architects, Chapter and Bishop should have been of one mind regarding the whole general character of a Gothic Cathedral."[72] Whatever role Satterlee might have played in changing the consensus is elided. His correspondence during this period is similarly scarce on the subject. The same goes for the board's minutes.

Working backward, one may find some clues as to what was going on behind the scenes. On December 29, 1905, Satterlee convened a meeting of the board of trustees. Prior to the meeting, he reminded the board members in a "strictly confidential" letter that "we can afford to make no mistake in so vital a matter as the choice of a plan for the Cathedral of our Church which is to stand for coming centuries in the Capital of the Country as a witness for Christ and as an inspiration for worship." Should the board be diverted into error on this most critical of decisions, the damage would be irreparable. Should the board choose well, on the other hand, financial support would "undoubtedly flow in." He followed these sentiments with this declaration: "I am sure . . . that the Gothic style of architecture appeals most strongly to the people at large for a Church building . . . therefore we may be most thankful that the Cathedral Board have already decided in favor of the Gothic style."[73] But there is no record that the board had met and arrived at this surprising agreement. Again, he communicated as though the choice were obvious and the matter essentially decided.

Satterlee was by all accounts a person of integrity. Were he a cynic, he might have stacked his advisory committee with only like-minded thinkers, but his handpicked advisors ranged from enthusiasts of the Gothic to lovers of the Renaissance; one advisor, Bernard S. Green, had overseen the construction of the Washington Monument, a marvel of an emergent modernism.[74] All of the evidence suggests that Satterlee was strong-minded and strong-willed but was also reluctant to strongarm his audience into assent. He was the type of person who regarded his views as self-evidently right—a function, perhaps, of a lifetime of privilege and affirmation. He presumed that people would naturally come around to share his view, or that God would so move them. In all things, his motives were pure, but his mind was intractable.

One of Satterlee's key practices was to get up close and personal with his target audiences. Satterlee was never known for soaring public sermons; Brent suggests his public oratory left something to be desired. "Line upon line, precept upon precept, here a little, there a little, was his method."[75] When he wanted to persuade someone of high standing or influence, he would get them alone, often take them on location to discuss the matter at hand, effect an almost deferential posture, and test their limits by asking leading questions or gently making assumptions to see where they might stand on an issue and whether they might be swayed. When he had rank, he might perform the same divide-and-conquer tactic, but he would assume a more austere posture, such as when he wrote the previously quoted note to his advisory committee. He used this tacking back and forth between intimacy and distance to his advantage. He would build a relationship, but within that relationship there were demarcations of place and authority that he would carefully exploit.

On one cold, snowy day in February, Satterlee insisted on bringing four of the advisory committee members to the then remote cathedral site to consider their reaction. In the "Private Record," he is not clear about any feedback he received in that instance. What is clear is that over time the committee was not shy about rejecting some of Satterlee's most cherished ideas, including how the cathedral would be situated on the close, his method for selecting an architect, and his preferred architectural style. One of those committee members would later admonish Satterlee in writing, stating that the mere fact that lots of people—meaning the public, not the committee or board members—preferred the Gothic style did not "seem reason enough for a choice. . . . We need correction of our tendency to settle things on the basis of our own private feeling."[76] After the February meeting on the close, Satterlee assessed the task he was up against. He recognized the complexity the relationships and perspectives involved. Unlike L'Enfant, however, he did not flail in the face of such complexity. Instead, he maintained his concord with the advisors and set about executing a long-term plan.

Two examples of his methodical approach come to mind. In 1896, the year of Satterlee's consecration as bishop, Flagg's designs came back with cost estimates, which were so high as to be disqualifying. Rather than task Flagg with reimagining his Renaissance conception in a more affordable way, Satterlee recognized an opportunity to undermine the consensus surrounding the design. After all, concerns over the prohibitive cost united those who preferred the Flagg design—Satterlee conveniently refers to the design as "tentative"—with those who opposed it. He reasoned that perhaps the board ought to table the idea until other, much more urgent matters were dispatched, such as erasing the overwhelming debt on the land and coming up with a more realistic construction budget, to say nothing of shoring up teetering relationships with the donors. As Jefferson had done with the L'Enfant plan, Satterlee leveraged practical concerns in order to conceal and advance his philosophical opposition.

He knew that this strategy might not deal a decisive blow to the Flagg design but that it could buy much-needed time to change the minds of key players. In his "Private Record," he declared with relief, "We were rid of all plans for the school and the Cathedral."[77] Satterlee did not report again on the matter of style for ten years, after the debt on the land was paid and construction could finally move forward. Not until June 1906 did he note with dispassionate finality that the board had agreed to consult Gothic architects only. "This cut off all who could draw beautiful plans but had had no actual experience in Gothic construction."[78] Indeed, all buildings on the close except for the Hearst School would be Gothic. That almost no mention of how this change was wrought was made by Satterlee or other board members in correspondence, journals, or public statements is a testament to Satterlee's quiet agility as a communicator.

Just as Satterlee harbored deep disagreements with the board's decision on the cathedral's style, he also opposed the land they had acquired for its construction. In the early days of Satterlee's tenure, the real estate market in Washington, DC, was extremely tight, and it was understood that the cathedral would be built on fourteen acres near Rock Creek Park that had been donated by Frances G. Newlands. This initial site was not ideal. It was sharply sloped and somewhat narrow, and it was farther from the city core than the organizers preferred, but it had the attractive feature of having been donated. Even so, this advantage seemed fragile. Early efforts to get the cathedral project going were in such disarray that board members feared Newlands would waver on his offer. Even the board members who were less enthusiastic about the Newlands site seemed resigned. It was the first, last, and only viable choice they had.

Satterlee, however, was in love with an unobtainable stretch of land at the top of St. Alban's Hill in the city's northwest quadrant. It was "the most beautiful and majestic situation in the whole District of Columbia for the coming Cathedral."[79] To him, it did not matter that the Newlands site was free. Its remoteness and layout were going to hamper construction. Plus, to accommodate the whole vision of the close, adjacent lots would need to be purchased at a premium, thus undercutting the advantages of a "free" donation. No doubt he tactfully highlighted these features when persuading the committee. What had been the cheapest—and therefore the best—option was growing less attractive every day. Meanwhile, there were indications that the St. Alban's property might be opening up for sale. "But, alas!" Satterlee lamented, "there were no funds in hand wherewith to purchase it."[80] Undeterred, he visited the site alone, "saw its magnificent view, and felt at once that this land on the corner of Massachusetts and Wisconsin Avenues was the site for the Cathedral."[81] Regardless of the foundation's existing commitments, the prohibitive costs, and the overwhelming logistics of changing sites, Satterlee was decided.

Satterlee knew of some board members who were, like him, unenthusiastic about the Newlands site, and he began to cultivate relationships with them. He also recognized that Phoebe Hearst remained perhaps the most essential piece to the entire puzzle. As the widow of the millionaire and former US senator George Hearst, her resources and influence had already proven invaluable. If the depth of her commitment could match the depth of her pockets, Satterlee reasoned, no challenge would seem insurmountable. She became the focus of his closest attention. Rather than allow the board to send her generic letters with updates or copies of minutes from the meetings, he made it a practice to write to her directly and to meet with her in person to provide updates, share concerns, and get her opinion on matters. In one key meeting, he took her to examine the Newlands site. Hewlett remarks that, during this trip, Satterlee "carefully led her to the conclusion that the land was unacceptable" and that she, not he, would need to persuade the board that it should be abandoned.[82] Satterlee's own record of the visit is oblique. He claimed that he did not share with Hearst his own feelings about the site but that she of her own accord remarked, "Bishop, the first time I saw this ground where they were going to put my school, I was sick at heart." He responded with characteristic deference, "I wish you would attend a meeting of the Cathedral Board and tell the trustees what you have told me." She replied, "I will do so gladly."

Satterlee described the board meeting that took place in the fall of 1897 when Hearst appeared and emphatically announced her opposition to the Newlands site. Once Hearst had her say with the members, effectively destabilizing all site planning, Satterlee rose to finish the job. Grimly, he peppered the board with numbers. The donated land came with costly and time-sensitive restrictions that would necessitate hundreds of thousands of dollars in spending. Only eight acres had been bought outright. Forty thousand dollars were already owed, a debt that he, as bishop, was responsible for seeing paid. And how could any bishop, he inquired, drum up the motivation to raise $40,000 for land about which neither he nor the project's chief benefactor felt anything but anxiety? The Newlands site was the one shred of structure to the whole plan for the Washington Cathedral; now it was disintegrating before the board's eyes. The mood in the room became gloomy. Board members who were already unsure of the project's future felt it was now certain to collapse. Outwardly, Satterlee remained grave, but inwardly he exulted. "Secretly, as the clouds grew darker, I felt brighter and brighter. We were free of any architect of the Cathedral plans, and now, if we could get rid of the land and start, ab ovo, with no obstacles in the way, I felt that the real movement was not at all backward, but forward."[83] Satterlee's optimism was well founded. Not long after the meeting, Hearst increased her gift to $200,000.[84] The task now was to find a site worthy of the project's magisterial vision. Satterlee set out in search of one, but of course he knew the destination beforehand.

Satterlee played the role of real estate agent brilliantly. Teaming up again, he and Hearst set off to examine more locations. The main reasons St. Alban's had not been an option earlier were, first, its unavailability and, second, even when it was rumored to be available, its high cost. But Satterlee wanted to show it to Mrs. Hearst. From the comfort of her private carriage, he treated her to the view and extolled the site's details: its command of the city, its expansive and relatively level ground, its anticipation of the city's most promising growth. Conveniently, a few of his cathedral colleagues happened to be nearby making similar observations. When they began to approach, Satterlee preempted them, exiting the carriage to make greetings while leaving Hearst inside and incognito, which was her wish. One of the colleagues said, ostensibly unaware of Phoebe Hearst's presence but easily within earshot, "Mrs. Hearst is reported as being a very generous woman; I wonder if she would not help us," implying that the site might be accessible with another dose of her generosity. When Satterlee reentered the carriage, he sheepishly asked Hearst if she had heard the comment. "Every word," she replied.[85]

From there it was on to Dupont Circle, near the heart of the city, where another property had opened up. Satterlee praised the location, but it was out of reach from the start. It was small and expensive, and another twenty lots adjacent to it would need to be purchased, requiring another impossible fortune. All said, it would cost upward of $400,000 just to acquire sufficient land to make the project possible. Whereas the Newlands site lived down to its low cost, the Dupont site, incongruously called "Widow's Mite," was lavish. Its location better approximated what L'Enfant had imagined a century earlier. Its proximity to the seats of power and to the city's most prestigious traffic could not be surpassed, but its expense was dizzying, and its odd layout would force another series of design compromises. Reflecting again in his "Private Record," Satterlee follows his observations of the property with an apologia: "If in future years people ask why we went so far away . . . for a site out in the country . . . , we can answer that we made every effort to secure the only available piece of land large enough for a cathedral within a mile and a half of the White House, but were prevented from purchasing it by circumstances utterly beyond our control."[86] In the end, the Dupont site served only as a foil. With the Newlands site and Widow's Mite as comparisons, Mt. St. Alban took on a Goldilocks-like appeal, and without implicating himself, Satterlee knew that Phoebe Hearst was now aware of the role she was invited to play.

These site visits took place in the fall of 1897. By December of that year, Satterlee, Hearst, and a couple of other cathedral officials were prepared to put an offer on St. Alban's. The asking price was $224,000, only $24,000 more than what Hearst had already pledged. Mrs. Hearst and the foundation confirmed that the balance could be covered. Just like that, Satterlee's dream location became a divinely bestowed reality. The Cathedral Foundation still had to extricate itself from the Newlands site, and the St. Alban's owner turned out to be less than accommodating in later negotiations, but the future of the cathedral was tangible again, even brilliantly so. Satterlee felt prepared to meet the full force of new, more profound challenges. It was time to imagine the cathedral's full message to the world, to compose and proclaim its mission, and to take on the overwhelming task of raising more money.

Addressing the External Problems

The main exigency in addressing the project's external problems was branding. The project had evolved from a new cathedral that would accommodate a growing population, to a grand headquarters for a new diocese in the nation's capital, to a kind of mother church for all Episcopalians. It was not clear whether each identity for the new cathedral superseded the one before it or whether each was supposed to be folded into the other.[87] Rather than try to achieve clarity by narrowing the project's scope, Satterlee launched it into the stratosphere. He introduced the cathedral's now-famous three missions: "a house of prayer for all people," "the chief mission church of the diocese," and "a great church for national purposes."[88] The first and third of these missions hearkened back directly to L'Enfant's century-old master plan, which was getting renewed attention in light of Washington, DC's turn-of-the-century urban boom.

Satterlee's vision, however, was different from L'Enfant's. Like L'Enfant, he wanted to build the nation's church. But in contrast to L'Enfant plan to build a civic pantheon to which the nation's sects would be conducive, Satterlee wanted to build an Anglican cathedral around which the nation's Protestant factions would unite as one and gradually be absorbed into the nation's mission. It would be a national civic temple like L'Enfant's, but on an Anglican basis.[89] Satterlee knew that Anglicanism had lost its hegemony with the advent of global democracy. By aligning its interests with the nation best positioned to lead in a democratic age, perhaps the communion could "retain spiritual leadership of the world."[90] In short, Satterlee's rhetorical strategy for addressing the external problems associated with the cathedral's mission boiled down to a reappropriation and strategic misreading of L'Enfant's long-orphaned idea. Satterlee supported the prohibition of state churches in the United States' Establishment Clause, but he saw no reason a church could not be the sponsor of the state. He was quiet about this intention at first. His reference to Major L'Enfant in his "Private Record," quoted previously, is representative. He kept such intentions close to the vest, but the three missions he chose for the cathedral were clues hiding in plain sight.

Satterlee's strategy was designed to succeed in three ways. First, broadening the brand of the cathedral allowed Satterlee to draw on the political momentum of Washington, DC's renewal. McKim, Douglas, and Paret had done much of the legwork, earning the cathedral its congressional charter and imagining its role as a major landmark, but Satterlee was the first to claim the legacy of the Federal District's first planner. That Satterlee's cathedral undermined L'Enfant's vision in significant ways was either unknown or unimportant to the cathedral's supporters. Second, Satterlee's vision transcended the church's identity crisis. Rather than alienating different interest groups within the communion by taking sides, Satterlee imagined the cathedral as containing the whole church and the country. Its mission would be above squabbles over revisions to the Book of Common Prayer, or the role of evangelism in the church, or the finer details of liturgy. Finally, Satterlee's strategy breathed life into a favorite object of Christian fantasy: the reunification of Christendom.

While all Protestant sects tended to enjoy the idea of Christian unification, the Anglican Church was especially well versed in the topic because it believed itself to have a claim to global Christian leadership. The Chicago Quadrilateral of 1886 was only the most recent text to raise the idea that the great schisms of the past might be healed. For decades, Anglican leaders had been imagining how they might find common cause not only with other Protestants but also with Rome and the Eastern Orthodox traditions. Reverend Patrick Kenrick was writing as far back as 1841 in favor of "a reconciliation with the Parent Church." Citing the "increased lustre" that the Catholic Church would bring to the Anglican and Protestant world, he exclaimed, "How great a triumph for the Gospel were all its professors as one great family, having but one heart and soul!"[91]

William Reed Huntington, a contemporary and favorite of Satterlee, had authored the Quadrilateral to promote a new catholicity that would thread Christians of all backgrounds together, but with a distinctly Anglican flair. He followed the Quadrilateral with a book titled *A National Church*, which gave concrete organization to what the Quadrilateral only intimated. Huntington argued for a national church with a federal structure, organized the same way Episcopal parishes and dioceses were organized, and based in forms of polity and worship that were distinctly Episcopal. He hoped that over time, possibly a full century down the road, the United States would formally adopt this church as the nation's own, a true state church. William T. Manning, S.T.D., also a contemporary of Satterlee, likewise imagined "a great synthesis in the whole of Christendom, . . . a union which is to include all of the historic branches of the Christian Church—Protestant, Roman and Greek."[92] In each case, the idea was that Anglicanism's lineal claims and its linkages between the Christian branches positioned it to administer the unity Christians were seeking.

Oxford Movement Anglicanism, which centered on the notion that the Anglican Church ought to emphasize its Catholic heritage more than its Protestant sympathies, was well known at the time. For much of the nineteenth century, this movement had led some Anglican thinkers to reconsider the schism that had split Christendom, first into Roman and Eastern; then into Roman, Eastern, and Anglican; then into so many dozens and hundreds of sects.[93] Henry Yates Satterlee, however, was not so sanguine. As I discuss in the following chapter, Satterlee drew on nativist impulses to frame the cathedral not as a sanctuary for all gods, as L'Enfant had wished, and not even as a sanctuary for all Christians, as many of his Anglican brothers wished, but as the shrine to a new Protestant hegemony, led by the Episcopal Church and the Anglican Communion. Satterlee was quiet about this detail at first. It made rhetorical sense to celebrate the principle of unity in the name of building L'Enfant's lost church, but in truth, the Oxford Movement was waning and nativism in the United States was on the rise.

In correspondence and public statements, Satterlee began to use the phrase "National Cathedral" as if the title were taken for granted, even though officially the church was still known as Washington Cathedral.[94] Likewise, Satterlee began to broadcast the cathedral's three missions, but he was vague as to their precise meaning. To use his own phrasing when expressing his feelings about the direction of the cathedral's architecture, he was expert at being "scrupulously noncommittal." Privately, however, both in his journal and his correspondence with trusted colleagues, he mused over the goal of building an institution that would unite the nation's Protestant factions and face down the Roman monolith.[95] This strategic ambiguity kept the terminology inspiring enough to win prominent endorsements and donations, but ambiguous enough not to merit too much scrutiny. It was a strategy that Satterlee and his successors adopted to great effect, biding their time until the notion that the cathedral would become the nation's cathedral, would become "America's Westminster Abbey," became a natural and public thing.[96]

Such was the idea in 1929, more than two decades after Satterlee's death but still sixty years before the cathedral's completion, when cathedral officials embarked on a capital campaign that would carry them through the following decade of construction. Taking their cue from Satterlee's visionary fund-raising efforts, foundation members sought the official endorsement of national figures. The list included six former, current, or future US presidents as well as a variety of other wealthy and prominent citizens. The endorsements were compiled into written statements, which were then organized and published as a book: *Eminent Opinion regarding the Cathedral at Washington.* Among the more striking features of this publication is the emphasis contributors placed on the cathedral as a national institution that was somehow essential to American democracy. Herbert Hoover, hoping to make the city of Washington an architectural inspiration to the country, wrote, "This hope will be achieved when there is a beautiful architectural expression of the fundamental aspects of our democracy. Certainly one of these aspects, because it is the deepest spring of our national life, is religion. Therefore, as a wonderfully beautiful expression of religion, I watch with sympathetic interest the growth of the great Cathedral on the heights overlooking Washington."[97]

James Gerard, the former ambassador to Germany, was even bolder: "Our nation, which will remain a nation only as long as the Christian religion is its foundation, needs a great focal point for its religious life—a Christian capitol as important as that which houses under its white dome the government of the nation. The great Washington Cathedral will be that capitol, the abiding place of the Christian ideals of our nation."[98] Daniel C. French, one of America's most famous sculptors, and the man who created the Lincoln statue that serves as the centerpiece of the Lincoln Memorial, spoke of the symbolic power of the architecture and location: "It is eminently fitting that this imposing temple to God and to the highest aspirations of mankind should stand guard—an enduring and constant influence—over the Capital of the Nation where the laws of the people are made."[99] John J. Pershing, the famous American general, stated that the cathedral would be a symbol of "the religion of the Republic" and a "demonstration of our common Christianity." Calvin Coolidge added: "The strength of our country is the strength of its religious convictions." Franklin D. Roosevelt reverently called the cathedral a "national shrine."[100]

These statements demonstrate several important themes. First, the contributors and those who solicited their statements promoted the cathedral as a national project. Its importance was found not in the need it filled for a diocese, a city, a bishop, or even the sponsoring church. It was relevant as a symbol of the country. Second, the cathedral was to be a fulfillment of destiny, a representation of the religious ideals purported to be endemic to the American project. That is, the cathedral was the realization of an idea already natural to mainstream religious and political traditions in the United States. Third, the cathedral was endorsed by the most "eminent" Americans, who spoke of its significance and pledged their unyielding support to it. The credibility of these voices was made all the more powerful by the spectrum of their political and religious backgrounds. Republicans, Democrats, Episcopalians, Methodists, Congregationalists, and others, except Roman Catholics, gladly praised the project for its centrality to American identity.[101] Cathedral leaders were only too glad to use *Eminent Opinion regarding the Cathedral at Washington* as a tool for the cathedral's far-flung capital campaigns. Part of the genius of Satterlee's rebranding was the fact that fund-raising for a truly national cathedral could be broadened to include donors from virtually any background. If one were a patriotic American, one could have a stake in this building. No wonder *Eminent Opinion* was the first official publication of the cathedral to adopt Satterlee's standard use of the phrase "National Cathedral."

In addition to rebranding the cathedral's mission, Satterlee became involved with its design. He made clear that the cathedral's iconography should depict scenes and words from US history, a history that he viewed as essential to American Protestants. In one letter to the cathedral's early principal architect, Satterlee wrote that the American historical scenes should be "intensely interesting" and "dear to the hearts of Puritans, Presbyterians and Methodists."[102] Satterlee expanded on these sentiments in other letters. Writing again to the same architect, he essentially whispered, "It is a National Cathedral, and sooner or later it will be in touch with the nation's life. . . . Certainly in some part of the Cathedral there should be statues and perhaps bas reliefs presenting different events of American history. You yourself have suggested Washington and Pen [*sic*]. I could add a great many other subjects. Some of them connected with our own Church, like the baptism of Pocahontas, Washington reading the burial service over Gen. Braddock, etc."[103] Satterlee implied that the cathedral would inevitably become, in effect, the nation's church. Although this becoming has fertile roots in Satterlee's own ideas and efforts, he was suggesting that this identity for the cathedral had a certain self-evidence that wanted only to be expressed.

The Peace Cross

The cathedral's first public event was an opportunity for Satterlee to set the tone for this "National Cathedral." Knowing the difficulty he would face in creating a national institution out of a sectarian cathedral, he wanted at least to ensure a "national image around which the Episcopal Church and other Christian churches could unite in one national and worldwide mission."[104] Just weeks before the 1898 General Convention, which would be held in Washington, DC, world leaders announced that the Spanish-American War was coming to an end. For such an event to coincide with the Episcopal Church's national convention seemed providential. The communion needed to be commemorated in a way that would disclose the cathedral's role as the nation's religious center. Satterlee's idea was to erect a large "peace cross" on the cathedral grounds (fig. 2.6). He believed that the ceremony, if designed strategically, could establish a pattern for the cathedral to sacralize events that were national in scope and significance.

Satterlee started to press President William McKinley to attend the event and say a few words. McKinley declined to make a speech, but he agreed to attend. Satterlee then convinced the Marine Band to play in full uniform, establishing a tradition that has lasted to the present day. Finally, once the event was over and the accolades began to flow, Satterlee saturated news outlets in and out of the church. He had two hundred copies of an article published in the *New York Sun* sent to all church bishops. Finally Satterlee commissioned ambassador-turned-writer Thomas Nelson Page to prepare a book on the event. Simply entitled the *Peace Cross Book*, the publication was sent to the church press and then mailed to all of the church bishops in the United States.

Satterlee wrote in his "Private Record" of the first moments in which the peace cross idea came to him:

> Then all suddenly, on the Sunday . . . while I was in the little Church in Twilight Park, the remembrance came back to my mind of the Communion service on Easter Monday of Bishop's guild, in which we had prayed so earnestly for peace. On that day the war with Spain was practically begun. Now it was practically over. Then came the remembrance of another service at Northeast Harbor . . . [where] we held a short thanksgiving service for the restoration of peace. This suggested the erection of a Cross of Peace as the first monument on the new Cathedral grounds with the inscription: "That it may please Thee to give to all nations unity, peace and concord, we beseech Thee to hear us, Good Lord!"[105]

Satterlee does not recommend proposals or generate ideas. He does not even "remember" events. Rather, events come "back to (his) mind," and these unbidden memories in turn lead to self-evident conclusions. Note how the agentive memory "suggests" the erection of a "Cross of Peace"—as if the memory and not the one remembering would thus entitle the sculpture. Satterlee's language implies that the memory is responsible for the proposed, lengthy inscription. Playing the role of revelator, Satterlee situates himself as merely the recipient of inspiration.

Note how Satterlee concludes his reflection on the Peace Cross idea: "At once I told the thought to my wife and daughter, also to Dr. and Mrs. Rives;

and Dr. Rives said at once he would give the Cross. We all agreed that no more beautiful beginning could be made of the National American Cathedral of the Prince of Peace."[106] Satterlee frames himself as the agent only when he is sharing the idea with other agents who might corroborate the inspired memory that produced the thought in the first place. No fewer than four other agents are consulted, and they in turn urge the idea forth. From this time forward, Satterlee becomes the active, anxious agent of God's will. "But no time was to be lost," he continues. "The next day I wrote to Mr. Gibson, the architect of the Hearst School."[107] Satterlee's agency in creating ideas is carefully obscured. His role is to receive and then dutifully evangelize the ideas of a will higher than his own.

The agentive elision is even more evident in Satterlee's subsequent appeals to President McKinley. Referring to the morning when he traveled to the White House to pick up the president, Satterlee recalls, "On the way out I said to him: 'I wish I could venture to ask the President to speak, notwithstanding his refusal.' He [President McKinley] responded: 'I should not venture, Bishop, for he might refuse again.'" Satterlee presses on: "This Cathedral is to last through coming centuries. One word from the President, if it were only a 'God bless this undertaking,' would make the occasion historic." At last McKinley provides an opening: "After your own speech is over you may appeal to me if you wish, and I will then decide whether or not to speak."[108] Although the address was short, McKinley included a sentence that undoubtedly pleased Satterlee: "Every undertaking like this for the promotion of religion and morality and education is a positive gain to citizenship, to country and to civilization, and in this single word I wish for the sacred enterprise the highest influence and the widest usefulness."[109] The most prominent national political figure had blessed the project as an advancement of national interests. Satterlee could not have been more pleased.

Satterlee then describes the unveiling of the cross. At first, the flag "envelops" the twenty-foot limestone cross. Then, as the flag floats down, it becomes "clouds of glory" out of which the cross rises. One symbol is not fully recognized without the other. Satterlee's final words on the event are explicit: "The first Service of the Cathedral was historic. The presence of the President of the United States and of our General Convention had nationalized the Cathedral of Washington. Henceforth it could not fail!"[110] At last, in a public way, Satterlee had effectively claimed and supplanted the vision of L'Enfant. His cathedral had been blessed by the chief priest of the American Civil Religion.

Fig. 2.6. Unveiling of the Peace Cross under the direction of Bishop Satterlee with President William McKinley in attendance, 1898. Washington National Cathedral Archives

Following the Peace Cross event, Satterlee embarked on an aggressive fund-raising campaign that included short tours to different cities, parlor gatherings, sermons, and individual meetings with wealthy and prominent benefactors. His thoughts were consumed with matters of money, promotion, and design. His "Private Record" reveals detailed ledgers of costs, revenues, expenditures, and funding sources, to say nothing of the copious personal reflections that gave shape to his anxieties as well as his hopes for the project. He recounts ideas for solving architectural problems, interactions he had with relevant parties, and his day-to-day worship activities. Incidentally, it was during these years that Pierre L'Enfant's name was making a comeback in Washington, DC, as the City Beautiful movement and the McMillan Commission exhumed the original planner's notes and ideas in an effort to make the capital the design gem it was always meant to be. But while L'Enfant's legacy was being celebrated by national luminaries, and while his plan was being reclaimed by the same office of commissioners that was once his bitterest rival, the Cathedral Church of St. Peter and St. Paul remained strangely silent about the capital's first planner. In his private reflections and public statements, Satterlee does not appear to mention L'Enfant.[111]

Fig. 2.7. President Theodore Roosevelt speaks at the Foundation Stone ceremony, September 29, 1907. Washington National Cathedral Archives

The Peace Cross event set the pattern for many similar events to follow, including the famous laying of the cathedral's foundation stone in 1907, which was attended by President Theodore Roosevelt and the bishop of London, each of whom made remarks. Roosevelt declared, "God speed the work begun this noon."[112] Hundreds of prominent clergymen, dozens of national dignitaries, and roughly ten thousand other people attended the ceremony (fig. 2.7).[113] Satterlee participated by tapping the foundation stone with the same gavel George Washington had used to set the cornerstone of the US Capitol Building just over a century earlier. The same pattern was evident more than eight decades later in the remarks of President George H. W. Bush at the dedication of the building, when he declared that the cathedral is "a symbol of our nation's spiritual life, overlooking the center of our nation's secular life," that it is "not just about faith but . . . also about a nation and its people," and that it is "our national treasure" designed "to strengthen the Nation's heart."[114] Satterlee could not have known the extent to which his rebranding strategy might work, but were he able to see the 1990 dedication remarks by Bush in light of the founding remarks by McKinley and Roosevelt, he would notice a pleasing symmetry.

❖

Today, the invocation of L'Enfant is habitual for those who describe Washington National Cathedral and its origins. Bloggers, scholars, presidents, even cathedral officials take for granted the notion that L'Enfant's grand vision was merely delayed until Satterlee brushed it off and set it atop St. Alban's Hill.[115] The problem with this view is the same problem we often encounter in general descriptions of the American Civil Religion. It presumes that there is some system of common meaning that transcends the competitions and dichotomies that define civic and spiritual life in the United States, when in fact the National Cathedral, like the American Civil Religion, is an ideal to which divergent interests lay claim. I hope this chapter shows that Satterlee's church never was and never could be the church of L'Enfant. Satterlee did not burnish L'Enfant's vision; he cloaked it in Anglican vestments and presented it to the nation and world as if it were immaculately conceived. The civil-religious vision of Henry Yates Satterlee was less a vision of the United States than it was a vision of the Anglican Communion and its destiny to lead the world into a new age of Christian unity. For Satterlee, L'Enfant's old vision of a national church served as little more than a trope.

For more than twelve years, Henry Yates Satterlee made the cathedral his obsession, but the months leading up to his death were especially busy. He continued visiting the parishes of the diocese, attending the October General Convention, traveling on other matters of diocesan business, and maintaining almost daily contact with the cathedral architects. During the first week of February 1908, he came down with a terrible cold. He nevertheless maintained a heavy schedule, including his monthly trip to New York by train to attend a meeting of the National Board of Missions, whence he traveled to Providence, Rhode Island, to fulfill a speaking engagement, and from there back to Washington through inclement weather and travel delays. As his cold worsened, he pressed on, conducting confirmation services at two missions for Black parishioners in Washington shortly after his return. All of this he did against the wishes of his family and doctors. As the days wore on, his cold turned to influenza, then to pneumonia. Informed by his doctors that he had passed the point of no return, Satterlee took to his private bedroom and reconciled himself to death. On February 22, at the age of sixty-five, he received

Fig. 2.8. Bishop Satterlee's sarcophagus in the apse of Bethlehem Chapel, Washington National Cathedral. Washington National Cathedral Archives

Holy Communion, gave a personal blessing to each of his family members who were present, and died.

Like L'Enfant, Henry Yates Satterlee did not live to see his vision realized. Barely one portion of one wall of the cathedral had risen above the ground at the time of his death. Interred first in the Little Sanctuary on the cathedral close, Satterlee's remains were later moved into the cathedral crypt, in an otherwise empty space partitioned behind the altar of the Bethlehem Chapel (fig. 2.8). If one did not know where to look, one might not be aware that anything lies in those shadows, but there resides the bishop's alabaster sarcophagus, cordoned off by rope, facing back-lit windows that depict the Nativity of Christ. That his remains were placed in this location was no coincidence. Bethlehem Chapel is the cathedral's first completed chapel. Beneath its altar lies the cathedral's foundation stone. Spreading out from its friezes and soaring above its vault ceiling, the cathedral continued to grow, stone upon stone, decade after decade, stretching outward and upward from the spot where lay the bishop's relics.

That it is an Episcopal cathedral is mostly unknown to Americans, and one must think this fact might please Bishop Satterlee. Like many other Anglicans of his time, he viewed the Communion as the one, true catholic religion, the best and foremost of all Christian approaches, and the church with the strongest claim to the lineal, universal faith established by Christ himself. Such a church should have no need to subordinate other faiths; its power must lie in its ability to be "assimilated by them."[116] Anglicanism was the best moral guide for society, and therefore society should come to adopt it naturally. He approached his rhetorical goals with this same view. As Hewlett remarks of Satterlee, he "had honed his natural ability to lead people through contentious issues in ways that would leave them with the impression that they, not he, deserved credit for what was accomplished. He was master at achieving his goals without alienating those who disagreed with him."[117] Satterlee's method was not to make his opinion dominate that of his interlocutor, but to make his ideas assimilable. Just so, Episcopalism would not command or explicitly seek to persuade; it would not absorb the Christian world. Rather, the Christian world, engrossed by this cathedral, would absorb Episcopalism, slowly assuming its shape, speaking its creed.

In his ability to communicate in this way, Satterlee was different from L'Enfant, and perhaps this difference explains why he succeeded where L'Enfant failed. Rather than lashing out at ideas he did not like, he waited—for years, if necessary—for opportunities to undermine them quietly, and to assign the blame to forces beyond his control. He also took pains to preserve relationships, even with those with whom he disagreed. Perhaps Satterlee was more like Jefferson, whose subtlety and patience outlasted the hope of a national church, then of a Capitol crypt, and even of a mausoleum. The great irony is that, in wiping the idea of a national church from the plan for the capital city, Jefferson, a heterodox Christian at best, created a vacuum into which Satterlee and the Anglican Communion righteously strode a century later.

It would be hard to argue against the success of Satterlee's strategy. Washington National Cathedral is by no means on par with Westminster Abbey, nor does it amount to the church L'Enfant and President Washington had in mind. The United States, more than a century after the publication of the Chicago Quadrilateral and the laying of Washington National Cathedral's Foundation Stone, is no closer to adopting a national church, let alone one with an Anglican basis; but there the cathedral stands, more prominent and powerful than ever. It hosts the national prayer services, presidential funerals, civil-religious sermons, and calls to social conscience that Satterlee undoubtedly envisioned. There in its crypt lie the remains of American luminaries, from Woodrow Wilson to Helen Keller. In its nave fly the flags of the nation's states and territories; on the floor of its narthex lie the seals of the states; throughout its nave and chapels stand the statues of US founders, thinkers, heroes, and heroines; and from its pulpit speak the priests and presidents of a still-striving and troubled nation. A close reading of the space itself is forthcoming in a later chapter. For now, we might simply acknowledge with awe the fact that this building exists at all, one of the largest cathedrals in the world, proudly announcing itself to be the nation's church, heir to L'Enfant.

CHAPTER THREE

The National Church in an Age of Nativism

The success of Bishop Henry Yates Satterlee's efforts is impressive by any metric. What other leaders tried and gave up and other churches dared not explore, he seemed to will into life—namely, the creation of what has become the nation's unofficial civil-religious sanctuary. Drawing on whatever means of persuasion were available, he raised money, political support, and public prestige despite overwhelming odds. To comb through Satterlee's correspondence, public addresses, and the careful work of cathedral archivists and historiographers is to get the sense of an authoritative and single-minded visionary. But such visions often obscure a complicated, underlying machinery. The cathedral's role as a "house of prayer for all people" with at least a nominally Anglican identity is bound up in nineteenth-century nativism.

It is no coincidence that the cathedral was conceived during a time of remarkable Roman Catholic growth.[1] This growth added powerful fuel to a rivalry between Roman Catholics and the American Protestant establishment. In this chapter, I argue that this rivalry expressed itself in multiple forms of violence: physical, political, rhetorical, even architectural. I conclude that the Protestant establishment achieved a victory that scholars of American religion have long overlooked. That nativism played a leading role in the cathedral's success adds a layer of complexity to our understanding of the American Civil Religion. Typically, the American Civil Religion is characterized in terms that glitter with unity and hope, but that same civil religion has always created exclusions as well as embraces.

Roman Catholic Growth and the Rise of American Nativism
Despite a Protestant bulwark that strove to blunt "papist" influence, Roman Catholic growth proceeded at a staggering pace almost from the first Euro-

pean settlements in the New World.[2] The tension between anti-Catholic sentiment and explosive Roman Catholic growth laid the groundwork for a nativist rhetoric that pervaded American Protestantism throughout the colonial period and well into the long nineteenth century. Beginning in the colonial period, anti-Catholic rhetoric was openly vituperative. It was perfectly acceptable to label the pope "demonic," the Roman Church a "whore," and for little children to play popular games such as "Break the Pope's Neck."[3] Lectures both in churches and respected universities pilloried Roman Catholicism in the name of "detecting and convicting and exposing . . . the idolatry of the Romish church; their tyranny, usurpations, damnable heresies, fatal errors, abominable superstitions, and other crying wickedness in her high places."[4] It was also during the colonial period that Protestant leaders instituted the most blatantly anti-Catholic laws, excluding Catholics from political access and sometimes from settlement altogether.[5]

Despite nativist invectives and laws, Roman Catholic growth only accelerated after the founding of the republic. This growth, which consisted mostly of poor immigrants from non-English-speaking countries, gave rise to a xenophobia unequaled in the colonial period. Catholic immigrants were labeled as "hordes" and "a menace," but still their numbers grew.[6] Even more troubling for the enemies of the Roman Catholic Church (RCC) was the expansion of more liberal laws. Anti-Catholic laws in Pennsylvania, Maryland, and Virginia, for instance, were replaced with laws of religious toleration. George Washington himself expressed the need for a policy of religious freedom, and he singled out Roman Catholics as a group in need of protection.[7] Meanwhile, the Reformation-born religious communities of the early colonial period, mainly the very Puritans to whom American settlement owed its anti-Catholic history, and the First Great Awakening revivalists who sought to quicken the waning faith of traditional Protestants, had become defunct or ineffectual by the time of the nation's founding. The spirit of Enlightenment pervaded the eighteenth century, and it set the stage for a neoclassical republic that resisted the trappings of Christianity.[8]

Despite the weakening of Christianity's hold and the increased diversity in Christian belief, nativism grew to unprecedented levels in the early republic. Sidney Ahlstrom observes that "xenophobia is . . . especially near the surface in a country which has only recently achieved full national status and which is vigorously engaged on many fronts in asserting its special character and destiny."[9] However, to note the nation was "asserting its special character and destiny" glosses over the fact that the country was still seeking a char-

acter to assert. By the early nineteenth century, the supposed Protestant establishment was in fact a hodgepodge of diffuse denominations, some high,
some low; some established, some radically unorganized; and all vying for
converts in a vacuum left by the collapse of the original colonial, Protestant
religious powers. It was a religious free-for-all, but rather than embracing
Roman Catholicism in the process, American Protestants turned to nativism
as one of the few tenets that united them. In spite of its size and growth, the
RCC was nudged still further to the cultural margins.

Still, it grew. Representing barely a single percentage of the white population at the time of the Declaration of Independence, Roman Catholics constituted nearly 20 percent of the population and were easily America's largest
denomination by the start of the twentieth century. Nativist laws became
more difficult to pass, and nativist rhetoric was forced to evolve. Whereas in
the colonial period, invectives were common, by the middle of the nineteenth
century Protestant leaders were obliged to couch their nativism in the style
of fair and polite argument, making dispassionate nods to constitutional government and, ironically, grand gestures to religious tolerance.

H. A. Boardman, pastor of the Walnut Street Presbyterian Church in Philadelphia, delivered a representative sermon against Roman Catholicism on
December 27, 1840. His sermon is noteworthy for embodying the generic
rhetoric and style of nativist insecurity. He begins by disclosing his own reticence: "The author of this sermon has never been an alarmist on the subject
of the increase of Romanism in the United States. He does not wish to be
considered as one now. But . . . a train of circumstances over which he had
no control, and the issue of which he could not anticipate, has led him within
a few weeks to careful examination of the subject."[10] Boardman then acknowledges that some in the American audience may feel squeamish about a
sermon in which another church is being assailed. So he assures them that he
will not controvert the principle of religious liberty: "Liberty of conscience is
a fundamental principle of Protestant Christianity. It is as uniformly recognized wherever a pure Protestantism prevails; as it is denied where Romanism prevails." He then links this "pure" Protestantism to the nation's sacred
founding documents: "It is incorporated with our national and state consti-
tutions; and forms one of the main pillars of our republic. . . . If the cause we
advocate cannot be maintained by truth and argument, it is not of God, and
deserves to perish."[11] Key to Boardman's strategy is the way he frames Roman
Catholicism as a foil, not merely against which a true Christianity is enshrined
but, more important, against which the country should enshrine its civil re-

ligion. The RCC is heretical because it violates the republic's civil-religious foundations.

Boardman's assertions were of course belied by the fact that Protestants were more often than not the ones who attempted to undermine the free exercise of religion. As R. Laurence Moore points out, from the beginning, Protestants not only assailed Catholics from the pulpit on occasion but also "created state-supported churches in America . . . , sponsored legislation that took the education of children away from families, . . . dictated standards of Sabbath behavior, and . . . sought to inject Protestant forms of worship into public ceremonies."[12] It was also a myth that notions of religious liberty and American character are a heritage of Protestant forbears. Moore reaffirms that Catholics played definitive roles in the colonization and cultural ideals of colonial North America.[13] Nevertheless, Boardman's brand of rhetoric had broad purchase in a culture that was itching for a worthy opposition. Roman Catholicism represented both a political threat for its ties to European monarchy and corruption and a theological blasphemy for its reverence of priests and rituals. As the following sections make clear, Henry Yates Satterlee drew on these same rhetorical tactics in building interest in and resources for the new cathedral project.

Building Nativism: A Battle of Symbols

Affecting polite argument was not the only way nativist rhetoric evolved during the nineteenth century. In his book *Gothic Arches, Latin Crosses*, Ryan K. Smith analyzes one of Protestantism's most subtle and least studied rhetorical strategies for blunting Roman Catholic influence. By around 1850, a clear shift had taken place in Protestant church architecture. Protestant houses of worship were adopting "entirely novel elements . . . representing customary Catholic approaches to the sacred through the senses."[14] The irony was hard to miss in Philadelphia, for example, where nativist emotions ran especially high: "Even as anti-Catholic rioters directed much of their wrath at buildings that represented the city's Catholic presence, many of Philadelphia's Protestant congregations began investing their own identities in sharply Catholic forms."[15] It is no surprise that the famous Gothic Revival in American architecture coincided with some of anti-Catholicism's most pronounced outbursts. The appropriation of altars, crosses, choirs, candles, vestments, robes, and so on reflected more than a broad shift in cultural tastes. The appropriation of Catholic style turned out to be another tactic of nativist rhetoric.

Protestant fears were well founded. Catholicism was indeed growing not only in numbers but also in popularity. As one Harvard University divinity professor concluded at the time, one major reason for the popularity was the church's material and ritual aesthetic. Its "bewitching charm has most powerful influences to address the eye, the imagination, and the feelings."[16] In other words, physical spaces had joined sermons, pamphlets, and songs as a rhetorical means to win adherents. What anti-Catholicism gave up with diminished legal violence—and gradually with diminished invective—it found in a rhetorical rivalry of aesthetics.

To understand how the RCC's aesthetics managed such influence, one need only revisit the growth statistics. The previously noted exponential growth of the Catholic immigrant population was underscored by a corresponding and equally impressive building campaign. From 1820 to 1860, the number of Catholic churches in the United States grew by 1,956 percent, a percentage three times greater than the next most prolific group (the Methodists), and a greater percentage than the next six religious groups combined.[17] This proliferation of churches began to undermine the popular caricature of Roman Catholicism as foreign or exotic. Americans could see Roman Catholic churches in their own neighborhoods alongside Methodist, Presbyterian, Baptist, and Episcopal churches. People were beginning see Roman Catholicism in the proverbial flesh and to experience its allure firsthand. The act of appropriating Catholic aesthetics thus became a kind of turnabout in which Roman Catholicism's own tools were used to undermine its appeal.

In the race to appropriate Gothic (read: Roman Catholic) overtones in their church buildings and worship services, Protestants had a worthy nativist heir: Episcopalians. Unlike the adherents of radically democratic, bottom-up movements of the Second Great Awakening, such as the Baptists and Methodists, Episcopalians were long accustomed to reverent, highly liturgical services and elaborately decorated spaces. Allen C. Guelzo examines the Protestant project of finding a reliable leader in the contest to outflank Roman Catholic influence in the nineteenth century. He notes that the Episcopal Church eschewed a strategy of evangelism in favor of a more High Church approach.[18] The Protestant establishment had become well aware of the need to consolidate allegiances, identify leaders, and exert influence in the interest of building an essentially Protestant civil religion at the heart of American life. Denominations competing among themselves while the "papist hordes" took over the country simply would not do. The Episcopal Church may not have been the populist exemplar some Protestants wanted, but at least it was not the enemy, and it was in a position to appeal to the sensibilities that were driving so many Roman Catholic converts. What is more, the Episcopal Church's wealth allowed it to move forward with Catholic appropriations. In contrast, churches with the fewest affinities to Catholic aesthetics (e.g., the Baptists) tended to adopt only the most basic features (e.g., the cross).[19]

In their collective push to rival Rome, the Protestant groups managed to maintain fairly strong alliances with one another. This dynamic has its analogue in the Church of England. During the late seventeenth century, the Church of England and its dissenters found common cause in the political interests of the nation itself. Calls for civil peace and religious tolerance took root, and by the end of the century people generally accepted that adherents of all faiths should be able to live in harmony so long as they could remain good subjects. The one stipulation was a thinly veiled exclusion of Roman Catholics, who were presumed incapable of fidelity to the crown by virtue of their loyalty to the pope. Thus, the inherent theological and political differences among Protestant groups in England could be subsumed within a unified front against popery.[20] The Roman Catholic threat in England was constructed as a foreign attack on the nation's sovereign interests.[21] The RCC's theological elements were objectionable only to the extent that they might undermine the state. Even in England, where a monarch reigned, Protestantism's consolidation within the Anglican Communion advanced as part of a broader political reform that embraced "constitutionalism and limited monarchy."[22] Again, the dangers of papism were framed largely in terms of civil-religious principles rather than in terms of sectarian theology.

As in England, so in the United States centuries later. The wedge between Catholics and Protestants had to do with civil-religious concerns. Protestants were historically aligned with poise, toleration, rationality, argument, and so on, while Roman Catholics were framed as the unthinking, emotionally attached subjects of a tyrant. Thomas Lessl, Charles Taylor, and others have examined Protestantism's claim as America's natural conscience.[23] Critiques of Roman Catholicism therefore tended to focus on its supposed intrigues and schemes. Consider, for instance, an 1846 address to the general bishops, clergy, and laity of the national Protestant Episcopal Church by John Henry Hopkins, bishop of Vermont. Motivated by the apostasies of several Episcopal bishops who had converted to the RCC, Hopkins lamented that previous measures enacted by the Episcopal General Convention had not effectively "checked and discouraged the progress of the insidious foe [Romanism], and that . . . the House of Bishops had distinctly declared the utter abhorrence with which our Church regarded the slightest approximation toward the corruptions of Popery."[24] Hopkins further alleged that the apostasies were the result of calculating papist sympathizers within the Episcopal Church and that while many had hoped "the climax of the peril had been passed, and that every mind which had been warped by the sophistry of this Romanizing party would recoil in disgust and dread from any farther dalliance with the system of abomination, . . . yet we have had lately some afflicting proofs that the infection continues actively at work among us."[25] Hopkins's strategy reveals a central theme of Roman Catholic othering during this period, which was to frame the RCC as a conspiratorial force seeking to undermine the true Christian faith, which emerged out of the English Reformation and grew deep roots in the soils of American liberty.

Washington National Cathedral as the American Westminster Abbey

Although the interreligious dynamics in nineteenth-century America were arguably more complex and certainly more numerous than those in England at the time, they bore some notable similarities with the English example. The Episcopal Church in the United States was under no illusion that it was the official state church. From the founding of the cathedral under Satterlee to the present day, leaders of the cathedral have been explicit in their rejection of an American state church while assuming a special guardianship of the nation's sacred and civic character.[26] Nevertheless, Satterlee's regular invocation of Westminster Abbey as a kind of model for the cathedral suggests ideological overlaps worth exploring. In chapter 2, I present the puzzle of why Satterlee would choose Westminster Abbey as his model, and I suggest several potential reasons. I also identify factors that may have gone into Satterlee's decision to embrace Episcopalism as his home faith once he determined to enter the ministry.

Here, I argue that Satterlee's decision to (1) embrace the Episcopal Church and (2) adopt Westminster Abbey as a model for Washington National Cathedral is tied partly to Anglicanism's hostility toward Roman Catholicism. Satterlee was not always shy about expressing his anti-Catholic feelings during his tenure as bishop of Washington, and he seems to have nurtured his prejudice since youth. Charles Henry Brent references Satterlee's "ingrained suspicion" of and "strong antipathy to the papacy," which Brent attributes largely to the influence of Cleveland Coxe, Satterlee's mentor following college.[27] Brent quotes letters in which Satterlee, serving as rector of his first parish, privately pans Roman and Orthodox traditions during one of his tours of Europe and the Holy Land. In one letter to his sister, Satterlee refers to an

Orthodox Easter ritual as "the most shocking imposture of Christendom."[28] Westminster Abbey may not have been an independent church in the way Satterlee envisioned for Washington National Cathedral, but it was a church that strove to keep its nation's civic life pure.

When Satterlee assumed leadership of the cathedral, his goal was likewise to create a national religious center that would keep the nation on the straight and narrow. To be fair, the bad blood between Anglicanism and Catholicism was not one-sided. In the same year Satterlee was made bishop of Washington, Pope Leo XIII declared all Anglican ordinations to be "absolutely null and utterly void."[29] There is a telling disconnect between Satterlee's enthusiastic embrace of the Chicago Quadrilateral of 1886, a document that implied a possible rapprochement between Rome and the Protestant world, and his rhetorical use of Roman Catholicism as a foil once he was installed as bishop and the fund-raising campaign was under way. In building the national house of prayer for all people, Satterlee made little or no pretense of embracing the Roman Catholic Church.[30]

To this end, Satterlee had two main strategies: brand the cathedral as national in scope; and raise the massive amounts of money required to construct a building equal to this brand. He understood that these two tasks were related. Douglas and McKim had come up with the idea of a cathedral foundation to appeal to Episcopalians from outside the Washington-area parishes. Satterlee's rebranding of the cathedral would allow him to broaden the fund-raising network to include the whole Protestant spectrum. This idea did not originate entirely with Satterlee. It was partly the product of advice he received from Senator George F. Edmunds of Vermont, who, in a letter dated January 25, 1898, wrote of the urgency of the religious competition taking place in the nation's capital: "If our brother Churchmen in every part of the country—especially those blessed with abundant means—could only realize the state of things, as you and I see it and know it, there would be, I am sure, no want of the material resources necessary to carry out the work with all of the rapidity of which it is capable. The capital of this great Nation is necessarily the pivotal point of national religious, as well as political, progress on the continent."[31] The letter makes a forceful moral declaration, but it also proposes a rhetorical strategy. Edmunds understood that cathedral funding would rely on whether potential benefactors understood the stakes involved. Donors would have to be shown that the cathedral would blunt the threat of Roman Catholicism and preserve the nation's civil religious character.

One notable detail about the Edmunds letter, which is explored in further

detail below, is its date. It comes almost two years after Satterlee's consecration as bishop of Washington. Prior to the letter, Satterlee received much
correspondence from powerful figures anxious to share their nativist concerns. After he received the Edmunds letter, Satterlee began to popularize
the idea of the cathedral much farther beyond diocesan boundaries. In doing
so, he regularly expressed concerns with, and sometimes openly inveighed
against, Roman Catholic expansion in the nation's capital. He wanted to create a stronger Protestant coalition around the cathedral project, and what
better way to build that coalition than with nativist canards? National Cathedral committees were formed in places such as Philadelphia and New York
to help facilitate fund-raising and speaking engagements, during which Satterlee often cited the Edmunds letter and argued that the Romanist Church
represented a national threat.

One must also consider the cathedral's first and still official name, which
tells a compelling story about its rivalry with the RCC. The name Cathedral
Church of St. Peter and St. Paul is unique in multiple ways. First, the cathedral is called after two saints rather than one, or rather than the popular "All
Saints" title so many other Anglican churches use. This choice suggests a
broader focus of identity than that of a typical Episcopal church, while avoid-
ing the genericism of the "All Saints" label. Why these two saints? And, more
particularly, why St. Peter? Of all of the cathedrals in the Anglican Communion, almost none adopts the eponym of Peter. In non-Anglo-Catholic traditions, the name is practically unheard of for cathedrals. Only two Episcopal
churches, other than Washington National Cathedral, use the name, and one
of them is, not coincidentally, in St. Petersburg, Florida.[32]

Douglas and McKim advocated openly for the unusual name because they
wanted to reclaim an important saint whose name had been too long the
prerogative of the Roman Catholic Church. "I want to proclaim to the Roman-
ists that we allow them no monopoly of S. Peter," Douglas wrote to Bishop
Paret in 1893, and Paret agreed.[33] By putting Paul, the principal saint associated with the Anglican Communion, and Peter, the principal saint associated
with Roman Catholicism, side by side, the cathedral branding strategy fanned
the flames of rivalry, appropriating not only the Roman Catholic style of architecture but also the "first pope" of the Roman Catholic Church. Satterlee
apparently embraced this name, though it was he who first experimented
openly with versions of the building's now-famous second name, Washington National Cathedral.

With the branding and mission of the cathedral effectively broadened, Satterlee undertook a large letter-writing campaign through which he singled out luminaries from across Protestantism. The purpose of the campaign was both to raise money from the wealthy and to get endorsements from the politically prominent. Denomination did not matter, so long as that denomination was not Roman Catholic. Copies of outgoing personal letters were not routinely made around the turn of the century; however, correspondence in response to Satterlee's appeals is available, as well as correspondence congratulating Satterlee on his ascension to the position of bishop. Several of these letters reflect the anxieties that Episcopal leaders harbored regarding Catholic growth and the lack of a unified Protestant front.

One letter from an S. M. Haskins from St. Marks Rectory in Brooklyn, New York, dated December 13, 1895, congratulates Satterlee on his election as bishop of Washington: "All good churchmen had cause to fear that in these days of broad thinkers, and canon breakers, and high ritualism, there might be an unwise choice. But thanks be to God their fears are now dispelled."[34] The phrase "high ritualism" appears to be a thinly veiled swipe at Catholicism and perhaps at the growing tendency among Protestants to appropriate the accoutrements of such worship. Once again, Catholic identity is automatically linked to other types of transgression, including the breaking of religious law and the weakening of religious commitment in the name, one presumes, of pluralism or tolerance.

Similarly, a letter from J. H. Gantt of Baltimore, Maryland, written the same week as the Haskins letter, uses the pretext of congratulations to provide some encouragement and coaching regarding the competition between Protestant America and the RCC:

> Permit me to say that nowhere has the American Catholic Church a greater [unreadable] than in Washington. The Washington multitude which [unreadable] from . . . all parts of the country need to feel the presence of a Church and a Bishop both of which are at once Catholic and American. The Romans and the Methodists are . . . at work to establish Universities so as to take advantage of the resources of political and scientific knowledge which are stored in various departments of the National Government.—The Church should be [unreadable]. For she alone is able to build up a holy . . . University at the nation's Capitol.—so . . . Christians can compete with the Roman Church in this respect—[unreadable] the American Catholic Church.[35]

Gantt refers to the never-to-be-realized hopes of an Episcopal university in Washington (the Cathedral School remained a secondary institution) as an ancillary to the establishment of a cathedral. For Gantt, the matter was not so much about educating Episcopalians in an Episcopal community as about an open competition between "Christians" and "the Roman Church" over which would make the best use of the nation's resources of "political and scientific knowledge." Gantt's reasoning draws a link between the responsibility to administer the nation's religious identity and the Episcopal inheritance of catholic (read: universal, *not* Roman Catholic) authority. Gantt's language suggests in microcosm the old anxieties about papal imperialism and colonization that go back hundreds of years. Episcopalians by legacy were called to face down the advance of Roman Catholic political power. This project was the essence of a proper civil-religious culture.

Such internal discourse did not find expression only in the moment of Satterlee's ascension or the exuberance of new plans. It continued during the cathedral's ensuing construction and institutionalization. The main publication of the cathedral, a serial called *Cathedral Age*, often reminded readers of the cathedral's role in asserting leadership of the nation's religious narrative. Referring to the country's growing infrastructural needs, one article links trends in American government and corporate bureaucracy to the need for greater Episcopal administration via the cathedral: "Government is meeting these new conditions through the establishment of great centralized administrative agencies, equipped for service and housed with a dignity befitting their importance. Business has created its skyscrapers, transportation its magnificent terminal stations, industry its impressive office buildings—and religion, facing similar problems, must turn to the cathedral, the institution which has proved itself through the ages the strong unifier of the spiritual aims of the people."[36] This excerpt is notable not simply because it sees American government and corporate and bureaucratic trends as useful analogs to the cathedral project, but also because the author sees these trends all as one movement to "unify" the nation. Centralizations of government, corporate, and transportation infrastructure suggest the Episcopal Church would not be doing its part were it not to consolidate the nation's disparate spiritual centers into a cathedral befitting the "spiritual aims of the people."

More and more, the cathedral project merged political anxieties with religious beliefs. Consider as part of the cathedral marketing campaign another piece published the previous year in the *Cathedral Age*. Written by Reverend Anson Phelps Stokes, canon of Washington Cathedral, the article is titled "Why a Cathedral at the Nation's Capital?" Quoting the late General John Kasson, a wealthy US ambassador who bequeathed the cathedral project more than half a million dollars, Stokes distinguishes between Episcopalians and Roman Catholics in "believing that the erection of a Cathedral of the Protestant Episcopal Church at the Capital of the Nation where the plain religion of Jesus Christ, unencumbered by obscuring rites and ceremonies, shall be preached to all people, will promote the true Christian faith and tend to elevate the standard of national morality and character."[37] Stokes's sentiments here reaffirm much about the rivalry between Episcopalians and America's Roman Catholics, including the sense that Roman Catholicism is a threat to true Christianity and, by extension, the nation's moral character; the sense that Protestant Episcopalians have a special right and obligation to share the true gospel with "all people" in the interest of rehabilitating that character; and the notion that Roman Catholicism is overly ritualized and obscure.

But the quote reveals more about the anxiety inherent in the Episcopal side of that tension. As indicated previously, the Protestant Episcopal Church was an in-between denomination. Heirs of the English state church, which was itself based on a post-Reformation ideal that resembled something like the churches of the Byzantine emperors, Episcopalians had to find a way to operate within a democratic religious marketplace. Mark Chapman observes: "What was perhaps most important in shaping the Church of England was a vision of a Christian nation upheld by a Christian monarch."[38] Within this construct, the divine right of kings claimed both spiritual and temporal responsibility over national affairs. As the American iteration of this tradition, the Episcopal Church at times appeared frustrated by its impulse to lead within a nation that denies a state church. Such is the story of the Church of England following the disintegration of the monarchical divine right from the eighteenth century onward: a spiritual hegemony in search of political authority.

Without such authority, affirming Protestant Episcopal control of the national soul became a matter of persuasion and self-promotion—a messy business but one that Satterlee was prepared to pursue. Asserting such leadership depended on one's ability to marginalize opposition, build attractive centers of influence, and educate the public in the proper character of a nation. Take, for example, Reverend Stokes's later comments in the same piece quoted above. Stokes sees the cathedral as a volley in an ongoing battle for rhetorical supremacy:

> the erection of a Cathedral under Protestant auspices at the Nation's Capital
> represent[s] a highly important project from the point of view of religion

and of patriotism. . . . The Roman Catholic Church is erecting in the city the
"National Shrine of the Immaculate Conception" and is pouring in for this and
other religious and educational purposes, millions and millions of dollars. . . .
But why should the Protestant forces, which are mainly responsible for the
foundations of the nation, and to which over three quarters of our people
belong, neglect their duty?

Furthermore the mediating position of our Church between the extremes
of Roman Catholicism and of Protestant Evangelicalism strengthens its position of vantage in this matter.[39]

Concerns over civic duty and authenticity are at the heart of Stokes's anxiety.
Note also that Stokes does not impugn the RCC for its own efforts to spread
influence. He simply urges the Episcopal Church to make more of an effort
in this regard. He also sees the Episcopal Church as a moderating force and
a pragmatic alternative to the extremes of Romanism on one hand and evangelicalism on the other. For Stokes as for so many others, the cathedral project was not simply a way of building a glimmering headquarters for the new
diocese, and not even an ecumenical house of prayer for all people. It was a
broadside in the contest for control of the nation's spiritual identity.

❖

Shortly after his consecration as bishop, Satterlee embarked on a series of
public talks and interviews to raise money for the cathedral project. Over the
course of the tour, he developed a rhetorical strategy in which the still-
unbuilt cathedral became a rampart against Roman Catholicism and a symbol
of Christian American culture. In one undated address to potential donors in
New York, Satterlee remarks, "I have been impressed more and more deeply
with the way in which [our cathedral] appeals, not only to the religious, but
also to the patriotic, instincts of our people."[40] This statement is followed by
a few sentences on the present and future greatness of the nation, which are
then followed by this statement: "Our Roman Catholic population since the
war with Spain has suddenly, in two years, been doubled. Through immigration and these causes the United States will soon probably take its place
among those countries where Roman Catholicism is most largely represented.
This fact has already been carefully weighed in the city of Rome itself, and
if we carelessly ignore it, it will be at the cost of another type of American
Christian life."[41] Satterlee then comments on remarks made by Roman Catholic archbishop John J. Keane, the former head of what is now named the

Catholic University of America. Keane had stated that the Catholic University was meant to be national rather than local in its influence. Satterlee notes this detail as though to suggest Roman Catholics were engaged in a campaign for political leverage: "I do not fear Romanism, in any way, as a growing spiritual power among us, but we must all recognize the fact that it will probably be a growing political power."[42] Like Boardman, Stokes, and other Protestant leaders quoted previously, Satterlee attempts to insulate himself against accusations of religious bigotry. Effecting to engage in polite arguments over political matters rather than open invective against a rival religion, Satterlee comes off as a champion of religious freedom who defends a particular American way of life. The issue, he implies, is not a sectarian one, but a civil-religious one.

Similarly, in an 1897 address to the annual convention of the Protestant Episcopal Church, Satterlee links the need for endowment funds to the rivalry between Protestant Episcopalism and Roman Catholicism. Lamenting the tendency among benefactors to endow colleges, universities, or other civic institutions rather than their own local churches, Satterlee argues that "the Church of God, whose history is an epistle seen and read of all men, must do more to earn the trust of those who would make bequests."[43] The statement seems like a standard appeal for money, but Satterlee abruptly transitions to what appears to be a non sequitur, "the Bishop of Rome." He notes that since the last convention, Pope Leo XIII has issued a bull, "declaring that the Anglican Orders are invalid." Satterlee continues by highlighting the essentially undemocratic nature of the bull: "It awakened that sense of equity which demands that no man, yes, no nation of men, shall interfere in the affairs of another without a righteous cause." One notes again the classic strategy of othering the Roman Church by affecting disappointment at its want of democratic values. Satterlee then takes the gloves off:

> The Bull of Leo XIII was instinctively felt by the sober-minded Clergy and Laity of our Church to be nothing less than an uncalled-for act of intrusion upon the home life of our national Churches of England and America; and it correspondingly touched in the breasts of our thinking men that innate feeling of self-respect....
>
> If he [the pope] speaks in the name of Christ, then, like Christ, he must "speak with authority and not as the Scribes." The letter of the Bishop of Rome does not sound this key-note. His thoughts do not move on this high level. He stands as a leader upon a much lower plane.[44]

Despite his characterization of the pope as a source of intolerance, it is not difficult to hear the dog whistles of nativism in Satterlee's choice of words: the contrast he sets between Roman Catholic power-mongering and the "sober-minded" instincts of Anglican leaders and laity; the way he paints the RCC as an "intruder" into the "home life" of otherwise free and autonomous Englishmen and Americans; the characterization of these Protestant victims as "thinking men" with "innate feelings of self-respect" in contrast, one presumes, to the slavish followers of the tyrant pope; and so on. The RCC, by virtue of its unwillingness to honor the orders of a Protestant faith, somehow becomes the embodiment of foreign threats to democratic freedom. To conclude, Satterlee makes the foil explicit: "It is not too much to say, that the Bishop of Rome, by his last act, has isolated the Papacy and cut it off from all participation in the coming reunion of Christendom. Furthermore, instead of accomplishing his own purpose, his letter will serve, on the contrary, to create a more general recognition and better understanding of the historic character of the Anglican Communion."[45] With that Satterlee makes an argument about the need for more bequests. To follow such an appeal with an otherwise puzzling censure of the pope's assault on free, sober, thinking Christians is to make his strategy rather plain. He sees the contest with Rome as both an exigency that calls for the cathedral and an opportunity to invest the cathedral with the energy and money necessary to claim the nation for Protestantism. Satterlee saw himself as an officer in the war over Christendom, and he believed that his cathedral would be among the most important conquests in the long history of that war.

Satterlee's Rhetorical Success

That Satterlee's nativist rhetorical strategy worked can hardly be contested. The almost overwhelming sums of debt incurred by the initial land acquisitions and other expenses to get the project off the ground were wiped away, slowly at first, but swiftly once Satterlee commenced his speaking circuit.[46] When he assumed the role of bishop in 1896, he faced what he called "the darkest of all the days of the Cathedral Foundation." Everyone seemed excited at the prospect of a new cathedral, but no one "proffered the material and financial help necessary to carry the project into effect."[47] With not so much as a single stone laid, the cathedral owed hundreds of thousands: $120,000 for the initial land acquisition, followed by more debt to acquire the outlying boundaries of the original plot on St. Alban's Hill. After receiving Senator Edmunds's letter in 1898, Satterlee's nativist rhetorical strategy began to take shape. During what was likely his most ambitious fund-raising tour, in 1900, Satterlee made it standard practice to quote from the Edmunds letter and to add his own views on the unsettling expansion of Roman Catholicism in the United States. By the end of 1905, all debts had been erased and major construction phases were ready for launch.

Additional evidence of the effectiveness of Satterlee's rhetorical strategy can be found in the failure of a competing, though lesser-known, project. In 1901, the *Church Standard* noted that Reverend Richard Lewis Howell, the founder and rector of a parish in Washington, DC, had announced his intention to seek contributions for the "World's House of Prayer and Praise in the Capital of the United States of America." Howell's idea departed from Satterlee's in at least one way: while Satterlee insisted on a cathedral of "Christian unity with an Anglican basis," Howell embraced a kind of radical ecumenism.[48] He viewed such a cathedral not as a place in which administrative prerogative would be centralized and filtered through a single denomination. Instead, it would be a place of leveling. Christianity would still be at its heart, but no faith group would be in charge, and non-Christians would be welcomed on equal terms.

Howell viewed Satterlee's Episcopal-centrism as problematic and promoted instead a national house of worship that would unite all churches without any sectarian pecking orders. Publicly, Howell made his position clear. His cathedral would be "controlled not only by one Church or sect, but by representatives from every Church or sect, forming a board of managers." His reasoning was that "this is a thinking age. All the churches while worshipping separately, nevertheless wish to get together on some common platform with no shibboleth of party."[49] Privately, he was even more grandiose. Writing to Satterlee, Howell reveals his intention for "a cathedral-like Edifice of Worship, planned by the best international talent procurable. It is meant primarily for a House of Prayer and Praise, for 'Jew and Greek, bond and free,' open every hour of the day and night throughout the year."[50] Howell's enthusiastic descriptions echoed in both tone and content the vision of Pierre L'Enfant a century earlier. For Howell, building a national temple meant building what was in essence a Pantheon in which all gods are welcome so long as they channel the citizens' convictions into a zeal for the country.

As the previous chapter shows, Satterlee was of a different make. For all his similarities to L'Enfant, including his flare for the quixotic, Satterlee was an effective politician. Where L'Enfant was impulsive and inflexible, Satterlee could be methodical and measured, even if his ambitions for the national church were no less grand. Satterlee responded to Howell with thinly veiled patronization, calling his letter "interesting" and praising his enthusiasm while questioning his Anglican bona fides. Invoking the Chicago Quadrilateral—for, in this case, it suited him—Satterlee makes it clear that only a less-than-loyal servant of God would dare strip the church of its inspired doctrinal mission: "I do not see how any loyal churchman can go beyond the New Testament truths, as they are laid down not only in the Prayer Book but by the Apostles themselves. It seems to me, that, in the intensity of your generous desire for a religious unity, and in the enthusiasm of the moment, you must have temporarily lost sight of those fundamental principles."[51] Satterlee's response underscores how he intended to resolve the tension between building a national church with an Anglican basis and building a house of prayer "for all people." In his view, he was building a church for everyone, because the Anglican Communion and the Episcopal Church were for everyone, especially Americans. The Quadrilateral, an endemically Anglican document, was the basis for a global Christian unity. To remove its Anglican core was to flirt with apostasy.

An Anglican Religious World Order

This vision of unity with an Anglican basis was not Satterlee's invention. It was rooted in a centuries-long political tradition. Among other thinkers, Richard Hooker, a famous sixteenth-century Church of England theologian, is credited with affirming the view of an Anglican via media, the notion that Anglicanism provides the ideal balance between Protestantism and Roman Catholicism. Hooker argued that the church ought to become part of the national lifeblood, such that its influence becomes essential to the nation.[52] Richard Hewlett notes that many nineteenth-century Episcopalians likewise came "to believe that the Episcopal Church had a distinctive identity that gave it a superiority over other American churches and made it an ideal form around which Christians of all denominations might be unified."[53] In this light, Anglican calls for unity were rarely calls for a true ecumenism. They were efforts to better organize the Christian world according to an Anglican vision.

Such sentiments were expressed diplomatically but openly at various Anglican conferences and in official encyclicals of the day.[54] They were also expressed in private communications, in which it becomes clear that while people like Satterlee were interested in greater unity with their fellow Protestants, they were not likely to abdicate what they felt to be a divinely appointed governing role. In private letters from 1907, over a decade after assuming the bishopric and just a year before his death, Satterlee took up correspondence with George W. King, a Methodist Episcopal pastor in Baltimore. King complimented Satterlee on his desire for greater unity with other Protestants, but he also chided the bishop, stating that it is the Episcopal Church that ought to come "more into sympathy with the rest of us in our hard work" and that whatever efforts Episcopal clergy are making should be made "in a larger degree."[55] Whatever message Satterlee was sending about ecumenism, it seems clear that some other Protestant leaders wondered about his motives.

Some of the bolder and more creative strains of Anglicanism assumed that the Church of England was the lineal descendent of the original Christian Church founded by Christ himself, and that English men and women were the literal descendants of Israel and the progeny of God's original chosen people. The claim of an ethnic heritage with the Jews may seem strange to modern ears, but it represents a not unfamiliar trope in the nineteenth century.[56] Precisely to what extent Satterlee believed the various rationales for Anglican supremacy is not clear. What is known is that he regarded Anglicanism as occupying a divinely ordained position of leadership among Christian traditions and that loyalty to Anglicanism therefore amounted to an expression of Christian devotion. It is also clear that he had little interest in ceding authority to other Protestants or in reconciling with the RCC. And yet Satterlee was never vicious in his critiques of Roman Catholicism. Like other Protestant leaders of his time, he couched his nativism in tones of polite argument, suggesting that divisions with Rome were accountable to Rome itself, which continued to fall short of the standard to which all churches ought to aspire, especially in a land of liberty, sobriety, and reason.

❖

In chapter 2, I argue that Henry Yates Satterlee's upbringing enforced a kind of paradox. His early life was a touchstone of social privilege, and he admirably and continuously worked to be worthy of it. However, while his behavior seemed beyond reproach, his way of viewing the world and interacting with it revealed a kind of apartness. He was present and involved in society, but he was also more comfortable in elevated roles. He preferred to interact with doting adults or to play with younger children, rather than to indulge with friends in what he may have viewed as more vulgar pastimes. He was a success in his studies and never an outcast, and yet he never seemed to blend among his peers. He embraced the role of exemplar.

Satterlee regarded the Episcopal Church in this same light. It was primus inter pares, called to chaperone Protestantism into a new era of unity. Throughout his career, Satterlee sought to alleviate suffering everywhere, minister to people from across faiths, and practice a universal Christianity fit for a noble nation. The condition, of course, was that this new Christianity be administered within the context of Anglican authority. For this reason, Satterlee gladly worked with other faiths, but he never saw himself as a true ecumenist. He drew widely on Methodist-style services when he felt his audience preferred it; and when it came time to design and build a baptistry for Washington National Cathedral, he insisted that one be built in a separate building on the close rather than in the cathedral itself and that the font be large enough to conduct baptisms by immersion. In this way, non-Episcopal Protestants could feel more comfortable taking part in cathedral-hosted rituals. Nevertheless, Hewlett finds no evidence that Satterlee ever took an interest in the ecumenist movement "or even knew of its existence."[57] Admittedly, this view is taken by most religions; they regard themselves as being best suited to the task of spiritual leadership in the world. What sets Episcopalism apart from others at the turn of the century is the presumption that this superiority called for a national church on the same order as England's Westminster Abbey. No other American faith was so bold as to claim the legacy of L'Enfant, or to do so with such a loose interpretation of what that legacy means.

I am always struck by the cathedral's resemblance to its builder and first bishop. Henry Yates Satterlee was by all accounts a genuine Christian who held himself to the highest standards, but like so many people of privilege, his view of political realities tended to be abstract. Somehow, he was both engaged and removed, immersed in Christian service yet insulated by patrician distance. Just so, the cathedral on St. Alban's Hill has for more than a century extended its hand of peace and healing to the whole nation while diplomatically guarding its boundaries. In its explicit conflation of American religion and politics, the cathedral has become a singular sort of grotesque. Like all grotesques, there is something both beautiful and precarious about it. One does not know whether to stand and admire it and even embrace it, or shudder and turn away.

CHAPTER FOUR

Francis B. Sayre the Prophet and Mariann Edgar Budde the Pastor

In the years following Satterlee's death, the cathedral project was beset with fund-raising and construction challenges. The national brand that Satterlee had worked so hard to cultivate continued to be useful because it allowed the Cathedral Foundation to seek support not only from Episcopalians but also from a variety of wealthy Americans who believed the nation needed a Protestant bulwark to confront the rise of Romanism and secularism. National leaders also continued to give the cathedral their blessing. In 1918, Woodrow Wilson attended a Thanksgiving service to mark the end of World War I. In 1921, Warren G. Harding led delegates to the Conference on the Limitations of Armaments to a service at the cathedral. In 1923, Calvin Coolidge declared that the cathedral had "already become both an adornment and an inspiration in the national capital" and that it stood for religion, which is "the foundation of all progress, all government and all civilization."[1] In 1928, Coolidge opened the services for the Episcopal Church's General Convention at the cathedral. In 1937, Franklin Delano Roosevelt attended a National Day of Prayer service following his second inauguration, creating a precedent for future presidents, including Ronald Reagan, George H. W. Bush, Barack Obama, Donald Trump, and Joe Biden.[2]

Despite these high-profile visits, the cathedral's progress in the first half of the century was blunted by two world wars and one catastrophic depression. Between Satterlee's death in 1908 and the eve of the Great Depression in 1928, only the cathedral's crypt was finished. The choir and sanctuary were completed in 1932, but by that time the Depression's grip was tightening and funds were drying up fast. Even in 1945, the year World War II ended, the building still lacked a nave, a south transept, and towers. There it was, forty years after the laying of the foundation stone, and the cathedral looked more like a ruin than a symbol of national faith.[3] Cathedral leaders did their best to promote the project, but without a grand space or any sense of when they would have one, their words seemed like just more glittering promises. The cathedral's mission, which had never been clearly defined even in Satterlee's day, was in danger of going completely fallow.

In May 1936, the Cathedral Council authored a report designed to revive the cathedral's sense of promise; specifically, it considered "how Washington Cathedral can best advance the Cause of Religion in the United States."[4] The report identifies three aspects of the cathedral's responsibility: "The first is to the city of Washington. . . . The second is to the Protestant Episcopal Church. . . . The third aspect is that of the relation of the Cathedral to the general cause of Christianity in America." In elaborating on these aspects, the report describes the council's vision of "the great Church being erected on Mount Saint Alban—whose Gloria in Excelsis Tower will guard the city on one side as the dome of the Capitol does on the other—as Washington Cathedral, a witness for Christ in the nation's capital."[5] The report repeatedly conflates *religion* with *Christianity*, declaring with reference to an unnamed Supreme Court decision that the United States is officially "a Christian Nation" that must pursue "the essentials of Christian faith and life." It adds that the very reason the cathedral project was launched decades earlier was to stand as a witness that "Jesus Christ is the Saviour of the world."[6] As Canterbury was to England and Santa Sophia was to the Eastern Empire, so, the authors openly hoped, "Washington Cathedral may ultimately come to mean to the United States."[7] Whatever the cathedral had become or would become, the report made clear that Christianity was its raison d'être.

Whereas L'Enfant's church would have drawn on religion to promote a particular nation, Washington Cathedral would draw on the nation to promote a particular religion. And yet, curiously enough, the authors of the report were not shy about claiming the legacy of L'Enfant just as Satterlee had done before them. "As is well known," they remind their readers, "L'Enfant's plan for the capital, made at Washington's request, provided for 'a church for national purposes such as public prayer and thanksgiving.' It did not prove possible to carry out this part of the plan, but Washington Cathedral has been trying, as far as possible under the changed conditions of democratic life, to meet the need."[8] The parenthetical is odd. What is meant by "the changed conditions of democratic life"? Perhaps it is an acknowledgment that although the church the Cathedral Council was building was different from L'Enfant's, it was a natural response to some new historical moment. To this day, however, the cathedral presumes the legacy. The cathedral's website proudly announces that "George Washington and Maj. Pierre L'Enfant cast the original vision for a unifying 'great church for national purposes' in the early days of the republic, though it was another century before the foundation stone was laid."[9] Speculation on the cathedral administration's interpretation of this relationship only raises several questions: Was L'Enfant's church supposed to be Christian? If not, what has changed? Has the nation's democracy come to understand the centrality of Christianity at last? It is not clear. What is clear is that this Christian cathedral is presented as the manifestation of a founding idea, the fulfillment of a request by Washington himself.

The report concludes with a reference to the cathedral's favorite foil, the Roman Catholic Church, which comprises "a little less than one-fifth of our population" and yet maintains a powerful religious and educational center in the nation's capital. Similarly, the report implies, the Protestant movement ought to have its influence felt under the leadership of the Episcopal Church.[10] As the cathedral faced its darkest days since the debacles of Paret, Douglas, and McKim in the 1880s, its leaders drew on Satterlee's old playbook: broadcast the cathedral's national mission, no matter how ambiguously; claim the legacy of L'Enfant, no matter how capriciously; and invoke the specter of papism. Whether the strategy worked is hard to say. The cathedral weathered the Depression admirably, reaching some important construction milestones along the way, even though it remained decades from completion; and, as noted previously, it managed to win the endorsements of national leaders. Following the report, however, it appears the cathedral did little more than maintain this holding pattern, and in time its lauded national mission fell back into obscurity. After 1937, the cathedral was involved in almost nothing of national significance.

Francis B. Sayre Resurrects the Cathedral

By the time Francis Bowes Sayre Jr. became dean of the cathedral in 1951, the project appeared to have no national mission at all. In a 2000 interview, long after his retirement, Sayre argued that the cathedral's administration had embraced a kind of parochialism and that his role was to renew the "focus on the national in Washington National Cathedral."[11] Between the Cathedral Council report in 1936 and his election in 1951, Sayre saw little evidence that the cathedral's leadership had exerted influence beyond the communion itself. Few if any Episcopalians qualified as national figures, yet the cathedral invited Episcopal preachers almost exclusively to preach from its pulpit. What

Fig. 4.1. Dean Francis Bowes Sayre Jr. preaches from the pulpit of Washington National Cathedral, c. 1951–1978. Washington National Cathedral Archives

was worse, the cathedral seemed indifferent to public affairs. Sayre explained this dilemma: "I started from zero at the Cathedral [inaudible]. I wasn't looked to, maybe I was looked to by some, but to be an influence on public affairs I had to learn how to be, why to be influential. Why was I Dean of this Cathedral for? What was the Cathedral being built for unless it could be helpful[,] to be useful for people who did want to have influence on public affairs and be non-parochial was a pretty good asset to the Cathedral. Nobody realized that before I went there, I don't think."[12] If the cathedral would not minister to the nation, the nation would not look to the cathedral for influence. For Sayre, this dynamic ran counter to the very purpose of the cathedral, which was to "change the soul of the nation."[13]

Sayre's interpretation of the cathedral and its mission speaks to what religious studies scholars sometimes refer to as the binary between prophet and pastor. A prophetic leader is one who thunders reform and calls the people to repentance. Such a leader may come across as a revolutionary or, at the very least, a visionary who views the world in broad and dramatic terms. This leader wants to reshape the cosmos to bring them into order with God's justice. A pastoral leader is one who is more concerned with the day-to-day work of ministering. Such a leader views their task as one of nurturing and seeing to the needs of the individual. Scholars understand that a leader can be both a prophet and a pastor, but whether they assume one role more than the other is a matter of context. It depends on what sort of leader they want to be and what sort of leader the historical moment calls for.[14] Sayre was an experienced and thoughtful pastor, but by virtue of his call to the cathedral, he embraced the prophetic mode.

Fortunately for Sayre, this focus on national mission coincided with a boom in the nation's economic and moral outlook. Following World War II, and under the leadership of Dean Sayre, the cathedral's ministry expanded along with the building's construction. The nave finally took shape. The south transept was enclosed. Dozens of stained-glass windows were installed. Sayre's notion of ministry began to take shape as well. A variety of preachers with national reputations were invited to speak from the cathedral's pulpit, including the archbishop of Canterbury, Martin Luther King Jr., Cesar Chavez, Billy Graham, and, remarkably, a number of Roman Catholic priests with whom Sayre had begun to form close friendships.[15] Sayre even authored a press release, published in the *New York Times* on May 3, 1960, in which he and several other Protestant leaders denounced the anti-Catholicism that had emerged in response to John F. Kennedy's presidential candidacy.[16]

Sayre also oversaw several high-profile interments, official visits, and installations. Woodrow Wilson, Sayre's maternal grandfather, was interred in the cathedral. So was Helen Keller. The cathedral hosted an array of international leaders, including the British queen, the Ethiopian emperor, the Indian prime minister, and presidents Truman, Eisenhower, and Ford. These three presidents, not to mention King George and Winston Churchill of England, were given memorial services in the cathedral following their deaths.[17]

Bays, chapels, and other memorials were dedicated to the nation's great events and leaders, from labor leaders to former presidents, regardless of their faith affiliation. Sayre was able to persuade someone at NASA to gift the cathedral a rock from the famous moon landing. That rock now forms the centerpiece of the cathedral's famous Space Window. The iconography filling the cathedral and the oratory flowing from its pulpit blurred religious and national lines with greater abandon than ever before.

Perhaps more than anything, however, Sayre's position on political debates made clear that he was not afraid to confront matters that were national in scope. Sayre was a liberal, and for nearly three decades he used the cathedral as a vehicle to speak out. During the 1950s he declaimed against school segregation and the machinations of Senator Joseph McCarthy, whom he called one of the nation's "pretended patriots."[18] During the 1960s, he marched with Martin Luther King Jr. for civil rights in Selma and Montgomery. In the 1970s, on the eve of Nixon's inauguration, he organized a concert of Haydn's *Mass in Time of War*, conducted by Leonard Bernstein, and he later joined the March of Conscience to protest the bombing of Hanoi and Hy Thong.[19] Throughout Sayre's twenty-seven years at the cathedral, he attempted to lead on matters of moral controversy, but he did so in a way that departed from the foundations laid by Satterlee and others. Whereas Satterlee drew on the political establishment to expand the influence of the church and cathedral, Sayre used the cathedral as a platform to challenge the political establishment. Whereas Satterlee solicited letters of endorsement from the nation's leaders, Sayre received letters from generals and fellow clergy excoriating his social positions and withdrawing support, and he was open about the fact that he was not on good terms with the likes of Truman, Nixon, and others with whom he had political differences, particularly when it came to war.[20] Sayre was redefining the mission of the cathedral according to his own theory of the American Civil Religion.

Satterlee and Sayre, Different but Similar

The differences between the two leaders do not tell the whole story, though. They were also alike. Like Satterlee's, Sayre's blend of pedigree and social mission made him attractive to a stalled cathedral project with a grand but nebulous mission. When the chapter elected him, it said with pragmatic relief, "Frank, you make sense."[21] Also like Satterlee, Sayre did not devote himself only to raising the cathedral's national profile; he also became deeply involved in its construction and planning. Under his leadership, the cathedral

reached 90 percent completion, including finishing the nave, the south transept, and the colossal Gloria in Excelsis Tower, the cathedral's three-hundred-
foot-tall centerpiece. He was also chairman of the building committee, and
he collaborated closely with designers on the cathedral's finer details, such
as the central tower's carved symbols, windows, and bells.[22]

Satterlee and Sayre were united by their boldness, their ambition, and
their attention to detail. For each, the cathedral was a means of advancing
something greater than the cathedral itself, something greater even than the
diocese or the city or the Episcopal Church. They both believed in a gospel
of social action. In one of his sermons early in his tenure as dean, Sayre asked,
in allusion to the prophet Elijah, "How long will ye go limping between two
sides?" He continued, "I am afraid we've been doing a good bit of limping
ourselves." Decades later, just four years before his retirement and after a career of activism, he had become only bolder: "Whoever is appointed the dean
of the cathedral has in his hand a marvelous instrument, and he is a coward
if he doesn't use it."[23] Not since Satterlee himself had a leader of the cathedral
been so ambitious in his efforts to define and promote the cathedral's national mission, and so involved in the details of the cathedral's design.

As I hope I have shown, although Satterlee and Sayre shared much in common by way of personality and method, their implied visions of the American
Civil Religion differed. Satterlee made the cathedral a lodestar of Christian
nationalism. In his view, the civic soul of the United States could be exalted
only insofar as it adopted an Anglican basis for spirituality. Doing so, he made
clear to planners, donors, and national leaders, would render the country
more rightfully Christian as the Lord used the cathedral to reunify His scattered sects and introduce a new era of peace. This version of civil religion,
like the vision of the Puritans and many others who followed them, presumed
that the nation's spirituality should be an extension of its Christian culture.
This vision of course ran in direct opposition to that of L'Enfant, which imagined a national faith in conjunction with but entirely independent of the
country's private faiths. The nation was never meant to be, in L'Enfant's view,
a constituent of Christianity; Christianity was to be a constituent of the national faith.

Sayre's civil-religious philosophy could almost not have been more different from Satterlee's. Notwithstanding his occasional endorsements of more
Christianity in the public sphere, Sayre's philosophy seems more like L'Enfant's. A reading of Sayre's public statements and even his sermons reveals
an aversion to sectarian language. He rarely if ever invoked the supremacy of

the Anglican Communion, and he tended to reference deity in a way that embraced non-Christians. He preferred the terms *God* or *Providence* to the name *Christ* in public discourse, and he regretted the medieval tendencies of the church to claim too much authority. "The sense of where man fits into the dispensation of God," he declared in a public statement following a presidential inauguration, "was a thing that centuries ago was thought to be almost exclusively the province of the Church to define. Therein lay the mystique of the Middle Ages in Europe." Sayre claimed that this mystique had vanished with the advent of democracy: "No such form of government could have been instituted if God had not been perceived to be at work, not merely among His priests, but in every walk of life, in every lively intelligence and gentle conscience that bears the image of creation. Thus was conceived the stunning notion that the Providence of history could well be entrusted to the universal suffrage of plain people, and the secular leaders of their election."[24]

Under Sayre, the meaning of the cathedral's national mission started to become more nuanced. An essay in the spring 1958 issue of the cathedral's signature publication, *Cathedral Age*, attempted to reaffirm the cathedral's unique role by reminding readers that it "is constituted by an Act of Congress a National Cathedral and a shrine in the nation's capital." An editorial footnote in the essay provides the following clarification: "More accurately this should read, The Protestant Episcopal Cathedral Foundation was chartered by an Act of Congress and, for many Americans, has become a national cathedral and a shrine in the nation's capital."[25] Sayre did not author the essay, but it is plausible that he influenced or even wrote the correction. Its sentiment jibes with his own civil-religious philosophy, and, as dean, he enmeshed himself in the details of the cathedral's mission. The cathedral exists to challenge institutional power, not to embody it.

None of this is to say that Sayre was squeamish about proclaiming his Christian faith or even affirming a "Christian heritage" for the nation. He regularly delivered sermons on conventional doctrinal topics.[26] However, Christian identity for Sayre was the means toward the cathedral's national influence rather than the end. He regularly drew on scripture to preach on subjects ranging from civil rights, to disarmament, to refugees, to the Cuban Missile Crisis and the Vietnam War. A 1971 sermon on the release of the Pentagon Papers illustrates how Sayre viewed the relationship between his Christian faith and the civic ills of his country. Beginning with a text from the Book of Jeremiah—he was fond of Jeremiah, the prophet who called God's chosen nation to repentance—he quoted: "The people that were left of the sword found grace in the wilderness. Therefore will I be God of the families of Israel and they shall be my people." Sayre's view of the United States was similar. "Have you considered," he asked prophetically, "that it might very well be God's will just now that if we, and most of the world with us, have chosen to hang on to all the old, man-made self-sufficiencies—all the old racial arrogances and familiar aggrandizements that have characterized our recent history, then God is going to just let us be shaken right apart. Let the old establishments come crumbling down—church and state and universities and political hypocrisies, the good with the bad, until at last we realize whose warfare this is—whose peace shall prevail!"[27] He concluded as Jeremiah would have, with a call for grace: "How shall we, in the paroxysm of our despair, find such grace?" He answered that the nation must embrace that "rare and strange thing to Americans . . . Humbleness," and that it must also embrace "Openness" and "Proportion" if God will "still deign to have us."

The address is classic Sayre. It begins from a place of scripture and doctrine, but it moves intrepidly into the issues of the day. His audience is no parish congregation. As he viewed the matter, he had been called to minister to the whole nation, so he targets its leaders: "I saw one day the look of utter agony on the face of the Secretary of Defense, as he peered out from behind the curtains in his office at the spot before the Pentagon where a young man had recently burned himself to death in protest against the falsehood of this war." Because such men make the decisions that impact the flow of history, he singles them out. They are the ones who demonstrate the exile of Israel, and they therefore are those who most need to return to grace, humbleness, openness, and proportion. Leaders of the cathedral since Satterlee himself were fond of commenting on the way the cathedral interacts with the Capitol in the landscape of the federal district, as in the following: "The Capitol and the Cathedral—symbols of Free State and Free Church," the latter symbolizing the conscience of the former.[28] Sayre viewed this relationship not as a union so much as a struggle. Just as the cathedral was a sermon in stone to the Capitol, so his words called the nation's leaders back to a sense of covenant.

Mariann Edgar Budde's Call to Decency

The line from Sayre's cathedral to the present-day cathedral is easy to trace. Beginning in the 1950s, the Episcopal Church began a cultural reformation that moved it "from the church of the establishment to a church of advocacy."[29] The Episcopal Church had always tended to be more progressive than its parent church, the Church of England, and it had always tended to favor social gospel initiatives, but in the 1950s this tendency gathered momentum. In its 1958 General Convention, the church passed a resolution recognizing "the natural dignity and value of every man, of whatever color or race, as created in the image of God." The church also called for the establishment of full equality in education, housing, employment, and public accommodations.[30] A year later, the Episcopal Society for Cultural and Racial Unity was established to break down class barriers. By the 1960s, church leaders were preaching openly on the struggle for racial justice and the need for civil rights legislation.[31] The church even began diverting a significant portion of its budget to facilitate empowerment initiatives in mostly black ghettos.[32] In 1970, women were admitted as delegates to the General Convention, and by the middle of that decade, women were being ordained to the priesthood.[33]

The list goes on. Through the 1970s, '80s, and '90s, the church pursued policies of liberation, inclusion, and activism. Conservatives reacted to the new policies with indignation. Many simply left the church, which resulted in a precipitous decline in membership beginning in the 1960s. Conservatives who stayed objected to the new policies by lamenting the church's involvement in social, political, and economic activities. To this day, tensions seethe. In 2009, many conservatives united in protest to form a new Anglican denomination called the Anglican Church in North America. In 2016, the Anglican Communion dressed down the Episcopal Church for its unilateral activism and removed the church's authority on decision-making matters within the communion for a period of three years. Undeterred, the church continued to raise its voice on the social controversies of its time.

Beginning in the early 2000s, those controversies tended to center on matters related to gender and sexual orientation, and Washington National Cathedral became a center for the Christian LGBTQ+ movement. Dean Sayre was not responsible for the transformation that began in the 1950s and 1960s, but he was very much aligned with it, and thus he aligned the cathedral. His successor John Walker was the first African American bishop of Washington and dean of Washington National Cathedral, a position in which he served from 1978 to 1989.[34] Walker had a global reputation for activism and was very much the heir to Sayre. Although the two leaders had personal differences, even open frictions, they both pursued reforms from a place of deep Christian faith and liberal politics. Their activism was a proclamation of their religion.[35] Between Sayre's high-profile reforms and the continuity provided by Walker's agenda, the cathedral placed itself in the vanguard of liberal Christianity.

The decades around the turn of the twenty-first century marked a period of whiplash, as the nation shifted to the right, first with the Reagan-Bush years, then again in response to the terrorist attacks of September 11, 2001, after which Americans seemed to settle into an aggressive polarization. Culture wars emerged with respect to LGBTQ+ rights and, specifically, the right of gay couples to marry; new tensions on matters of race erupted when Barack Obama became the first Black presidential nominee from a major party and then served two terms as president. A counterculture going by the name Occupy Wall Street rose up to protest unchecked capitalism and income inequality. Political differences seemed increasingly like moral lines in the sand as Americans sealed themselves off from each other.[36] Cathedral leaders were forced to reconcile the cathedral's tradition of unapologetic social justice with its mission to remain a house of prayer for *all* people. Plus, liberal denominations like the Episcopal Church were coming under fire for what seemed their partisan activism, and they were hemorrhaging membership. Conservatives needed to know that they too were welcome in the "nation's church."

When President George H. W. Bush blessed the completion of the building in 1990, he signaled a renewed partnership between the political establishment and the cathedral. That is not to say the cathedral's administration had abandoned its social justice activism, but only that they would begin to take a more conciliatory approach to the institutions of the day. Cathedral leaders began to focus on outreach in the form of public programs, which included musical education and performances, theological training, cultural events, and conferences. The cathedral hosted George W. Bush's National Day of Prayer address following the September 11 attacks, in which Bush introduced a radical civil-religious vision that authorized preemptive war. It also hosted state funerals for conservative icons Gerald Ford and Ronald Reagan. Bishop John Bryson Chane, who led the cathedral beginning in 2002, was an advocate for LGBTQ+ rights, but he focused his most high-profile initiatives on international and interfaith relations.[37] In other words, the cathedral's administration had begun to tread more pragmatically. Although the cathedral's identity as a liberal Christian institution was settled, and although cathedral leaders maintained support for progressive initiatives, they increasingly resisted the trappings of partisanship and played nice with the establishment. They wanted the cathedral to be a force of stability in a nation of unrest.

Chane's ecumenical initiatives seemed a smart way for the cathedral's mission to move forward. He had become a global leader in interfaith dialogue, and thanks to the ties he had built with the Islamic Republic, he was even

Fig. 4.2. Right Rev. Mariann Edgar Budde, bishop of Washington, preaches from the pulpit of Washington National Cathedral during the service celebrating the life of Neil Armstrong, Thursday, September 13, 2012. NASA Image Collection/Alamy Stock Photo

instrumental in freeing American hikers who had been taken hostage in Iran. He also presented papers at numerous human rights conferences across the globe and won several national and international distinctions for his efforts. And yet, while his own profile grew, the Washington diocese continued to struggle. Parishes were facing financial hardship, membership was down, and the profile of the Episcopal Church itself was no better off. Cathedral leaders had gone some way to correcting the cathedral's partisan image, but they seemed to be neglecting its local mission.

When Chane retired in 2011, the Episcopal Church found an ideal candidate for his replacement. Mariann Edgar Budde, the unassuming former rector of St. John's Episcopal Church in Minneapolis, Minnesota, was a woman of fifty-one and the first female bishop of Washington (fig. 4.2). She had a diminutive physical presence but a style of communication that blended competence and experience with compassion and patience. She smiled broadly and spoke in measured and inviting tones. She often came off like a school principal who approaches an overwhelming job with the serene fortitude that comes only from having spent years doing the groundwork herself. Budde described her leadership approach accordingly: "I have learned that anything worth doing takes time. Leading a parish well, raising a family well, being faithful in any realm of life and ministry takes time, perseverance and faith. . . . I am called to leadership more than prophecy, . . . taking small, steady steps to transform our lives."[38] Budde signaled that her style would not be one of bravado or Jeremianic indignation. It would be more scrupulous, patient, and local.

When she accepted the position of bishop of Washington, Budde made it clear that her approach to national politics would be couched within her role as the pastoral leader of a diocese. "The temptation is greater," she told the Episcopal News Service, "to focus on what's happening on the federal side of the government. . . . I'm not a chaplain to the government; I'm the pastor of pastors and a leader of congregations. I tend to pick my issues carefully." She also made it clear that she would not take the approach of her predecessor, John Chane, who, she insinuated, embraced the world stage to the neglect of the more local and pastoral elements of the job. She believed the cathedral needed someone who would focus on the cathedral's "congregational life and vitality."[39] Reflecting this focus on ministering in more local ways, Budde is more explicitly Christian in her public statements than many of her predecessors were. She regularly invokes the name and mission of Christ, she frequently quotes from Christian scripture, and she freely speaks of her sectarian commitments as an Episcopalian. Her two published books underscore these priorities. Her first, published two years before her election as bishop, is titled *Gathering Up the Fragments: Preaching as Spiritual Practice*. It is an empathic appeal to fellow pastors and priests on how to preach to their congregations "with authority, clarity, and humility."[40] Her second book, published eight years after her election, is *Receiving Jesus: The Way of Love*.[41] What attracted the cathedral to her, and what she has emphasized in her ministry since assuming leadership, is her focus on a worship community's inner life.

Budde's priorities appear to be born not only of her personal philosophy as a Christian but also of the exigencies facing the Episcopal Church. She took the helm roughly a decade after the schism that resulted in the Anglican Church of North America. With conservatives leaving in droves and liberals becoming less enamored with religion generally, the Episcopal Church boasted fewer than two million members at the time of Budde's appointment. This number represents the fewest members of the church in modern history. Budde's focus on nurturing congregations seems like pastoral triage as much as it does theology. One of her first resolutions as bishop was to travel the diocese and speak to a new Episcopal congregation every Sunday, attempting to use her position at the cathedral to revitalize the communion locally.

More and more, Budde's style appeared to be a correction of the political broadcasting of her predecessors. When pressed, she sometimes struggled to articulate the relationship between the cathedral's diocesan identity and its more nebulous, national mission. In a 2011 interview with National Public Radio, she responded to a question about the cathedral's role in national life: "There wasn't one—there was no—the creation of this cathedral is a miracle. And the sustaining of it is the stewardship responsibility of our time. . . . The cathedral has a base of ministry and a scope of ministry that is national in scope. My predominant ministry will be for the renewal and revitalization of this diocese."[42] Budde's oscillation between accounting for the cathedral's local and national identities is not solely the result of her ambivalence on the subject; it is the consequence of the building's origins in the nineteenth century when Paret, Douglas, McKim, and, later, Satterlee all struggled to articulate a mission that would be targeted enough to meet the needs in Washington, DC, yet grand enough to assert influence over the Protestant Episcopal Church, the United States, and Christendom itself. The ambivalence of her answer belonged to the cathedral, not to her. As long as she was the leader of the diocese, she could tamp down the cathedral's role in national life and focus instead on her own priorities as shepherdess of her flock.

The Problem of President Trump

Budde's reserved approach would be stretched to its limit in July 2019, when then president Donald Trump was accused of fanning the flames of racism by publishing a series of tweets directed at congresspeople of color. To be clear, Budde was not opposed to taking public stances on matters of social justice. She often took to social media in support of LGBTQ+ rights, gun law reform, and immigration reform. However, she curated her public persona in such a way that these positions seemed ancillary to her revitalization efforts within the diocese itself. It was very deliberate, then, when she decided to raise her voice in denunciation of the president's rhetoric. The Trump administration was facing criticism for its treatment of refugees at the US-Mexico border, because, according to reports, refugee children were being separated from their parents, kept in cages, undernourished, unbathed, and forced to remain in their own filth.[43]

Members of Congress protested the conditions. Representative Elijah Cummings of Maryland was especially vehement in his criticism. In a congressional hearing before the House Oversight and Government Reform Committee, which he chaired, Cummings reamed Department of Homeland Security head Kevin McAleenan: "We are the United States of America," he shouted at McAleenan. "We are the greatest country in the world. We are the ones that can go anywhere in the world and save people, make sure that they have diapers, make sure that they have toothbrushes, make sure that they're not laying around, defecating in some silver paper."[44] Trump responded to McAleenan's dressing-down with criticism for Cummings's home district in Baltimore. Calling the district "a disgusting, rat and rodent infested mess," Trump claimed it was "the worst in the USA." He also insinuated that the reason for its struggles had to do with corruption and that an investigation ought to be launched into its use of federal funds "immediately."[45]

Trump's comments might have been passed over as just more bluster, and the implication of racial divisiveness might not have come up, except that earlier that same month Trump tweeted that certain " 'Progressive' Democrat Congresswomen"—presumably the four Democratic congresswomen of color known as the Squad—ought to "go back" to the "crime infested [countries] from which they came."[46] He had demonstrated a pattern of ridiculing whole districts represented by racial minority members of Congress, though he would do the same to Nancy Pelosi later the same month. He had also demonstrated a pattern of deflecting criticism against his own immigration policies not by defending his record but by seeking to alienate the source of the criticism and even presuming, falsely, that his critics were not from the United States. Indeed, three of the four congresswomen targeted by Trump were born and raised in the United States; the other, Representative Ilhan Omar of Minnesota, was a naturalized US citizen who had come to America as a refugee twenty years earlier.

Trump never made explicit reference to the skin color of his critics, but the dog whistles of racism and xenophobia were evident, and an indignant chorus rose up in response. One of the most clarion voices in that chorus was that of Bishop Budde and Washington National Cathedral. In a rare national press release titled "Have We No Decency? A Response to President Trump," Budde, along with Dean Randolph Hollerith and cathedral canon Kelly Brown

Douglas, rebuked the president: "This week, President Trump crossed another threshold. Not only did he insult a leader in the fight for racial justice and equality for all persons; not only did he savage the nations from which immigrants to this country have come; but now he has condemned the residents of an entire American city. Where will he go from here?"[47] Gone was the tranquil and forbearing voice that Budde had been cultivating for years. Gone was the philosophic patience. Gone was the olive branch to the nation's executive. For the moment at least, Budde the pastor became Budde the prophet: "We feel compelled to ask: After two years of President Trump's words and actions, when will Americans have enough? . . . When does silence become complicity? What will it take for us all to say, with one voice, that we have had enough?" Budde had never invoked her role with the cathedral in such a forceful and public way. The statement is conspicuously devoid of any sectarian identifiers. It does not reference Jesus Christ, Christianity, the Episcopal Church, or even "religion." It uses variations on the phrase "faith leaders," and it references "the sacredness of every single human being," but beyond these generalities, there is nothing to mark its theological commitments.

At the heart of the statement is an allusion to a famous moment in 1954 when US Army attorney Jack Welch went on television to defend his client against the fatuous accusations of Senator Joe McCarthy, who had been going around the country claiming to have evidence of a vast Communist conspiracy within the federal government. Filled with indignation, Welch looked McCarthy in the face and asked: "Have you no sense of decency?" The moment somehow helped the nation wake up to McCarthy's bullying. People began to see his words as the craven and reckless behavior of a demagogue. Budde and her colleagues, however, turned the call for decorum onto the audience itself: "The question is less about the president's sense of decency, but of ours." The collective voice of the cathedral was calling on Americans themselves to rise to a moral standard that should define them as citizens. In an environment where words can trigger violence, the president's words suggesting that largely Black or Brown cities and countries represented an "infestation" called for a renewal of civic dignity.

That statement brought Bishop Budde out of the pastoral shadow of the diocese and into the national spotlight for the first time. She was interviewed on national television and in national newspapers. A year later, when Trump used tear gas and police in riot gear to clear away protesters for a photo opportunity in front St. John's Church in Lafayette Square, the historic "Church of the Presidents" that resided within the Washington, DC, Episcopal Diocese,

Budde was solicited for comment and freely gave it. "I am outraged," she said in a seething tone. "Everything he has said and done is to inflame violence. We need moral leadership, and he's done everything to divide us."[48] The breakdown of the nation's civil-religious standards seemed to hail Washington National Cathedral back into the public sphere.

Despite the clarity of Budde's response to President Trump, the renewed attention on the cathedral raised questions about what the building's purpose and mission really were. Does the cathedral leadership speak for the nation? To the nation? And if so, does it have a unique authority to do so? Should pundits invite the response of cathedral leaders on matters of citizenship and morality? After the riots in DC, Budde was interviewed, along with several other religious leaders, on the *Diane Rehm Show* for National Public Radio. When questioned about the role of faith in healing the nation's divides, she repeatedly went out of her way to couch her responses in her faith. "As a Christian," and "for those of us in the Christian faith" were typical disclaimers. Never did she embrace a role as a spokesperson for civic morality beyond what her faith dictated.[49] Similarly, questions were raised about Budde's allegiances when she did wade into public debates. The blog for the Institute for Religion and Democracy wondered whether Budde was participating in "selective outrage" as part of her "partisan" sympathies.[50] Budde had spent nearly a decade ministering to the diocese when she found herself called into the public arena because of the dual mission of the church where she kept her seat. She was, whether she intended to be or not, both a minister to the diocese and a custodian of the nation's civil-religious life. In the end, she could not deny the legacy of Francis Sayre and others whose outspokenness had been a natural extension of their Christianity and their link to the cathedral, and she never seemed settled in this split identity.

An Enduring Confusion

When the cathedral was completed in 1990 and President George H. W. Bush gave his famous dedicatory remarks, even then, after more than eight decades of planning and construction, the cathedral's mission was not clear. A draft document called the "Planning Context for 1990" had been prepared in 1988 as a lead-up to the dedication.[51] As an exercise in preparing for the future, the document grapples with the very same questions that animated tensions between the cathedral's earliest planners. "Who are we?" the document's authors asks. "What is important to us? What do we think the world

will be like when we dedicated [*sic*] the cathedral?" The document then outlines what it believes are the cathedral's main purposes: "To be a symbol of
the nation's religious life: An example to others"; "To be an important part
of religious life in the Nation's Capitol [*sic*]"; "To be a major institution in the
PECUSA [Protestant Episcopal Church of the United States of America]";
"To be a place of learning and spiritual enrichment." The document's authors, known simply as the Program Committee, were in charge of preparing
the cathedral for its "year of consecration." They admitted that their discussion was "loose and unstructured" and that the "boundaries between concerns were fuzzy." Their effort to clarify the cathedral's role in the nation and
world, however, did little to mitigate that fuzziness. Not listed among the
purposes was the fact that the cathedral was—and was always intended to
be—the chief mission church of the diocese. There is no mention of local
pastoral care for Episcopalians. While it is clear that the cathedral's leaders
ought to work to raise the profile of "religion in the public square" and serve
as an example "to the broader Christian community," there is no sense of
what shape these efforts should take. The document points the cathedral to
problems such as "world poverty and hunger," "the widening gap between
rich and poor," "relations between superpowers," and the "acceleration of
technology and scientific development" but does not explain how the cathedral ought to situate itself in relation to these problems. It simply calls on the
cathedral to "play some part in influencing the nation's response to national
and world problems." So, when President Bush stood in the pulpit and declared, "Here we have built our church," his meaning could not have been
less clear.

From Dean Sayre to Bishop Budde, the cathedral's leaders have striven to
navigate this ambiguity, whether by planting themselves directly on the national and global stage and making their voices heard, as did Sayre, Walker,
Chane, Hall, and others, or by exploring more quietly inward, as has Budde
and a host of bishops and deans not named in this book, because they delimited the scope of the cathedral's mission in the interest of more local and
pastoral priorities. There seems much to recommend them all, and much
to recommend the cathedral itself, but I have not come away with any sense
that the cathedral as an institution is something anyone can put a finger on.
It is a tabula rasa that a given leader might shape according to their own values and objectives. Many organizations are this way, and this complaisance
would not be a concern, except that the cathedral's leaders make a uniquely

bold claim to the world, that Washington National Cathedral *is* something—specifically, that it is something Americans can fundamentally rely on for a sense of direction in a world of disorder.

In May 2016, I interviewed Preston Hannibal, the head of pastoral care for the cathedral. During the interview, Hannibal stressed the cathedral's Episcopal identity, and he admitted that the meaning of Satterlee's (and before him L'Enfant's) phrase "church for national purposes" is different today than it was a hundred years ago. Today, the national mission is a constituent of the cathedral's Episcopal ministry.[52] To put it another way, today's cathedral does not invoke its Episcopal identity as a call to consolidate Christendom under its purview, as Satterlee would have had it. Rather, it invokes Episcopalism as a call to bring greater peace and harmony for the nation and world. Fair enough, and noble, but cathedral leadership continues to wrestle with what this process looks like. The cathedral is divided between its diocesan commitments and its strain to be something like Westminster Abbey. This confusion marked the debates into which Satterlee entered more than 120 years ago, and it does not seem to have been resolved. Meanwhile the diocese, the church, and the nation itself seem to be heading toward schism.

My thoughts here may read like a critique of the cathedral, but a larger concern lies at the root of its role in the world. When Thomas Jefferson jettisoned the idea of a national church, both in the form of a national pantheon and, later, a crypt in the Capitol Building, he created a vacuum, and competing interests have been trying to fill it ever since. Preston Hannibal's response to the question of why we need the cathedral underscores this point. "Americans needed a sacred space to call our own," he says. The idea seems lofty and reassuring, but it points to an anxiety. Why do we have this lack to begin with? Why do we need a supplement to our civic life? And if Americans need a place to call their own, why is that space a cathedral of the Protestant Episcopal Church and not a public temple dedicated to a coherent set of civic ideals? We might point to the National Mall, the Washington Monument, or the Capitol as the real spaces of our civil-religious life, but they rarely host funerals, inter heroes, or call the nation to prayer and meditation. The Capitol is the possible exception here, as it does in fact host annual prayers, and the bodies of heroes do, from time to time, lie temporarily in state within its rotunda; however, it remains mainly a place of political business, and Americans do not cognize it as a sacred space. This fact is regrettable, since, in appearance, the Capitol Rotunda strikes me as the sort of awe-inspiring shrine to the nation L'Enfant himself might have imagined (fig. 4.3). From its statu-

Fig. 4.3. View looking up to the ceiling of the Capitol Rotunda with statue of George Washington in foreground. Photo by Brandon Kopp

ary to its murals to its reliefs, all the way up to its ceiling fresco, "Apotheosis of Washington," the rotunda seems a monument to L'Enfant's dream rather than a realization of it. Sadly, such government spaces underscore the fact that Washington and L'Enfant's idea was never realized and that, as a corollary, the American Civil Religion has never felt resolved.

PART TWO

RHETORICAL POSSIBILITIES

CHAPTER FIVE

Philip Hubert Frohman's
Fourth Dimension

A Close Reading of Washington National Cathedral

The first half of this book was devoted to the history of the idea of a national church and particularly to the manifestation of that idea in the form of Washington National Cathedral. I attempt in chapters 1–4 to show that the vision of Washington National Cathedral relies on the civil religious ideals of Pierre L'Enfant and George Washington but that it departs from those ideals in significant ways. For more than 120 years, the cathedral has struggled to articulate the extent to which it is local, national, or global and what role its sectarian commitments ought to play in its broader ministry. I also argue that this confusion of identity may be less the result of the cathedral's own uncertainties than the result of the nation's failure to establish a coherent civil religious vision for its citizens, a failure that first occurred in the debates over the planning and design of the Federal City dating all the way back to the late eighteenth century.

It is no wonder that in its attempt to administer the American Civil Religion, Washington National Cathedral often seems like a charioteer holding the reins of wrangling horses. Its effort to pilot the horses, or at least to keep them civil to one another, is admirable but tragic in a way. The cathedral is both religious and political, sectarian and nonsectarian, local and national, private and public. For over a century, it has tried to reconcile these priorities, to rein the horses into a kind of harmony. For instance, the cathedral argues that its Episcopal identity amounts to a call of universal mission. In this sense, its social and political interests are outgrowths rather than contradictions of its sectarian function. Of course, all churches that enter the realm of political discourse adopt this rationale. Their faith calls them to leaven the worlds they inhabit. Yet it is just the one church—the one that sits atop St. Alban's Hill—that calls itself the National Cathedral and presumes a special relationship with the nation's leaders, institutions, and traditions. In pursuing this unique role, it hosts competing personalities and interests, and in its effort to nurture the nation's manifold soul, it struggles to manage its own diocese.

I argue that the cathedral's exertions point to a weakness in the nation's civil-religious bedrock. Wittingly or not, the cathedral allows us to recognize the existential distance between Americans and to consider the possibility that shared premises might never be possible. In this second half of the book, I consider the various voices and agendas that the cathedral has engaged. My point is to examine the historical tensions and theoretical ruptures that continue to undermine the American Civil Religion. By analyzing a variety of rhetorical texts, I consider the way these voices have presented competing theories, or theologies, of the American Civil Religion, and how these theologies appear to be on a collision course with one another. I begin with a close reading of the cathedral itself.

Philip Hubert Frohman's Fourth Dimension

The chief architect of Washington National Cathedral was Philip Hubert Frohman. Frohman assumed the role in 1921 as a thirty-two-year-old prodigy. He took over for George Bodley and Henry Vaughan, who were exponents of the fourteenth-century Gothic style and favorites of Bishop Satterlee. Frohman honored Bodley and Vaughan's vision. "We believe you will find that the greatest harmony and beauty in the final effect of the chapel will be realized if all of its appointments are carried out in accordance with the ideals of its designers," he wrote to a colleague;[1] but he did not shy away from making revisions that he felt better captured the spirit of the project, and he remained the principal architect for more than fifty years, all the way to his death in 1972.

Frohman was also a kind of philosopher of architecture. In letters and an unfinished treatise on architecture, he articulated an approach to building that sought to capture what he called a "fourth dimension," an experience in which the worshipper loses all sense of time and space and becomes co-present with God. This approach to architecture requires a commitment on the part of the designer that holds nothing back. They are attempting to create, after all, another world. Frohman often faced critics who felt he was "lavishing" too much time on minor elements of the building's detail. The costs of his efforts, both in terms of time lost and money spent, were becoming extravagant. Frohman wrote to one such critic: "Had we not expended

Fig. 5.1. Philip Hubert Frohman, architect of Washington National Cathedral from 1921 to 1972. Washington National Cathedral Archives

this amount of our own time in striving to obtain that interest and refinement of detail which is one of the distinguishing marks and superiorities of real Gothic architecture, . . . we would have felt that we had betrayed our trust and that we had failed in doing our best in fulfilling our duty to . . . Him for whose glory and worship this chapel has been built."[2] Frohman saw time as something that ought not to be measured, certainly not at the expense of the quality of the finished product. Time was a secular construct that, if catered to, would betray trust and fail God. A cathedral is no quotidian structure; it should be built with an eye to time*less*ness.

In his unpublished manuscript "The Fourth Dimension in Architecture," Frohman writes: "When designing a church building an architect should realize that he is confronted with the singular problem of creating a structure which will enclose space in such a manner as to suggest infinity and eternity."[3] Since eternity cannot literally be produced by a designed structure, the architect must rely on an ability to manipulate the viewer's response *to* the structure. Frohman continues: "By the disposition of its material substance it must enclose those who enter it in a way which will produce an effect upon their minds which will cause their spirits to feel the presence and the reality of that which is not material and which can not be seen by the mortal eye."[4]

What Frohman is describing is akin to the concept of *kairos* that I outline in the introduction. Kairos is a theory of time and space that is based on notions of revelation, when chronos, or linear time, is interrupted by a special opportunity or sacred event.[5] Kairos was originally depicted as the youngest son of Zeus flying about with wings on his heels and a forelock on his head. If captured, Kairos blesses the moment with the opportunity for change. The concept has found traction in both rhetorical theory and theology as a way of describing how the quality of time and space shifts based on unique situations or sacred hierophanies. What is possible in one place or moment is not possible in another. Temples, cathedrals, and shrines are means of holding these kairotic moments and sustaining their rhetorical charge. The worshiper experiences a dimensional shift that allows them to recognize a Truth that the profane, chronic world denies. They experience their surroundings as a divine manifestation. For Frohman, kairos was the energy that sustains the fourth dimension, and nothing could more purely channel this energy than a grand Gothic cathedral.

The Exterior

Standing atop the highest point in the northwest quadrant of Washington, DC, Washington National Cathedral is like the stone of Jacob writ large, a central axis point linking a chosen nation to the God who ordained it. The tallest of its three towers stretches thirty stories into the air. Its nave from front to back spans the length of two football fields. Builders took nearly a century to shape its raw materials into what is now the sixth largest cathedral in the world.[6] If one were to look north from the rotunda of the Capitol Building, one would see a tree-covered incline leading up to the church. As John Ander Runkle writes of cathedrals generally, they "seek to show us a vast unity that transcends our everyday categories, inviting us to see ourselves as part of an encompassing oneness of self and cosmos. They seek to inspire in us a vision of a world held together by unity of purpose embodied in the sweeping harmony of architecture and faith."[7] Mt. St. Alban is home

Fig. 5.2. Aerial view of Washington National Cathedral, nearing completion in September 1983. Washington National Cathedral Archives

to the cathedral close, a campus of gardens and buildings designed for worship, reflection, education, performance, assembly, and administration. At the center of the close rises the monolith with its soaring archways and flying buttresses. The southern approach to the cathedral is blanketed by the Olmsted Woods, about which Frederick Law Olmsted himself remarked: "The great charm of approaching the Cathedral through and up a wooded hillside, leaving the city far behind and below, helping one to forget the hurly-burly, and busy-ness of a work-a-day world, must be taken advantage of to the fullest extent . . . [s]o that one at last reaches the Cathedral cleansed in mind and in spirit."[8] Like Satterlee, Olmsted had in mind a sanctuary set apart from the city, standing like a sentinel in a heavenly remove. Someone who ascended to its entrance would leave the profane world behind.

When the cathedral marked its centennial in 1990, the same year President Bush dedicated it, it sponsored a publication celebrating the symbolism of the building's location "at one of the highest points in the city, overlooking the halls of government, the monuments, the signs and symbols of a nation's life. Indeed, a visitor to the nation's capital would see a city presided over by two prominent hills, on one the U.S. capital, where the destiny of the country is shaped, and on the other higher promontory the nation's house of prayer."[9] Clearly, the designers had a rhetorical agenda. They wanted the cathedral to appear as if in a symbiotic relationship with the halls of government, to stand as a symbol of the soul that animates the nation's civic body. Far more than evidence of one religion's presence in the nation's capital, went this thinking, Washington National Cathedral should announce itself as the spiritual axis point of the United States, a stake in what Mircea Eliade called the "larval modality of chaos."[10]

The façade of the cathedral is dominated by two massive towers, each rising 234 feet into the air. At the north corner of the entrance stands the Tower of St. Peter (fig. 5.3). Near its base is a canopied, life-sized statue of the apostle himself. His hair, face, and robe appear to be windblown. His jaw and lips are clenched. Over his shoulder he clutches a fisherman's net, but his gaze is set on something distant and, judging by his expression, a bit alarming. His eyebrows are furrowed, his mouth is slightly open, as if he wants to say something but his voice and words fail. Although he leans slightly back, he cannot train his eyes away from whatever specter he sees. To the viewer at street level, Peter exists somewhere else, lost in some other time. He is not aware of the cathedral goers who walk by him or the giant church at the base of which he stands. He is, instead, on the shores of Galilee, caught in a moment of sublime pause, and one is left to wonder what compels his view so dramatically.[11] He is a fisherman, burdened with day-to-day responsibilities, but he finds himself enthralled by a heavenly vision (fig. 5.4).

The Peter statue is hardly alone in communicating this message of blended awe and terror. A viewer who approaches the cathedral entrance may experience something similar. The viewer faces three portals, but the portals do not invite the viewer in without sending a strong message first. Above each portal sits a large tympanum relief. Sculptor Frederick Hart named the largest relief "Ex Nihilo" (fig. 5.5). Its dimensions are massive, dwarfing an average-sized person and spanning the width of the middle arch that frames the main doorway. The human figures in "Ex Nihilo" are depicted in a storm. They seem to be born from a massive, cosmic cloudburst. Their expressions communicate a kind of abject terror. Naked, male and female, they swirl in the mist. They are the perfect, pre-Fall humans: innocents suspended by some transcendent force.

Fig. 5.3. Main, west front entrance of Washington National Cathedral, with Tower of Saint Paul on left and Tower of Saint Peter on right, 2016. Zeytun Travel Images / Alamy Stock Photos

The figures in "Ex Nihilo" are not autonomous agents. They are constituents of a divine reality. They seem not to be conscious at all, and yet they are expressions of a kind of perfection. Frederick Hart's comment on the sculpture is telling: "The figures emerged from the nothingness of chaos, caught in the moment of eternal transformation—the majesty and mystery of divine force in a state of becoming."[12] Hart adds: they are "caught in the moment," a moment created for the purpose of something both mysterious and divine.

Fig. 5.4. Canopied statue of St. Peter at base of Tower of St. Peter, west front of Washington National Cathedral. Author photo

This entrance is more than a hole in a wall. It is an opening in time and the threshold to another world.

The entrance bears many other elements that communicate otherworldliness, each emphasizing an interface between two worlds. Elsewhere on the exterior one finds angels, saints, chimeras, grotesques, arches, spires, all of which help to generate a tension between the worldly outside and the heavenly inside. The idea behind a Gothic cathedral's entrance is not to suggest a seamless, stressless movement from outside to inside but to highlight the anxious contradiction between earth and heaven. When one ascends the steps and passes below the soaring archway and through the shadowed portal of a Gothic cathedral, one is said to ascend the "mountain of God" and enter the "Gate of Heaven."[13] As with all seductions, the building cautions the onlooker even as it coaxes them forward.

The Interior

Crossing through the portal and into the narthex, or interior entryway, viewers forget the sheer limestone towers of the outside. They look out into the

Fig. 5.5. Frederick Hart's renowned tympanum birth-of-humankind sculpture "Ex Nihilo," above the central main entrance to Washington National Cathedral. Craig Jack Photographic / Alamy Stock Photo

yawning expanse of the nave (fig. 5.6). Their immediate impression is probably consistent with what one might experience in other great cathedrals. Magnificent arches rise upon each other into ever higher strata until they dissolve into the curvature of the ceiling more than one hundred feet up. The glow through stained glass dapples the walls with spectral colors and shadows. The giant piers and archways that flank the nave look elegant—even delicate—from a distance, but the view is beguiling. Up close, their bases are between fifteen and twenty feet in diameter, each column a bind of colonnettes rising more than ten stories to the ceiling. Looking straight east toward the back wall, or chancel, the observer is treated to an uninterrupted view more than five hundred feet long into the nave and, ultimately, the choir, above which is lofted the rood beam and the carved image of the crucified Jesus. Behind this image is only black space. The void has the illusory effect of a giant cavern. One cannot know where exactly the cathedral ends.

The nave's iconography follows Gothic building conventions. Its images are designed to educate the viewer about the Christian story. The Creation is

Fig. 5.6. A view from the floor of the nave of Washington National Cathedral, looking up toward the Rose Window, above the cathedral's west entrance. The flags of the fifty states line the balcony above the lowest arches. Felix Lipov / Alamy Stock Photo

depicted in the west end—recall the façade and "Ex Nihilo"—while the story of redemption is represented in the east end. Christ's sacrifice on the cross is represented above the High Altar reredos, where the cathedral's symbolic narrative more or less culminates. The building is filled with images and texts taken directly from scriptures. Stained-glass windows, almost three hundred in number, portray the parables of Jesus and the miracles he wrought as recorded in the New Testament. Walls are inscribed with lines from sacred text. Reliefs and sculptures portray ancient prophetic acts. The cathedral, in short, is a place where time stops and Christian revelation fills the void. It is an exemplary Anglican kairos.

What I have described so far suggests the same sort of cathedral one might encounter in any other major city with a well-established Christian population; but if one returns for a moment to the cathedral's entrance and looks again, one finds another, more peculiar narrative taking shape. Immediately inside the same west entry, on the floor of the narthex, are the seals of the nation's fifty states as well as the seal of the District of Columbia. They are laid

Fig. 5.7. Statue of George Washington inside main entrance of Washington National Cathedral. Wirestock, Inc./Alamy Stock Photo

evenly around the larger Great Seal of the United States, which, incidentally, happened to be designed in part by Pierre L'Enfant. To one's right, about forty feet away, framed by great columns, stands a heroically sized statue of George Washington (fig. 5.7). To one's left at approximately the same distance is an equally large statue of Abraham Lincoln. It is telling that the Washington and Lincoln interior statues correspond almost exactly to the St. Peter and St. Paul statues on the exterior. The viewer is flanked by apostles while entering, then by presidents once inside. One cannot even look heavenward in the cathedral without noticing the flags of all fifty states lining the vaulted ceiling. Even before one has stepped into the nave, one is treated to a mosaic that makes it impossible to separate American destiny from Christian providence.

The apostolic and presidential statues show a juxtaposition of Christianity and American politics that is unusual for a church building of such prominence, but the cathedral contains elements that do more than juxtapose politics with religion. For instance, inside the cathedral, on the landing of the parclose stairway that leads down into the crypt, sits a statue of Abraham Lincoln kneeling in prayer (see fig. 5.8). From a distance of forty to fifty feet,

Fig. 5.8. Statue of Abraham Lincoln in prayer by Herbert Spencer Houck, in parclose stairway of Washington National Cathedral. Author photo

one cannot tell what the statue depicts. It almost appears to be a silhouetted priest or missionary, deep in prayer for his flock. It is only upon closer examination that one recognizes the bushy brow and gaunt shoulders of the sixteenth president. The image is every bit Lincoln. His whole body communicates a resignation; he carries a weight so heavy that it has driven him to his knees. There is no other option but prayer. One also sees that what may have seemed a cassock or priestly robe from afar is a riding cloak and that the president is wearing boots. He is clearly meant to be outdoors. As the story goes, the sculptor, Herbert Spencer Houck, was inspired to create the figure because of a family legend. Houck's father had been a chaplain in the Union army during the Civil War. After coming home from battle, he claimed that while walking through the woods near Gettysburg, he accidently came across the solitary president kneeling in supplication to God.[14] The story is entirely hearsay, but there the image resides in bronzed perpetuity.

Houck and the many hundreds of other sculptors, architects, stained-glass artists, wood carvers, painters, and masons who worked on the cathedral recognized implicitly that they were designing something for a strategic emotional impact rather than an accurate historical reading. The statue of Lincoln in prayer is tucked away in a corner of the cathedral, but what it suggests about the union of politics and religion is important. The cathedral, taken in its totality of history and design, more than juxtaposes religion and politics. It does not merely argue that the two spheres can productively coexist. It assumes that they exist as one, in the same pregnant image, space, and moment. As I observe in chapter 2, it was Bishop Satterlee's idea from the beginning that the cathedral's iconography should depict scenes and words from US history and that these scenes ought to capture the hearts of other Protestants.[15] Satterlee set out to tell the nation's story within the literal and theological framework of Protestant Christianity—to build an American *axis mundi* and, in so doing, call American citizens to a new recognition of their divine destiny in the world.

The Stained Glass

Possibly the most explicit expression of Satterlee's vision is found in the stained glass. Author Elody Crimi and cathedral archivist Dianne Ney have documented in considerable detail the building's stained glass, accounting for the history and interpretive breadth of many of the tens of thousands of images embedded in the windows.[16] The images blend politics and Christianity in various ways. One prominent window, visible from the nave, depicts the temple of ancient Israel crumbling into ruins. It is overgrown with vines; its walls have begun to crack and collapse. One man, a priest of some sort, appears to be single-handedly replacing the stones. In one hand, he holds the Torah high. In the multifoil one sees an image of the United States Supreme Court building. At the bottom of the window are the words "We, the People of the United States."[17]

Another window visible from the nave highlights the executive branch of the US government by depicting the White House in its multifoil continuing the quote of the Constitution's Preamble: "in Order to form a more perfect Union" (fig. 5.9). The primary images in the window, those that run across the lancets and proceed from top to bottom, are taken again from ancient Israel. Moses is shown leading the exilic Hebrews through the wilderness. Crimi and Ney write that the images represent "the persistent faith of the Hebrew nation during its forty-year journey through the desert, as well as the faith America places in the leadership of its president."[18] A third window in the series highlights the legislative branch of American government. Its explicitly religious elements highlight the story of the Good Samaritan. The

Fig. 5.9. "Faith of the Hebrews" stained-glass window, with White House depicted in the window's multifoil window. Elody Crimi, photographer. Courtesy of Washington National Cathedral Archives.

victim is shown bleeding on the ground. Other figures pass him by, but the Samaritan cares for him. In the multifoil is an image of the US Capitol. This coupling reflects the Founders' belief that members of Congress "would provide a voice for the least powerful and most in need."[19]

Farther down the nave is a window titled "Servants of God." This window is subtler in its depictions of political life, but Crimi and Ney provide a thorough explanation. The authors point out that the first three male figures in the window are, respectively, William Penn, a proponent of religious freedom and humane treatment of Native Americans; King John, who was forced by popular demand to sign the Magna Carta, decreeing rights for all citizens of England; and Stephen Langton, the English bishop who organized the "barons" to demand their rights. To the right of these figures appears John Marshall, chief justice of the US Supreme Court. Marshall is credited with defining the court as the legal body that interprets the Constitution. He is shown in full robes holding a copy of the Constitution. Below him are two unidentified men standing before the Supreme Court building. The authors conclude: "The mythical Phoenix rises in the cinquefoil above, representing the justice of God being renewed and brought back to life through his servants on earth."[20]

Other windows go still further in blurring the lines between Christian allegory and American history. One window, called "Wings of Courage," places an American military general known for his service and faith in almost the same stained-glass image as biblical abstractions. Deep blues and reds represent the sturdiness and power of religious courage. Flowering plants and trees symbolize the journey from war and misery to faith and grace. If one looks closely enough, one can also see an image of the US Air Force Academy chapel. Some windows emphasize the political and make only subtle reference to the religious. For example, the window titled "Abraham Lincoln's Mother and Step-Mother" shows Nancy Hanks Lincoln standing with a grave expression on her face. Below her is a covered wagon, as if to represent the remoteness and simplicity of life at the time. Finally, at the bottom of the window is an image of Sarah Bush Lincoln, Abraham Lincoln's step-mother after his mother's death. Her arm is placed around the future president's shoulders as he performs family chores. The only explicitly religious symbol in the entire painting is the Bible in Nancy Lincoln's hands.

The list of political images goes on almost indefinitely. Two prominent windows, titled "America the Beautiful I" and "American the Beautiful II," depict natural scenes from across the North American landscape. Inscribed within the windows are words honoring an American colonel "whose loyalty did not fail nor his prayer that upon this nation God's grace be shed and brotherhood be won from sea to shining sea."[21] Another series, this one called "Humanitarians," shows images of educator George Washington Carver, prison reformer Elizabeth Fry, and medical missionary Albert Schweitzer. Another window, titled "Universal Peace," celebrates US senator and secretary of state Frank Billings Kellogg. Two other windows, which were recently removed, honored Robert E. Lee and "Stonewall" Jackson.

The stained-glass windows mingle the symbols of church and state in ways that can best be described as consubstantial. This method of knitting unlike things together in stained glass is not entirely unique. Designer Douglas Strachan has been credited with accomplishing a similar feat in Scotland. In the windows he designed for the Scottish National War Memorial in Edinburgh, Strachan weaved folk heroes, biblical narratives, and contemporary Scottish personalities together to reinforce the image of Scotland as a member of the British collective. He evoked a harmony of history, folklore, religion, and myth through the medium of glass and sacred space.[22]

Like the windows of the cathedral, the windows of the Scottish National War Memorial are arranged in seminarrative style. On the left side of the apse, the windows "recount the birth of war and incorporate scenes from the Book of Genesis. In the windows opposite, the havoc and terror of war are displayed, intertwined with the idea of salvation drawn from the Book of Revelation."[23] Within such contexts, stained glass becomes a powerful mode of rhetoric. The percipient no longer makes distinctions in time or place. As Philip Frohman's theory would have it, the past and present, the terrestrial and celestial are collapsed into an eternal here and now. In the case of the Scottish War Memorial and Washington National Cathedral, this collapse is a merging of faith and nationality. In terms of Frohman's fourth dimension, these identities are not only merged but also taken up into a realm where earthly reasoning has no place, a kairotic realm where one's beliefs take on the import of revelation and one's actions take on the force of divine mission. Supreme Court justices and congressional representatives are barely distinguishable from priests and prophets of the Judeo-Christian scriptures. Citizens become votaries more than voters.

The Inscribed Walls

The walls, too, tell the story of America's divine calling. Various bays are inscribed with quotations which assume that calling. One of the most telling

Fig. 5.10. Woodrow Wilson's tomb, nave of Washington National Cathedral. Washington National Cathedral Archives

inscriptions is tucked away in a middle bay just removed from the south side of the nave. It was only after reading the inscription that I turned around and noticed the giant stone tomb that encases the remains of Woodrow Wilson (fig. 5.10), whose words are those on the wall: "The stage is set, the destiny disclosed. It has come about by no plan of our conceiving, but by the hand of God who has led us into this way. We cannot go back. We can only go forward, with lifted eyes and freshened spirit, to follow the vision. It was of this that we dreamed at our birth. America shall in truth show the way. The light streams upon the path ahead, and nowhere else."[24] The excerpt comes from Wilson's 1919 submission to the Senate of the Anglo-Franco-American Peace Treaty. Wilson planned a national tour that would take him across the country, promoting the treaty as central to American values and greatness. He drew upon time-tested readings of American destiny to make his case. Note the way he, like Satterlee, sets a "stage" that "discloses" "destiny." He situates

the nation within a conceptual space irrevocably linked to divine imperatives. He acts as a kind of revelator, a sharer of the divine will. Rather than
appeal to logic, he points to destiny.

Participants in the cathedral experience go through a process that changes
not only their sense of self but also their sense of the world and its realities.
My own experience is representative. Although the cathedral did not move
me to some sort of ecstasy of religious conversion, even after many visits, my
openness to a different view of the world expanded. Progressing from one
iconographic detail to the next, I gradually stopped trying to make sense of
each individual artifact and its placement in the building. Items did not need
to make perfect historical sense on their own terms; they needed to make
sense only in terms of the cathedral's overall mission. Richard T. Feller and
Marshall W. Fishwick, writing of the power of cathedral iconography, note
that "symbols are visible signs of invisible ideas or qualities. They compress,
convey, and release emotions better than any other device of communication."[25] Symbols best perform this function, according to the authors, through
"blending." Statuary, reliefs, tapestries, quotations, windows, monuments,
and other individual objects become textures in the fabric of a reality that
refuses to make distinctions between one thing and the next. Juxtapositions
of religious tradition and politics become unities in Washington National
Cathedral.

This view of the cathedral is consistent across its history. As Dean Sayre
remarked: "Cathedrals do not belong to a single generation. . . . They gather
up the faith of a whole people and proclaim the goodly Providence which has
welded that people together as they have hoped and suffered and believed,
across the centuries."[26] Cathedrals "weld" their objects together and cause
time to collapse by the power of "Providence." Ney writes, "Eternity lies at the
heart of a cathedral. This is the gift of Gothic architecture: a sense of *kairos*,
of non-linear time that allows reaching across the centuries to bring all into
communion in prayerful awe."[27] Samuel T. Lloyd III, dean of the cathedral in
the early 2000s, would have made Frohman proud: Lloyd wrote for the cathedral's centennial in 2007: "Cathedrals are acts of extravagance. They seek
to show us a vast unity that transcends our everyday categories, inviting us
to see ourselves as part of an encompassing oneness of self and cosmos. . . .
Cathedrals offer a vision of heaven for people to experience in the here and
now—all of life held together within the embrace of a loving God. And so in
our age of fragmentation and disconnection, glimpsing such soaring grandeur
and beauty can be exceedingly powerful."[28] The cathedral claims to be the

confluence and voice of that broader history. Its project is a "struggle to express, in tangible materials and inadequate proportions, ineffable and transcendent realities."[29] The cathedral's visionaries, with Satterlee leading the way, did not set out to create a museum of different narratives, trajectories, traditions, histories, and so on. They set out to build the "spiritual home for a robust young nation."[30] The cathedral's endeavor of identity creation grew out of an impulse to affirm a religious conscience for an entire people.

❋

Richard T. Feller, one of Satterlee's successors, once found himself having to justify the extravagance of the cathedral in light of the world's abundance of poverty and sickness. In a letter to one of his critics, Feller declared that we must build these structures so as to keep our "conscience." He argued that creating these kinds of spaces will always be "an act of worship."[31] The arguments the cathedral makes are not so much about defending practical policy as about building an identity, for the cathedral as well as for the worshiper. Rhetorician Edwin Black introduces a related principle he calls the "second persona," which references the audience hailed into being by a text. By the telling of who they are, auditors are constituted as *a people* with a particular worldview. As the text creates their identity, so they assume and perform it.[32] In its simplest form, the second persona may imply, for example, an audience of environmentalists by using phrases like "as stewards of the natural word" or "protectors of our children's future." The thrust of Black's theory is that persuasion is most effective when the target audience persuades themselves; this feat can be accomplished only if the audience believes itself to be a certain way, to have a certain destiny.

A cathedral is ideally suited for such a rhetorical project, since its workmanship is "an elaborate and carefully crafted performance of identity, experience, and values."[33] As this performance unfolds, the worshiper transforms from observer to participant, an agent of the worldview constituted by the text.[34] Satterlee once remarked that Washington National Cathedral "unites every congregation in every place, with the people of God in all ages."[35] Architectural historian Christopher Rowe elaborates that theme: "When a pilgrim in a Gothic cathedral gazes upon an image of Moses delivering the tablets of the Law they are not merely evoking the event through 'memory' . . . but are, in kairos, actually participating in the event itself."[36] It is not as if the cathedral has ferried the worshiper back in time so much as it has collapsed time into an eternal now, a kairos. In the case of Washington National Cathedral, the act of citizenship in the here and now *becomes* an act of transformative worship.

This principle is at the heart of Frohman's theory of the fourth dimension: the worshiper has felt themselves transformed by the space. In the case of Washington National Cathedral, however, this transformation takes on an explicit politics. As uncomfortable as it may be to admit for some, Satterlee's masterpiece is a monument to Christian nationalism; it frames the United States as being bound to biblical history. The Supreme Court Building may as well be a Christian temple. Abraham Lincoln may as well be a martyred saint. The term "Christian nationalism" has many meanings, from the inclusion of Christian art in the public square to the passing of laws that favor a Christian worldview to—hypothetically—the open declaration by the federal government that the United States is a Christian nation. Although Satterlee advocated the legal separation of church and state, his cathedral clearly falls somewhere along this spectrum. As I strive to make clear, the building is at its root an effort to create a pan-Christian world, centered in Washington, DC, and fueled by American empire. To explore Washington National Cathedral today is to see Satterlee's vision concretized by a half-century of Frohman's work.

Satterlee's successors—Sayre, for instance—have reinterpreted the cathedral's relationship to the nation. The mission of the cathedral today seems no longer to involve Christendom as a political project. It promotes a "generous-spirited Christianity" based in principles of tolerance, compassion, and the social justice ideals of Jesus Christ, which makes exploring the cathedral space that much more confusing.[37] There remains something ungainly about the fusions. Often, visitors are not even aware that the cathedral is sectarian, that it is owned and operated by the Washington, DC, diocese of the Protestant Episcopal Church. Hearing only that it is called the "National Cathedral," they are drawn to it, but upon entering, they find it difficult to make sense of the space: the apostolic and presidential statuary, the biblical and constitutional imagery, the medieval-looking tapestries and the state flags, the Christian crosses and the state seals, a stone from Mount Sinai and a stone labeled GITMO donated, for some reason, by the Guantanamo Bay naval base. As soon as one begins to feel the pull of the holy, one stumbles across another political artifact that seems out of place.

Perhaps the most disorienting iconography is found in the Stonewall Jackson and Robert E. Lee bay windows. I discuss these windows and their contested removal later in the book, but they embody the cathedral's confounding essence and thus deserve mention here. The windows depict various scenes from the warriors' lives—leading soldiers in battle, teaching students in the classroom, conferring on horseback. In one panel, Jackson is shown piously kneeling and reading the Bible. In another, Lee is shown in regalia before what appears to be the main building of Washington and Lee University. His arms and palms are passively open like Christ revealing his wounds to his disciples. Etched in stone beneath one of the depictions of Lee are the words "A Christian soldier without fear and without reproach," and under Jackson: he "walked humbly before his Creator whose word was his guide." In the culminating panel, one of the generals—Jackson, it appears—is rendered in a state of resurrection before the cross, his arms outstretched, a royal blue cloak flourished about his neck and back. The words "So he passed over and all. The trumpets sounded for him" are etched into the glass.

To its credit, the cathedral tried for many years to recontextualize the windows, to frame them as part of the cathedral's role as "a repository of American memory," or to use them as a starting point for difficult discussions about race.[38] But the removal of the windows after more than a half-century in the heart of the nave reveals the cathedral's fraught project.[39] It struggles to contain, let alone to harmonize, the voices that compete to inhabit the American soul. It is *not* ultimately a repository. Museums are repositories. The cathedral is a kairotic opening into the fourth dimension. What it enshrines speaks with the voice of prophets. In many spots, its effort to blend the sacred and the civic results in beautiful combinations, such as in its niche statues of Dionysus of ancient Greece and Kagawa of Japan, or in its Humanitarian Bay, which depicts scenes that furthered human rights and includes a stained-glass window featuring George Washington Carver. In other places, however, the combinations do not result in such beautiful mosaics; instead, they come off as grotesques—brilliant but unsettling and perhaps nonsensical. The moment Henry Yates Satterlee determined to thread the American story into the walls of his Christian cathedral, he foreordained this incoherence.

CHAPTER SIX

Martin Luther King Jr.'s Sacred Time

On March 31, 1968, Martin Luther King Jr. delivered what would prove to be his final Sunday sermon. It was a mild Sabbath morning, the air filled with spring. King had been invited by Dean Francis Sayre to preach at the cathedral as part of a traditional worship service. Sayre had developed a close relationship with Reverend King, and for the better part of the decade he had shown support for the kinds of civil and economic reforms King advocated. Sayre had attended the March on Washington for Jobs and Freedom in 1963, hosted the American Indian Capital Conference on Poverty in 1964, and celebrated the passage of the Civil Rights Act of 1964 with a Service of Thanksgiving and Commitment at the cathedral. He had also marched in Selma for civil rights in 1965 and advocated passionately from the cathedral pulpit and in the media for social justice.

When he extended the invitation to speak, Sayre knew that King was preparing for the Poor People's Campaign, a massive march that would be held in Washington the following month.[1] Given the political nature of King's plans in the capital and Sayre's affinity for activism, there was some trepidation among Cathedral Chapter members. They wanted a Sunday homily, not a political screed.[2] The cathedral also received dozens of letters of protest from other members of the community.[3] One representative letter, handwritten by Eleanor K. Harbinson of Baltimore and addressed directly to Dean Sayre, reads: "As a confirmed Episcopalian in good standing, I feel compelled to protest your offer of the Washington Cathedral for Martin Luther King's purposes. If this were truly for the Brotherhood of man, I would go along with you. However, it appears obvious that King's purposes are definitely racial (one group only) and that the goal is to stir up more racial Tension & anxiety which can only lead to disaster. We are all living under Tremendous strain

Fig. 6.1. Martin Luther King Jr. delivers his last Sunday sermon, from the pulpit of Washington National Cathedral, March 31, 1968, five days before his assassination in Memphis. Dennis Brack / Alamy Stock Photo

in our country today & we don't need to add to these."[4] Harbinson and others like her hearken back to the white moderates King had famously critiqued in his "Letter from Birmingham Jail" five years earlier and whom he critiques in the very speech I quote below.[5] Like Harbinson, those moderates were uncomfortable with the timing of King's cause, implying that he should just wait while the world worked its way out of its present turbulence. They framed themselves as sympathizing with calls for racial justice, but they were critical of King's provocative rhetoric and direct action. King had been answering such critics for years, and anxieties like those expressed by Harbinson were unlikely to faze him now.

Nor were such letters likely to affect Dean Sayre, who had made his views on racial justice clear since his installation as bishop. As far back as 1953, just before the *Brown v. Board of Education* decision, Sayre had been public about his support for desegregation as well as for a "non-gradualist" approach.[6] As Teresa Morales observes, in response to his public views, Sayre was accustomed to receiving letters far nastier than the one written by Harbinson, including missives admonishing him to keep his nose out of politics, lest he encourage race mixing and the destruction of the country.[7] In other words, letters protesting King's appearance were not likely to change any minds. What they reveal is that the cathedral remained a contested space. For some, it represented a kind of civil-religious retrenchment whereby the nation circumscribed and defended its spiritual identity. For others, it represented a civil-religious disruption—or, perhaps better, a civil-religious *ir*ruption from a protected sacred space into the profane world. The purpose of the first interpretation is to conceive of the cathedral as retreating from the menace of the world. The purpose of the second is to conceive of the cathedral as confronting the world. Letters or no letters, nothing prevented one thousand people from jamming the cathedral to hear the famous preacher and activist deliver his sermon.[8]

True to his message, King spoke of revolution, activism, and justice, but there were no prominent complaints following his appearance. Chapter members were satisfied and the public seemed happy. Nevertheless, five days later, King was assassinated. In his honor, the cathedral held a service of mourning that same day, and thousands of people spilled out of the nave onto the Pilgrim Steps to show their support. King's death threw a light back onto the sermon he had delivered from the Canterbury Pulpit just days earlier, and his words took on a new significance. In this chapter, I discuss how King managed to package his revolutionary message for a Sabbath-day audience and how, in the process, he crafted a theology of the American Civil Religion that drew on the spirit of the cathedral. This theology takes its cue from Frohman's fourth dimension and imagines a set of political positions as having the force of revelation. For King, the American Civil Religion requires a sense of kairos, an urgent moment and space of opportunity that moves the nation to reform. King does not merely ask the nation to change its mind; like the prophet Jeremiah, he calls the nation to repentance. In his view, God has opened up a space in history for righteous revolution. Americans who do not inhabit this space remain in a profane world where injustice prevails.

A Note on Delivery

The title of King's sermon is "Remaining Awake through a Great Revolution." He engages topics ranging from war and nuclear arms, to economic history and political isolationism, to land grant colleges and farm subsidies, and even to child poverty in India. So much for the notion that his only purpose was "definitely racial," as Harbinson worried. But, although it is not exclusively "racial," it is plainly political, even revolutionary. The radicalism of King's message, however, is softened by the style of his delivery.[9] The sermon is about "remaining awake," yet King's pacing is arduously slow; his tone is mournful. At times, it almost seems as though he is trying to put his listeners to sleep. Absent are the rises and falls that are typical of his more public addresses—the bombast before marchers in the South, for example, or the anthemic calls on the National Mall. Here, in this church on a mild Sunday morning in early spring, he sets himself and his audience apart from the world of noise.

His face, too, is impassive, almost as though he is not speaking to the audience in the church but instead communing with his own thoughts or some other power. His brow is furrowed, his eyes often gaze downward in thought. Sometimes his gaze moves upward into the air above the pulpit, such as when he describes Paul on the island of Patmos. His voice breaks in odd places, at the end of transitive verbs or midway through clauses. The address is marked by deep pauses, as, for instance, when he introduces the title of the address: "I would like to use as a subject from which to preach this morning [four-second pause] remaining awake [three-second pause] through a great revolution," or when he quotes scripture, "Former things are passed [two-second pause] away." His whole delivery—his vocal quality, facial expressions, and body language—communicate a sense of remove. There are dips out of time and long periodic sentences that are given such sober delivery, they seem etched rather than spoken. His strangely timed and unusually long pauses underscore this sense of remove. His most extended pause comes at the very beginning of the address, a full fifteen seconds following the end of the hymn. During this silence, he looks down at his notes, then around the room with dour reverence, before finally beginning his remarks at the ponderous rate of one hundred words per minute. Not until seventeen or eighteen minutes into the forty-seven minute speech does his voice begin to take on some more life and, occasionally, a quicker pace; his hands begin to gesture more too, but the ethos he established up front has already set the tone. He dips into and out of time, taking his listeners with him into small caesuras, like little retreats from chronos.

Given the solemnity of his delivery, it is easy to forget that King's message was not like most Sunday sermons. It is striking that such a radical address could sound so much like a traditional homily. To hear him speak like a subdued priest about, for example, US alienation from other nations—"There is not a single major ally of the United States of America that would dare send a

troop to Viet Nam, so the only friends we have now are a few client nations"—
is a strange thing, but this way of speaking serves two purposes. First, it dis-
arms those listeners who are anxious that they are going to be harangued
politically. By all sounds and appearances, they are experiencing a Christian
sermon. They sit reverently and silently in pews throughout the address. The
choir members and other viewers behind King show faces of introspection,
their hands in their laps. Like an incantation, the sermon invites the listeners
into the fourth dimension, where they understand King's ideas as being revealed rather than proposed. From here, I consider the content and language
of the speech, and the way these elements, like King's delivery, create removes
into sacred time and space. I divide the analysis into three parts.

The Van Winkle Problem: Time Passage and Time Stoppage

Throughout the speech, King draws on kairotic conceptions of time and sacred notions of space to imbue his claims with a sense of leverage and moral
import. In the early part of the sermon, King refers repeatedly to time stoppage. Most of his early comments to this end appear rather casually: "It is
always a rich and rewarding experience to take a brief break from our day-
to-day demands and the struggle for freedom and human dignity and discuss
the issues involved in that struggle with concerned friends of good will all
over our nation" (1.2).[10] Here discourse fills the void. The abstract space created by the "brief break" creates an opportunity for discussion. To take a *brief
break* is to step momentarily outside of temporal continuity. The normal, linear movement of time has been interrupted, and the interruption has created
a space in which to "discuss." The reader will note how the *break* to which
King refers is not an opportunity for rest (the purpose for which we generally
conceive of breaks) but a reason for poise, an exigence to discuss further action. The audience, though in break, becomes poised to listen to the "issues
involved in [the] struggle." I will not claim that King's apparently casual references to time and space in this first paragraph are all so calculated as to
reinvent the audience's notion of time and space. Rather, I assume that the
conceptual foci of these sentences is consistent with—and the natural consequence of—King's ongoing project to separate himself and his audience from
the lull and drone of a world that is not in "pause," a world being swept along
in the current of chronic time.

Having deployed these preliminary metaphors about pause, King pivots
into a full, conceptual frame for the discourse. The fourth paragraph introduces the Washington Irving fable about Rip Van Winkle with these words:

"I am sure that most of you have read that arresting little story from the pen of Washington Irving." The Rip Van Winkle story, which is about time passing one by, is meant, in King's words, to "arrest" us—in effect, again, to give pause. By highlighting the importance of time stopping, King demonstrates the danger of time passing. The implication is that if we stop time, we might understand the import of the moment and the necessity for wakefulness.[11]

The listener may further observe how this later reference to stoppage is more assertive than the earlier ones. To *arrest* certainly seems more insistent than to *pause* or merely *take a break*. Comparatively, then, the next reference to time stoppage is downright violent: "Modern man through his scientific genius has been able to dwarf distance and place time in chains" (2.5). A complete explication of this line would make an interesting read, but for the purpose of this chapter, it is enough to acknowledge here that King's use of metaphor as a means for referencing pause has become progressively more graphic. The notions of *arrest* and *chains* speak volumes to an audience that is acutely susceptible to the pathos of slavery and segregation, but King seems to be inverting these notions so as to make them creative of justice. In his use of the term, *to be arrested* means not to be unjustly detained but to recognize something important (as illustrated in the story of Rip Van Winkle). Likewise, when he remarks that our technology has the power to "place time in chains," he suggests that this power is a good thing, because it is an indicator of how far we have come and how interconnected we are as a species. It also points to a thesis he develops more deeply as the speech unfolds: time must be stopped for progress to be made.

It is from this point that King begins to turn from stopping time to changing its trajectory. He says that we are "caught in an inescapable network of mutuality" (2.6), which he follows shortly with this reference: "John Donne caught it [meaning, the realization that humankind is an interdependent collective] years ago and placed it in graphic terms—'No man is an island entire of itself'" (2.7). King's repeated references to being *caught* comport well with the metaphors of *arrest* and *chains*. To be *caught* or to catch, as in the case of Donne, suggests a moment of realization. Apprehension becomes a means of comprehension. King then qualifies the reference to Donne by commenting, "We must see this, believe this, and live by it if we are to remain awake through a great revolution" (2.7). For King, to *see* is to capture (or be captured by) a moment of realization. Donne *caught it* and, by implication, could *see*. Likewise, when we *pause, break,* or are *arrested, chained,* or *caught,* we are woken from the Van Winklean slumber of ignorance.

What I seek to demonstrate at this point in the reading is simply that King makes repeated reference to various notions of pause and that these references suggest that pauses may create spaces or moments of import; or, at the very least, these references suggest that the notion of pause is essential to the realization of opportunity. For King, we do not pause to rest. We pause to comprehend and then to do something. We pause to express delight and appreciation, discuss important events, or experience or affirm realizations. For the sermon, then, a pause is desirable only if it is filled with something productive of action.

Here, in the earliest part of the sermon, King's metaphors of pausing, breaking, stopping, arresting, catching, and chaining connotatively heighten our yearning for release. The hour is stark; it is "the most segregated hour in America" (3.2). In this way, King indicates there are two kinds of pause: the inert sleepfulness of the foolhardy Rip Van Winkle and the poised ripeness of opportunity, or kairos. In the first example, time exists, but it moves along unqualitatively. It contains nothing of import for the person who is asleep, but it provides essential opportunities for the person who is poised. The poised person will recognize the qualitative character of time and apprehend the opening it presents. King now proclaims that "the hour has come . . . to work to get rid of racism" (3.3) The *hour* of segregation becomes also the *hour* of opportunity. Some scholars have noted that King makes a similar move in his "Letter from Birmingham Jail."[12] The jail becomes no longer a symbol of static defeat; it is the very situation of influence. Similarly, for King *chains* are no longer the dreadful yoke of chronic imprisonment; they are the means of capturing time. To *pause* is not to sleep, but to wake. To be *caught* is, in effect, to apprehend. By deploying this series of paradoxes, King's rhetoric transforms the weapons of slavery into the means of justice.

The Dives Problem: Space Making and Space Filling

King characterizes injustice as a division between X and Y. Injustice is not merely the tyranny of one race over another but also the chasm that lies between them. King spends much of his discourse (not only in this speech but in most of his speeches) lamenting the notion that Blacks and whites cannot or should not live together. King, though arguably more radical than popular history has noted, does not advocate Black Power so much as he seeks productive racial convergence. His repeated telos of integration is underscored by his metaphors of space. If his goal is to link the extremes into a network of interdependence and harmony, his metaphor is the bridged gulf.

King begins the second half of the sermon by recounting Jesus's parable of Lazarus and Dives. The parable indicts the rich Dives, who refuses to aid the impoverished Lazarus. Once dead, Dives finds himself in hell, "and there were a fixed gulf now between Lazarus and Dives" (6.1). This quotation is the first of four references to a "gulf" in the space of seven short paragraphs within the sermon. King notes that Dives failed in his "opportunity to bridge the gulf that separated him from his brother" (6.2). King goes on to state (6.3) that "this is America's opportunity to bridge the gulf between the haves and the have-nots." Then he remarks: "[We are calling] attention to the gulf between promise and fulfillment; to make the invisible visible" (7.1). This last reference is especially salient because it reinforces King's inclination to reconcile paradox. Just as imprisonment becomes power and pause becomes poise, so the invisible becomes visible. It is through these metaphorical inversions that King drives home his notion that where there is lack, there must be fulfillment, and where there is ignorance, there must be revelation.

I choose the word *fulfillment* here for its biblical connotations. My claim that King's delineation of space represents a need to fill (or fulfill) the opportunities those spaces create is rooted in a reading of Paul's letters. Paul tells the Ephesians that "[God] hath put all things under his feet, and gave him to be the head over all things to the church, Which is his body, the fullness of him that filleth all in all."[13] In Ephesians 3:19, Paul similarly states that the faithful "might be filled with all the fullness of God." Repeatedly thereafter, Paul's letters equate Christ himself with the very notion of fullness.[14] For King, as for the early apostles, the notion of a gulf is anathema to God's justice. It is for this reason that Paul also says, this time to the Romans, that to accept God's will is to receive "a fullness of the blessings of the gospel."[15] To bridge the gulf, then, is to fill a space with God or, more abstractly, to fulfill a divine opportunity, a kairos.

So again King links the exigence (the gulf) with the opportunity (the bridge). The gulf is no longer just a terminal space; it is a mandate for fulfilling God's purpose; it is a kairos to build a bridge. These seven paragraphs in the sermon are also crucial for understanding the essential relationship between *kairotic* time and space. In order to remove from chronos time and enter kairotic time, the rhetor must build spaces of suspension and poise that represent opportunities to reconceptualize the world. For King, a revelatory rhetor, these spaces have the potential to negate the prevailing order of things (chronos) through the suspension of natural laws. Emile Durkheim refers to this potential as "the supernatural" because such spaces take on the divine imperatives of godly action.[16] They become the sanctified realms wherein God's time takes effect. Richard McKeon calls them "spaces in which things come to be or to be known according to transcendental principles."[17]

Perhaps it is no coincidence, then, that King's rhetoric routinely characterizes his abstract enemy as the *disease* or *sickness* of racism. The myth of time as chronos is inflected in the metaphor of the disease of racism as chronic. "[There] is the notion," King says,

> that only time can solve the problem of racial injustice. And there are those who often sincerely say . . . "if you will just be nice and patient . . . the problem will work itself out." [The answer to this myth] is that time is neutral . . . and can be used . . . constructively or destructively. . . . And it may well be that we will have to repent in this generation . . . for the appalling indifference of the good people who sit around and say, "Wait on time." Somewhere we must come to see that human progress never rolls in on the wheels of inevitability. It comes through the tireless efforts and the persistent work of dedicated individuals who are willing to be co-workers with God. So we must help time and realize that the time is always ripe to do right. (3.4–6)

King most explicitly attacks chronos time in the final paragraph, quoted above, in which he denies the inevitability of human progress. I note this line for the way it returns to the themes outlined earlier in the address. King situates us in space (*somewhere* rather than *somehow*) to herald the recognition (*come to see*) of human progress. But of course, once the apprehension of the idea of progress is accomplished, action imperatively follows (i.e., progress comes "through the tireless efforts and the persistent work of dedicated individuals"). So we move from pause, to recognition, to action. Accordingly, King proclaims later in the speech that "the nation doesn't move around questions of genuine equality for the poor and for black people until it is confronted massively, dramatically in terms of direct action" (7.1). Paul Tillich conceives of kairos as "the eternal breaking into the temporal," which is remarkably consistent with what King suggests here. We "help" time by stopping its progress and confronting it with divine justice.

The Revelator's Solution: Filling in the Time and Space of Poverty

Before I summarize the analysis and suggest some implications, it is worth noting that there is an overall prepositional emphasis on space—not only in the beginning of the speech but throughout it. King's use of the preposition *in* during his opening paralipsis and throughout the speech in various metaphors of and references to space and time reveals a rhetoric rich in kairos. The notion of pause is central to kairotic apprehension and, subsequently, to action, because it is within the time(lessness) and space of a pause that one "sees" (i.e., realizes) the exigence of a given situation. King further highlights this point with an even more striking preponderance of the preposition *in* beginning midway through the sermon.

Consider the point (4.6) where King transitions from a discussion almost exclusively about racism to a broader critique of poverty in the world. He acknowledges that racism and poverty are closely linked, then he launches into a litany of observations regarding impoverished places and circumstances throughout the world. The following excerpts are illustrative:

> In Bombay more than a million people sleep on the sidewalks every night. They have no beds to sleep in; they have no houses to go in (4.7). . . .
>
> As I noticed these things, something within me cried out, "Can we in America stand idly by . . . ?" And I started thinking of the fact that we spend in America millions of dollars a day to store surplus food, and I said to myself, "I know where we can store that food free of charge—in the wrinkled stomachs of the millions of God's children all over the world who go to bed hungry at night." (5.1)

As these and the following short paragraphs reveal, King finds himself filling space and coming to *see* (i.e., "notice" or "know") the reality of the situation around him. There is a robust back-and-forth between the preposition *in* and the verb *see*. Importantly, the spaces typically referenced with the word *in* tend to be empty spaces, which, in a just world, would be filled. Houses and beds are meant to be filled, and people are meant to fill them. The "wrinkled stomach" of an impoverished child ought to be filled with food. Notice also that what follows King's initial observation in the first paragraph of the above quote is the realization "I noticed," and the implied call to action: "Something within me cried out, 'Can we in America stand idly by?'" One sees King's three-part rhetorical sequence: the pause, the recognition, and the movement toward action. One further observes that this movement toward action is not constructed deliberatively, but out of a transcendent, moral imperative.

King continues:

> Not only do we see poverty abroad; I would remind you that in our own nation there are about forty million people who are poverty stricken. I have seen

them here and there. I have seen them in the ghettoes of the north; I have seen
them in the rural areas of the south; I have seen them in Appalachia. I have just
been in the process of touring many areas of our country and I must confess
that in some situations I have literally found myself crying. (5.2)

Perhaps the most distinctive element of this passage is its forceful use of
anaphora. Like his more famous "I have a dream" anaphora, the repetition
of "I have seen . . ." increases the stress of a single point, which is in this case
that poverty affects people everywhere, and King has seen it. He has authentically "been there." He has entered the spaces of injustice, realized the nature of the problem, and been moved to tears. In this way, King situates himself rhetorically at the cross-section of time, space, and recognition. This
maneuver illustrates King's ability to build suspension and enact release.

Religious spaces are called *set apart* or *sanctified* because they are places
of removal from the outside world and its constraints. The cathedral is designed as a space of suspension wherein God's will fills the consecrated moment with recognition and impels the audience toward release. King reinforces this with his emphasis on transformational spaces:

I was in Marks, Mississippi, the other day, which is in Whitman County, the
poorest county in the United States. I tell you I saw hundreds. . . . And I saw
mothers and fathers who said to me. . . . And I was in Newark and Harlem just
this week. And I walked into the homes of welfare mothers; I saw them in
conditions—no, not with wall-to-wall carpet, but wall-to-wall rats and roaches.
I stood in an apartment and this welfare mother . . . pointed out the walls with
all of the ceiling falling through. She showed me the holes where the rats came
in. . . . Living in conditions day in and day out where the whole area is con-
stantly drained without being replenished. (5.3–5)

Significant in this excerpt is the graphic nature of the spaces King inhabits.
Initially, he places himself in poor communities, but the descriptions funnel
down to the concrete details of the homes and people who live there. In describing these particularized moments, King seems especially occupied with
the unjust "holes": the passageways for rats, the untrue walls that cannot
sustain ceilings, which in turn "fall through." The last sentence is perhaps the
most revealing: the area where these people live is "drained without being
replenished." For King, space, like time, is neutral. A space can be either bad
or good, secular or sanctified. It depends simply on how it is framed and,
subsequently, filled. Through King's reconceptualization, a jail cell is rhetor-

ically transformed from a place of powerlessness to one of influence. A pulpit and the church within which it sits are not symbols of escape from the world; they are spaces wherein the will of God is poised for action in the world. Similarly, impoverished communities become exigencies for the advance of justice.

King's implied claim is ultimately that spaces for justice can be created from the isolation of racism and poverty. Very near the end of the speech (9.8), he deploys what may be the most impressive metaphor of the discourse: "With this faith we will be able to hew out of the mountain of despair the stone of hope." Hope is created out of the same stuff as despair. King's rhetoric throughout the speech has drawn congruence from incongruence and, in so doing, carved openings for productive action. In hewing the stone of hope out of the mountain of despair, King creates yet another opening for faith from what would otherwise be an impenetrable mass.

King concludes the speech with a reference to John the Revelator: "Thank God for John, who centuries ago out on a lonely, obscure island called Patmos caught vision of a new Jerusalem descending out of heaven from God, who heard a voice saying "Behold, I make all things new—former things are passed away" (10.1). Earlier (2.1), King noted John's words without mentioning the Revelator by name, let alone where he (John) was when the revelation was received. King simply stated: "Changes are taking place and there is still the voice crying through the vista of time saying, 'Behold, I make all things new, former things are passed away'" (2.1). The words provided a fitting theme, which King then used to build his own sermon about change, but it is significant that King waits until the end of the speech to provide the context for John's words. Just as King began the speech by acknowledging his own temporality and space (the pulpit, the cathedral, Sunday morning), so he ends it by placing John on the lonely island of revelation "centuries ago." Both places are set apart and sanctified for the purpose of suspension, realization (or revelation, if you prefer), and the impulse for action. In both instances, suspension moves to insight, which in turn moves to the accomplishment of divine justice. In both instances, God speaks through an oracle. In this way, the speech begins and ends with a divine rhetor who is situated within a sanctified space and suspended within the fourth dimension. John's revelation is separated from King's oration by thousands of years and miles, but the message is unchanged. John's exile, the "Negro's" slavery, King's own imprisonment, and God's pulpit are all bound up in the same project of justice: to move faithfully from old to new.

❧

King's vision was as it should be for a preacher or prophet: idyllic. It is to be expected that his view of change started with revelation and ended with faith in a future marked by universal peace, brotherhood, and prosperity, just as the Bible prophesies. From a civil-religious standpoint, this idealism can be troubling. It can lead us to believe that we are fated for a future that is just and peaceful. King, of course, was not so naïve. He called prophetically on the nation to make the changes that need to be made. He held all parties accountable, but he too was tempted by utopic visions. In another one of his concluding metaphors he declared, "With this faith, we will be able to transform the jangling discords of our nation into a beautiful symphony of brotherhood." It is now cliché to talk of diversities as symphonies. Sometimes the differences really are too great to overcome. King spoke more than a half-century ago, and Satterlee spoke a half-century before him. In both cases, the leaders had civil-religious visions of a country that would at last become a space of harmony and order according to some divine vision. They had different ideas about the means of achieving this harmony. Satterlee pursued his vision by creating a cathedral that could hail the nation into a heavenly space. He made sure the walls and windows would proclaim this order with the authority of God's truest church. King created rhetorical spaces, pauses in time that he filled with his own version of godly justice and order. Both rhetors understood that there was something about the nation's moral core that had never matured. Satterlee had recognized the vacuum left by L'Enfant and the founders, and he believed with near certainty that that space ought to be filled by the Episcopal Church. King recognized the moral vacuum simply by looking at the interminable pain suffered by the nation's marginalized peoples. "Great documents are here to tell us something should be done," he remarks (33.10). He adds that the leaders of the nation have always been presented with recommendations for economic justice and moral renewal, and yet—he repeats the statement several times—"nothing has been done" (7.1–2). Both rhetors recognized a spiritual lack, a civil religion that was never built.

Just as there is something unsettling about the efforts of the cathedral iconography to bring America's disparate voices into harmony, there is something that seems always to resist the symphony of which King speaks. Despite the nation's hard-fought progress, a confusion of values continues to plague American civil-religious culture. In the same culture that King sang of a coming symphony, other priests of the civil religion have harangued the nation into war, inequality, and other discontents. There may be everything right with King's civil-religious vision, but his rightness is not my point. There seems to be something wrong with the quality of the civic space he inhabits. It is too broad, too contested, always too baffled and frustrated for a symphony. Within such a space, even a vision that strikes the right chords is liable to be shouted down or, in time, forgotten.

CHAPTER SEVEN

The Bush Presidents' Rock of Religious Faith

Washington National Cathedral's official timeline lists only two major events between the years 1990 and 2001: the completion of construction, which led to the dedication service when President George Herbert Walker Bush offered concluding remarks; and the National Day of Prayer and Remembrance service following the 9/11 attacks, when President George Walker Bush, the former's son, led the nation in mourning. Bush Sr. was a lifelong Episcopalian with ties to Washington, DC, going back a quarter-century. It was a coincidence that he became president at the time of the cathedral's completion, and he delivered his remarks with a sense of felicity. He viewed the building as a national shrine and a moral compass for Americans everywhere. As his remarks show, he also had a command of the building's history, purpose, and important players.

Bush Jr. was raised in the Episcopalian faith of his father, but he converted to Methodism when he married his wife, Laura. His Methodism was only nominal, however, until he met Billy Graham, who challenged him to make his faith real. Bush Jr. had struggled with alcohol for most of his adult life, and his faith had always been patchy, but he accepted the challenge from Reverend Graham and experienced a life-changing conversion. Bush Jr. was able to quit drinking, devote himself to his family, and feel God's love in a permanent way. He read the Bible daily and publicly spoke of his belief in Jesus Christ in evangelical terms.[1] By the time he stood in the cathedral pulpit after 9/11, he was already regarded as "the most openly religious president in generations."[2]

In this chapter I consider these two speeches as articulating different civil-religious visions. Bush Sr.'s speech represents an establishment approach to the American Civil Religion, a vision that embraces the nation in its wholeness but naïvely overlooks the gaps in its civil-religious bedrock, gaps through which leak the nation's discontents. Bush Jr.'s speech represents a civil-religious vision that aligns in alarming ways with Christian nationalism. Bush Jr. promotes Christianity, not in explicit ways but obliquely. He implies an apocalyptic Christian framework to promote a war that would last more than a decade, wreck his reputation, and damage the global standing of the United States. The two speeches are related in that the first represents the anemic civil religion that was left over from the failure of Washington and L'Enfant's federalist vision, while the second represents the sort of civil-religious vision that preys on that anemia.

George H. W. Bush's Moral Compass

Bush Sr.'s address from the cathedral on September 29, 1990, presents a beautiful symmetry. Just as Theodore Roosevelt had done eighty-three years before to the day, Bush stood as the nation's chief executive and chief civil-religious priest to bless the work of the cathedral. Roosevelt had presided over the laying of the foundation stone in front of roughly ten thousand people. It was a day of optimism and faith. The Marine Band played, representatives of the government and dignitaries from other countries attended, and of course leaders of the cathedral and the Anglican Communion were there to consecrate the work. Bush punctuated his remarks with a comment on the similarities:

> What an extraordinary moment this is. Eighty-three years ago this day, this hour our predecessors here laid a cornerstone, and now, eight decades later, we look at Mount St. Alban and say—here, we have built our church.
>
> Not just a church: A house of prayer for a nation built upon the rock of religious faith.[3]

Here Bush references the cathedral's mission. This building stands alone as "our church," a "house of prayer for a nation built upon the rock of religious faith." Bush accepts the premise that the United States is a nation that is endemically religious, and presumably Christian. The line about "the rock of religious faith" may allude to Plymouth Rock, where Puritans seeking to escape religious prejudice first landed in the New World. It may also be an allusion to Christ's words to Peter in the New Testament, "Upon this rock I will build my church."[4] In either case, the allusion implies a Christian cosmos.

Fig. 7.1. President George Herbert Walker Bush observes details at the dedication of Washington National Cathedral, September 29, 1990. Washington National Cathedral Archives

And why should it not? Bush stands in Satterlee's church, the very sanctuary that was designed to be the foundation of a new Christian hegemony that would spread across the globe on the wings of American progress.

Like most presidents of the modern era, Bush is careful not to speak too forwardly about the details of Christian theology. He does not reference Jesus, favoring the term "God" rather than "Christ," and he refers to "faith," "prayer," and "spirituality" rather than terms that might denote sectarian commitments. Of course, when he quotes or alludes to scripture, it is Christian scripture, and the sanctuary in which he stands is a cathedral of the Episcopal Diocese of Washington. None of this is to say that Bush would leave out other faiths, if he could, but only that in calling this building "our church," there is a telling absence. It is not a mosque or a synagogue or a temple, or for that matter the Basilica of the National Shrine of the Roman Catholic Church just across town. It is a Protestant Episcopal church that, as part of its ecumenist mission, offers its patronage to other faiths. Nearly a century earlier, Bishop

Henry Satterlee envisioned a spiritual axis point that would captain a new Christian unity in America and beyond, allying with other sects but never ceding its executive role in the nation's spirituality. Bush does not go so far, but he accepts that the role of this church is to serve as the nation's moral compass. He continues—:

> A nation whose founding President, George Washington, said: "No people can be bound to acknowledge and adore the invisible hand—which conducts the affairs of men—more than the people of the United States."
>
> And so we have constructed here this symbol of our Nation's spiritual life, overlooking the center of our Nation's secular life. . . .
>
> A symbol that carries with it a constant reminder of our moral obligations. Whenever I look up at this hill and see the Cathedral keeping watch over us, I feel the challenge reaffirmed.

At this early point in the address, Bush Sr. affirms the standard narrative of Washington National Cathedral: that it is the realization of the vision of Washington himself. Of course, Washington never suggested a Christian cathedral as the "great church for national purposes." Even the language of Washington that Bush Sr. quotes is more ambiguous with respect to deity than the words of many modern presidents. The phrase "invisible hand" is practically a deflection rather than an affirmation of any one God or doctrine. As a colonist, Washington had been a baptized Anglican, but his presidency never suggested Anglicanism should be some sort of spiritual archetype for the nation. This detail is overlooked in the narrative of Washington National Cathedral that Bush repeats. Bush also reinforces the dynamic Satterlee had in mind. The cathedral "overlooks the center of our nation's secular life." For Bush as for Satterlee, the cathedral exists at a righteous remove from the city, as if it were a judge on a bench enforcing the nation's moral code.

He continues by establishing his metaphor of the compass: "[W]e must govern by the moral imperatives of a strong moral compass. A compass based on the kind of purity of vision and values that inspired our early founders. . . . And a compass oriented to the words of St. Paul, who looks down on us from the left, 'And now abideth faith, hope and love, these three; but the greatest of these is love.'" The language here is presidential and *epideictic*, which is a genre of rhetoric in which "the speaker tries to establish a sense of communion centered around particular values recognized by the audience."[5] The occasion is one of celebration, so it is to be expected that the discourse be generalized. Bush is not here to outline new policies. He is here to praise and commemorate the achievement of the cathedral. Rhetorically, he is doing well what he is expected to do, given the occasion. Beneath the surface of his address, however, there resides a series of questions and puzzles over which he himself has little control. What is the challenge he feels is reaffirmed by the cathedral? In what direction precisely does this moral compass point him? Does he suggest that it points unambiguously in the same direction for all Americans? Further, if all Americans are expected to abide in "faith, hope, and love," whose version of these ideals are we to accept? St. Paul's? In other words, in saying roughly what most presidents would say in this situation, Bush Sr. reveals the facile nature of America's civil-religious character. What, after all, is the moral code by which this church would direct us?

As the address unfolds, these gaps in meaning become only more taped over. Further on in the speech, Bush celebrates the many Americans who

> caught the exhilaration of the dream that seized those who envisioned this Cathedral—and yet who didn't live to see it a reality.
>
> Men like Pierre L'Enfant, [whose] 1791 plan for Washington included "a great church for national purposes." Or Henry Satterlee, this city's first Episcopal Bishop, who yearned for a place "forever open and free." And the members of Congress who voted the 1893 charter of foundation.

As Bush outlines it, the history of this national church is a seamless progression from Washington and L'Enfant to Satterlee to the present day. The completed cathedral is the culmination of a civil-religious endeavor that was always there, just never enshrined in this "astonishing place of stone and light, a massive 300-million pound mountain of Indiana limestone" (paragraph 9). In referencing the dream caught by the Founders, Bush merges past, present, and future, building in text the kind of kairos Satterlee built in tangible materials. Just as Washington and Lincoln inhabit the same world as Peter and Paul; just as a visitor to the cathedral today inhabits the same world as a medieval pilgrim or a biblical Samaritan or an ancient Israelite priest, so L'Enfant and Satterlee inhabit the same national cosmos. They are cut from the same civil-religious cloth.

Bush revels in the building's iconography, in which "mosaics of the Great Seal of the United Sates and the State seals are set into the floors. Where bays honor Washington, Lincoln, Stonewall Jackson and Robert E. Lee." He speaks of the cathedral's memorials to everyone from Herman Melville and Alexander Graham Bell to Harriet Tubman and John F. Kennedy. He details the mesmerizing effect of the stained glass. In what is the speech's most eloquent moment, he references the cathedral's purpose in time and space, declaring that the cathedral embodies a sacred space:

Where an unexpected shaft of sun can leave a stunning memory. . . .
Where the history of the Cathedral and the history of the country have been interwoven. . . .

And a sacred time:

When we need to grieve—we come here. . . .
When we want to understand—we come here. . . .
When we want to celebrate—we come here. . . .

Bush describes the cathedral in terms that would have pleased L'Enfant. It is a place of beauty, memory, patriotic fervor; a place of national mourning, education, and celebration. For all his eloquence, however, there is something still uneven about Bush's ideals. I do not blame Bush. He is a president speaking at a public gathering; but he unwittingly reveals a project that is still unfinished, even if the Grand Finial is to be placed atop the Pinnacle of the St. Paul Tower that very day.

L'Enfant never had the chance to develop the national church idea. As I establish in chapter 1, the ignominy of his departure and the emergence of Jefferson's anti-Federalism ensured that a national church would be tabled. Like the city itself, L'Enfant's church was far from ever being realized. Bush does not seem to understand that the history he valorizes is an enigmatic one. Washington National Cathedral may be all of the things Bush says it is, but how we define those things remains a matter of one's own experience and conviction. Americans come here to grieve, to understand, and to celebrate, but how? As he concludes the address, Bush assumes the matter is settled: "And now that our national treasure is complete, how will it fit into our lives? I would love to see the entire country discover this Cathedral as America's resource, refuge, and reminder. Somewhere to strengthen the nation's heart. We should consecrate this place in the words of Isaiah: 'For mine house shall be called a house of prayer for all people.' All people. For all Americans" (paragraph 27). The sentiment is sincere and laudable, but for Bush Sr., grieving, understanding, and celebrating may take certain forms, while for someone else they may take other forms. Throughout the address, Bush Sr. speaks of the cathedral as the nation's "moral compass," but in a nation of competing gravitational pressures, this metaphor loses direction fast. We have not settled on the limits of this great church or, for that matter, of the national faith it claims to look after.

George W. Bush and the Terror of History

George W. Bush as president was first and foremost a man of faith. He made as much clear during his first campaign for the presidency and his first months in office. In ways unprecedented in the modern presidency, Bush framed himself in evangelical terms, as a leader guided by faith and prayer. In his memoir *A Charge to Keep*, published just a year before his election, he speaks of his life-changing meeting with Billy Graham: "It was the beginning of a new walk where I would recommit my heart to Jesus Christ. I was humbled to learn that God sent His Son to die for a sinner like me. I was comforted to know that through the Son, I could find God's amazing grace."[6] As candidate and president, Bush did not shy from such affirmations, and he quoted Christian hymnody and scripture frequently. According to Kevin Coe and David Domke, Bush, more than any other president in the modern era, used the "prophetic mode," a form of presidential discourse that evokes the United States as a divine means for freedom in the world.[7] Like the prophetic mode of religious leadership discussed in chapter 4, the prophetic mode in presidential terms is about broad visions of good and evil more than concerns over policy or context.

The nation as a benevolent hegemony fits with the prophetic mode, and it suits those in power. If one is raised in privilege and if one fills a position of influence, it is a comfort to know it was likely God's will that put you there as part of a cosmic destiny. In his first inaugural address, Bush declared, "We are not this story's author," and then, in allusion to the nation's founders, "an angel still rides in the whirlwind and directs this storm."[8] To make such references to a Christian worldview serves at least two purposes for Bush. First, it establishes him *as* a Christian, and therefore as a representative of the Christians of America, who were largely responsible for his election and would likely be so again. Second, it imbues his administration with a sense of destiny, suggesting that whatever its outcome, his record will be merely an extension of divine grace. Little did Bush know how useful this rhetorical worldview would become.

Once 9/11 occurred, Bush marshaled his Christian rhetoric in the starkest terms of his public life. No longer the folksy Christian evangelist of compassionate conservatism, he embraced the apocalypse. The world became a

Fig. 7.2. President George W. Bush delivers remarks from the pulpit of Washington National Cathedral on the National Day of Prayer and Mourning, September 14, 2001, three days after the September 11 attacks. PF-(usna) / Alamy Stock Photo

cosmos of good and evil, friend and enemy, God and godless. His infamous statement to the joint session of Congress, in which he declared that "[e]very nation, in every region, now has a decision to make. Either you are with us, or you are with the terrorists" prefigured a holy war into which he, the nation, and the world were being called.[9] Rhetoricians and scholars of the American Civil Religion have long regarded presidents as "national priests." Once they assume the mantle of moral leadership, they must be able to "interpret, communicate, and exemplify the right pieties with respect to America's founding myths."[10] When a president brings a Christian worldview to this responsibility, that priesthood becomes bound up with a whole separate eschatology that carries the weight of thousands of years of history and prophecy. This merging of the nation with a Christian narrative is of course the whole purpose of Christian nationalism. When Bush spoke from the Canterbury pulpit three days after the September 11 attacks, he evoked the cathedral of Henry Yates Satterlee. The United States had been hailed into the arc of history. Bush made it clear to the world that the United States would answer the call.

Bush's much longer and more widely viewed State of the Union address to the joint session of Congress on September 20 is often considered the president's definitive post-9/11 speech. The cathedral address nearly a week earlier, however, is where Bush introduces the so-called "Bush doctrine," his policy of preemptive war in the name of fighting terror. In the cathedral speech, he frames the doctrine in religious terms, as a conflict between good and evil. He had already declared the day of his address to be a National Day of Prayer and Mourning, and it was expected that his remarks at the cathedral would befit a religious service. So, when he pointed Americans in the direction of more bloodshed, Bush came off less as a politician or even a commander in chief than as a prophet. The State of the Union address and the many interviews, press conferences, and speeches that followed merely echoed and developed in more diplomatic terms the quiet ferocity of the cathedral address.

The Middle Hour

Bush begins the address with a temporal reference:

> We are here in the middle hour of our grief. So many have suffered so great a
> loss, and today we express our nation's sorrow. We come before God to pray
> for the missing and the dead, and for those who loved them.
>
> On Tuesday, our country was attacked with deliberate and massive cruelty.
> We have seen the images of fire and ashes and bent steel.[11]

Like my reading of the MLK sermon in chapter 6, my analysis of Bush's address focuses on notions of time. We are suspended in "the middle hour of our grief"—a phrase that asks to be unpacked. Literally, a middle hour is a turning point between beginning and end. The service began, fittingly, under wet gray clouds, around noon, and Bush rose to the pulpit at about 1 P.M. Bush does not say *we are here this afternoon*. He calls the moment the middle hour *of our grief*, as if from this point or some point near at hand the sun will emerge. Caught in this immortal present, that moment that Aristotle says is without time, we are removed from chronos.[12] In my reading of the 1968 King speech, I show how King worked to remove his listeners from everyday time and situate them within a charged moment ripe for change. This sort of rhetoric rejects notions of past and future, which are constructions of time that would merely have us wait. This sort of rhetoric embraces kairotic time, the moment of revelation, when the opportunity to claim one's destiny emerges.

As a memorial address, the speech also falls under the same broad genre as Bush Sr.'s address delivered barely more than a decade earlier. It is epideictic: rhetoric that concerns itself with uniting communities around shared values, whether in celebration, mourning, or some other special occasion. Rhetoricians Lawrence Rosenfield and Dale Sullivan have independently argued that a true epideictic rhetoric may also act as a religious experience, like a revelation of divine truth.[13] In this sense, epideictic rhetoric is often kairotic. By reinforcing communal values and revealing new truths, epideictic rhetoric can set the stage for change. Aristotle noted that epideictic rhetors trade in the present, but they are not uninterested in the past or future. They "often make use of other things, both reminding [the audience] of the past and projecting the course of the future."[14] In other words, the past may be a delimited repository of events, but it is through the prism of our present values that we interpret its meaning. Rhetorician Dale Sullivan has argued that epideictic rhetoric occurs when "rhetor and audience enter the timeless, consubstantial space carved out by their mutual contemplation of reality."[15] Speeches of celebration and mourning, praising and blaming constitute a genre that attempts to define its audience according to a set of *existing* values, what George Kennedy calls "timeless virtues."[16] The future may be an abstraction, but it is shaped according to the things we hold sacred in the here and now.

Bush's beginning is perfect for the occasion. By isolating his audience in the middle hour, he controls the mechanism of movement from past to future. Americans have not come here to this church to adjudicate the reasons why the attacks occurred, a genre of rhetoric Aristotle calls forensic, or whether war is the correct response, or, if so, how that war ought to be prosecuted, a genre of rhetoric Aristotle calls deliberative. As Bush puts it, they have come "before God to pray." They are here to remove themselves from the profane world and to reconstitute themselves according to the values they hold in common. When airplanes plunged into the World Trade Center and Pentagon, Americans were forced to contemplate a new reality together. They entered the cathedral and listened to their president in the faith that he would reveal some way to orient them to this reality.

When in his second paragraph Bush references the "massive cruelty" of the attack and the "fire and ashes, and bent steel," his language reminds Americans of the hellscape they now face, reinforcing the sense that they have been removed from quotidian life and now inhabit something otherworldly. One of the most defining emotions of the 9/11 attacks was the confusion they entailed. *Why did they do it? Why do they hate us?* was the refrain. Americans wanted answers that would restore order to the cosmos. They looked not for theorists or adjudicators or policy makers, but for prophets and seers. Like Sayre and King, Bush embraces the prophetic mode. Having acknowledged the chaos and injustice of the events, he begins the work of framing a new, more just order. As part of this project, he takes the traumatic details of the attack and begins to give them a sense of order:

> Now come the names, the list of casualties we are only beginning to read: They are the names of men and women who began their day at a desk or in an airport, busy with life. They are the names of people who faced death and in their last moments called home to say, be brave and I love you. They are the names of passengers who defied the murders and prevented the murder of others on the ground. They are the names of men and women who wore the uniform of the United States and died at their posts. They are the names of rescuers—the ones whom death found running up the stairs and into the fires to help others. We will read all these names. We will linger over them and learn their stories, and many Americans will weep.

Bush attempts to mitigate the abstract trauma of the attacks by assigning names to casualties and placing them in discernable categories (e.g., "men and women who began their day at a desk"). The rhetorical construction of the section reinforces this sense of order. He is fond, like King, of anaphora, the repetition of phrasing at the beginning of successive clauses: "They are the names. . . . They are the names. . . ." There is a patience and orderliness to his arrangement, as if Bush is doing with language what a builder might do after an earthquake: slowly, methodically taking the collapsed stones, raising them up into view, and pressing them into place. Bush is charged with emotion, but he remains composed and purposeful in his speaking. Rather than try to extinguish the inchoate rage and grief of the moment, he gives it composition and voice, assuring Americans that the chaos of the attacks will be controlled.

This portion of the speech bears several resemblances to the style of King's address. Anaphora is employed throughout. The "names" become symbols of a past that now hovers all around us. We cannot help but think of the "names" as representations of ourselves. They were people doing quotidian things, like sitting at a desk waiting for the clock to tell them they could go home, but when faced with a violent transformation, they became heroes who defied death in the face of evil. Rhetorician John Murphy points out that the images of heroism Bush describes are not simply evidence of goodness and determination; these images represent "the biblical test of a chosen people."[17] Each microprofile is an exemplar, depicting an average person who has been thrown into a timeless struggle. In this interpretation, the great benefit to the listener is, again, the sense of order out of chaos. If we can process the deaths of regular people like ourselves as though they are part of a grand narrative, we can make sense of our own place in this world. We, too, have destinies.

What also compares well with King's style is Bush's impulse to situate his audience within emotionally charged spaces, and to do so repeatedly. Just as King situates his audience within the spaces of poverty, framing each image with the phrase, "I have seen . . . ," Bush transports his audience to the spaces of terror ("They are the names of . . ."). The exigencies may be different, but the strategy is the same: giving a past event the urgency of the present. The audience feels copresent with the images presented to them, and they are moved to action. Bush ends this segment in the future tense: "We will read these names." Just as he has joined past to present, so now he joins present to future.

"And I assure you," Bush continues, "you are not alone. Just three days removed from these events, Americans do not yet have the distance of history, but our responsibility to history is clear: to answer these attacks and rid the world of evil." This statement is conspicuous for several reasons. First, it marks the only time when Bush refers to himself in the singular first person. Almost invariably choosing the plural pronoun over the singular "I," he presents himself in synecdoche, as a part standing for the whole; his voice is the *vox populi*. His grief, his resolve, his answer to the attacks become not his at all, but "ours," and *our responsibility to history is clear*. Just as his voice has become *vox populi*, so *vox populi* becomes *vox dei*. Bush's statement also explicitly reminds the audience that they stand within a uniquely timeless moment, without "the distance of history." For the moment, at least, we remain in the middle hour, the pause between past and future, but Bush implies we will have that distance in time. Kairos has a complicated relationship with chronos. It is a different dimension in which chronos is eternally erased. On the other hand, kairos is often charged with the power to crash into chronos and change its trajectory. Heaven, likewise, is a dimension of both removal from and interaction with the temporal world. Divine imperatives are filtered into the world in order to correct its offenses and change or slow its progress toward oblivion. This relationship between chronos and kairos is what Bush invokes when he reveals "our responsibility to history." He does not propose a new political policy; rather he reveals a divine imperative: we must "rid the world of evil."

At this point in the investigation of the 9/11 attacks, Americans were still largely unaware of who Al Qaeda were, why they existed, and to what extent they were responsible for the tragedy. The fact that the origin and meaning of the attack were not yet clear did not deter Bush from stating that our responsibility was clear. It may seem a reach to presume that we can rid the world of evil, but Bush makes it clear that these attacks mean not a war against a particular enemy but a war against evil itself. To fight evil is to fight an abstraction, a force that has no definition, no boundaries, and no temporality. It requires a spiritual comprehension of the world. Within such a framework, politics have little place. They may be leveraged since they serve the higher purpose of God, but that is the extent of their usefulness.

Bush's next lines reveal a subtle conflation of God and the United States: "War has been waged against us by stealth and deceit and murder. This nation is peaceful, but fierce when stirred to anger. This conflict was begun on the timing and terms of others. It will end in a way, and at an hour, of our choosing." Bush's description of "this nation" bears a striking resemblance to the biblical God. When God, or "the Lord," is characterized in scripture as angry, he is overwhelmingly described as provoked (e.g., Deuteronomy 4:25, 6:15; Isaiah 1:4, 65:3). Left unprovoked, he speaks "peace unto His people" (e.g., Psalms 85:8). That is, the God of the Bible promotes peace except when his wrath is kindled, in which case he unleashes terrible furies. Most modern nations likely see themselves the same way, as peaceful until attacked, but Bush's language has a biblical ring. Words like "stealth," "deceit," and "murder" connote the Evil One, or the chief priests and scribes, who "sought how they might take [Jesus] by craft and put him to death."[18] Similarly, Bush's United States is peaceful until stirred to anger, in which case the nation becomes a warrior against evil.

The implications of Bush's reference to time in this section become clear when considered in light of the Bible. Bush invokes the United States of America as the force that will determine the nature and timing, even the "hour," of the end. This declaration seems oddly conceived, given the mystery that still shrouded the conflict at the time. The notion that we could choose the terms and end-time of a war against an enemy whom we did not know is ambitious, perhaps unrealistic. Bush's claims, however, are consistent with a view of the USA as an omnipotent force against evil. God is likewise the chooser of hours. Matthew states that no person knows the hour of the end when God will come again and peace will reign. No one, "not even the angels," knows God's chosen moment to crash into the temporal realm and end unrighteousness. God alone knows and he alone chooses.[19]

Bush's fusion of the United States and God may seem less problematic within the context of the cathedral, where prophets and presidents, biblical narratives and American history, and the flag and the cross are all broadcast in tandem. But here is where I think Bush's rhetoric departs from King's. King saw himself and his audience as "helpers" of time, servants of a God who promotes a new time and a new history. Admittedly, Bush is more constrained than King when invoking a relationship to God. Were he to become overly sermonic, Bush's address would transgress the conventions of presidential discourse, even in an epideictic speech on a day of mourning. Bush, however, takes the role of national priest a step further. In the passage above, God is not explicitly invoked; he is embedded. Characterizations of the nation seem like characterizations of the all-powerful being. God and the political end are one and the same.

Here again is the difference between a civil religion like the one L'Enfant and Washington envisioned and a Christian nationalism like the one Satterlee envisioned. In the former, religion serves the purpose of the national interest, whereas in the latter, the Christian God becomes the national interest. David Domke's critique of Bush is apt here. For Domke, a scholar of presidential language strategies, presidents are well within the limits of their genre to invoke God in language, but Bush's invocations of God have a tendency to move directly into imperatives for political and militaristic action. This impulse, in Domke's view, is Bush's great transgression. "The president and his team," writes Domke in reference to the Bush administration, "consistently utilized communication approaches that merged a conservative religious worldview and political ambition in pursuit of controlling public discourse, pressuring Congress (and the United Nations) [and] engendering a view of its actions as divinely ordained."[20] I would take Domke's assessment even further. Bush does not merely imagine a country that is the object of a divine will; he constructs a nation that is the very source of divine will.

Almost immediately after his statement regarding the inevitable conflict, Bush moves into a conciliatory tone, promoting comfort and assurance through prayer:

> There are prayers that help us last through the day, or endure the night. There are prayers of friends and strangers, that give us strength for the journey. And there are prayers that yield our will to a will greater than our own.
>
> This world he created is of moral design. Grief and tragedy and hatred are only for a time. Goodness, remembrance, and love have no end. And the Lord of life holds all who die, and all who mourn.

The statements on prayer at the beginning of this passage direct the listener away from the statements about war and toward supplication to God. We are taught to get through "the journey" by yielding our will to another, one "greater than our own." Having just announced a radical position with respect to American power, Bush leaves no room to explore the implications of his statements. Instead, he retreats to the prayer encomium, reminding us that the world we inhabit is a moral one. "Grief and tragedy" are tied to "time," while "goodness, remembrance, and love have no end." We also find comfort in "the Lord of life." The gospel of John teaches its reader that "in me ye might have peace. In this world ye shall have tribulation, but be of good cheer, I have overcome the world."[21] When we exist *enkairos*, we are held within the bosom of God, and we are assured that the outcome of our struggles is divinely conceived. Our obligation is not to kick against the pricks, but to assent to the revealed will of a force "greater than our own."

Bush concludes the address by stating that our response to the attacks of 9/11 is a divine charge: "Our unity is a kinship of grief, and a steadfast resolve to prevail against our enemies. And this unity against terror is now extending across the world. America is a nation full of good fortune, with so much to be grateful for. But we are not spared from suffering. In every generation, the world has produced enemies of human freedom. They have attacked America, because we are freedom's home and defender. And the commitment of our fathers is now the calling of our time." Panegyrics to unity are common fare for presidents. In this case, Bush crafts unity by antithesis. There are those who love freedom and there are those who hate freedom, and the United States is "freedom's home and defender." Therefore, those who hate freedom attacked America. The formula is simple. If one is not to be considered an enemy to freedom, one is to get in line behind the USA. This unity, Bush observes, "is now extending across the world." By extension, this means America's leadership is extending across the world.

The outcome seems inevitable. We have moved from the past, with its wrecks of time, into the kairotic present, with its revelatory order, and finally into a future full of destiny. It is all part of a single eternal arc. When Bush says "the commitment of our fathers is now the calling of our time," he brings the past to bear on the present as though we are here to pledge a sacred trust. It is fitting that the last line is spoken from the cathedral pulpit, the very pulpit for which Bishop Satterlee himself acquired the stone. Surrounded by the iconography of American history and Christian destiny, and just three days removed from the attacks, Bush summons Americans to the fight. For a time, it worked. Post-9/11 Americans were looking for a revelator who could make quick sense of a world frozen by tragedy. They felt not so much that they were at the threshold of an endless, complicated war as that they were joining a timeless struggle.

❖

In a visceral sense, Bush's cathedral address is moving. It comforts mourning Americans by remembering those who were lost, celebrates the values they embodied, and reconstitutes the character of the nation as a whole. Bush's delivery also seems inspired. He speaks with gentle resolve; he takes his time, makes eye contact, furrows his brow, and sets his jaw at just the right moments. His inflections have the cadence of a prayer. His whole countenance seems moved by *energeia*, the ancient rhetorical figure in which the speaker embodies the emotions they are trying to communicate—in this case, the grief, the fervor, the resolve. In the subsequent weeks and months, Bush would continue to lay the rhetorical foundation for which he broke ground that day at the cathedral. The United States seemed determined to go to war anywhere as soon as possible without respect to the constraints of time and space and the inherent messiness of it all. "My job isn't to nuance," Bush once said. "My job is to say what I think."[22] The audacity of this statement implies that one does not need to conform to constraints, since one is the force of constraint itself. Bush's America becomes the voice of divine will, the vanquisher of evil, and the chooser of hours.

Domke refers to Bush's worldview as "political fundamentalism," which he describes as "an intertwining of conservative religious faith, politics, and strategic communication. It is conceptualized as consistent with, yet substantially distinct in societal implications from, civil religion." Domke adds that the Bush Jr. administration after September 11 was able to transform "a religious paradigm into a political one by choosing language and communication approaches that were structurally grounded in a conservative religious outlook but were political in content and application."[23] This is why Bush Jr.'s administration and rhetoric always felt so religious, even though Bush refrained from making explicitly sectarian references most of the time. His political worldview was the mirror image of a fundamentalist religious worldview. No wonder the nation took on such an ominous pall. It was not just the smoke and ash of the terrorist attacks themselves that overshadowed the early 2000s; it was also America's apocalyptic response. Eye must answer for eye; fire must fight fire. What is more, the dark work of war is the surest means to prevent non-Christian nations from gaining ground in a shrinking geopolitical landscape. Christian conservatives were only too happy to get behind Bush Jr.'s vision. The Moral Majority that took root in the Reagan years, which is where Domke locates the birth of modern American political fundamentalism, blossomed under Bush Jr., as Christian fundamentalists extended their fight for family values, criminalization of abortion, prayer in schools, and sexual orientation and gender conformity to a military crusade against Islamic fundamentalists both at home and abroad.[24]

Like Satterlee's, Bush's vision of global unity is unsettling. Satterlee was just as much a believer in unity as anyone else, but he believed that unity in the world would be best achieved under the aegis of the Anglican faith, with the National Cathedral as that faith's home and defender. Bush assumes that the unity of grief that binds Americans together will extend throughout the world, thus uniting civilized nations everywhere. He indicates that the banner under which these nations will unite is the American flag, since it is the United Sates that will choose the terms of this crusade. Although the enemy is abstracted as "evil," the principal role is assigned to a single nation. It was a doomed strategy. The world is, in fact, a complicated place. As rhetorician John Murphy commented somewhat presciently in 2003: "'[E]ternal perdurance' . . . [is] a nice place for presidents to visit, [but] it is not a good idea for them to live there. . . . Sooner or later, President Bush will discover the world's resistance to simple answers."[25] Despite the traumas of 9/11, the international community could not accept wholesale the United States as the new source of divine will.

Where Bush had expected an overwhelming global alliance, he managed a comparatively ramshackle "coalition of the willing," which pursued the War on Terror in fits and starts over the following decade.[26] Many nations provided logistical and political support, but many others, perhaps spooked by Bush's bellicosity, did so only in exchange for increased aid from the United States. The United States accounted for more than 80 percent of War on Terror troops, with only three other countries participating in combat operations.[27] Bush's approval rating peaked in the months after the attack at over 90 percent, but as emotions settled and his war dragged on, that percentage plummeted. By the time he left office, his rating hovered around 20 percent.[28] The nation's favorability in the eyes of the rest of the world also tumbled in the first decade of the millennium.[29] Perhaps Bush learned of the world the same lesson Satterlee's successors had learned of the nation. Complex communities balk at master plans. It may be tempting to take an external theology and try to impose it on a civil-religious community that is as amorphous as that of the United States, but it will not remain in place for long.

Both of the Bush presidents were careful not to apply an explicitly Christian worldview to their leadership of the country, but they implied it with great force. Bush Sr. validated the mission of Washington National Cathedral, doing what so many presidents before him had done. He praised its role in bringing morality to the nation, and he argued without nuance that the cathedral could apply a moral code to a country entangled by dilemmas. The question that gets overlooked by this presumption is, Why did we need a private church to supply this morality in the first place? What were we missing, and why were we missing it until this church came along and supposedly filled the gap? Part of the answer to this question is to point out that this church, noble though its efforts have been, cannot supply the code Bush took for granted. To be a "house of prayer for all people," it must give voice to a host of moral incongruities. As Americans, we often like to point out that incongruity is one of the principles we hold most sacred. It is our inalienable right to disagree that merits reverence, and the cathedral is where that right is enshrined. Fair enough, but I do not believe this notion is what Bush Sr. had in mind when he spoke of a moral code and a rock of religious faith. Even if he had, he did so beneath the rood beam and the crucifix of a Christian cathedral, under the gaze of the apostles and prophets. To suggest that this building, rather than, say, the Capitol or the Mall, is the sacred ground of American diversity would be disingenuous.

Even within this Christian identity, the cathedral is not sufficiently articulate. Bush Sr. may have affirmed a particular kind of faith for the nation, but he did so in oblique ways. To suggest that a Christian, Anglican cathedral was "our church" as a nation was too narrow to be an accurate statement, and yet Bush Sr.'s message was also too generic to give shape to the kind of religious rock of which he spoke. By not acknowledging the discrepancies between the visions of L'Enfant and Satterlee and their successors, Bush Sr. left gaps in the nation's civil religious mortar. So, when Bush Jr. rose to the pulpit on that rainy September day in 2001, his Battle Hymn did not seem any less natural in the shadows of that nave than Reverend King's message seemed decades earlier. Like King before him, Bush Jr. called for what amounted to a moral crusade, but whereas King had drawn upon the cathedral to promote an end to war, Bush implied a call to holy war. There is a strangeness and incoherence to the voices that haunt this cathedral, not just in speech but also, as I have shown, in the iconography, statuary, even the location.

I am not suggesting that any civil religion must impose strict orthodoxy upon its public. There will be debates, passionate ones, but there ought to be a sufficient number of premises that a nation can agree whether or not it is Christian and, if so, in what way it is so. Americans cannot even get that far, and the history of this cathedral is proof. To its infinite credit, today's Washington National Cathedral would be just as willing to welcome an atheist as an Anglican into its chapels, but as cathedral officials have admitted, this come-as-you-are Christianity is still Christianity. The cathedral is called to "love they neighbor," because it is Christian, *not* because it is American. At its best, this Christian sense of calling is ennobling and inspiring, and truly an invitation to all. The cathedral's "walk" of this mission merits the highest praise. I would nevertheless continue to push against the idea that the American Civil Religion and its professed temple should be an outgrowth of any sectarian faith. As the Bush speeches show, the dream of L'Enfant is yet to be realized.

Both presidents Bush regarded the United States of America as a nation founded upon religious principles—"the rock of religious faith," as Bush Sr. put it. In the sense that some early Americans settled in the New World to escape religious persecution, this notion is true, but even from its earliest colonists, the United States has been a place of diverging and competing motivations. Whether one points to the Puritans of Plymouth or the capitalists of Jamestown or the slaves of Point Comfort or the soldiers of the Castillo de San Marcos or the missionaries of Santa Fe, or even the revolutionaries of Philadelphia, the notion that *a* religious faith united them, let alone one so singular as to be founded upon a rock, just does not hold up. It was *because* of these diverse headwaters that Washington and L'Enfant had envisioned the capital as a great estuary. They yearned to build something wholly new, not simply because they wanted distinction but because they knew that the nation was already something original, confounding even. Old models would not do here.

CHAPTER EIGHT

Civil Seership

The Revelatory Project of Cameron Partridge and Gene Robinson; or, The Revelation of Matthew Shepard

On June 22, 2014, the Rev. Dr. Cameron Partridge, an openly transgender chaplain of the Episcopal Church, delivered a sermon from the pulpit of Washington National Cathedral. Having made national headlines one year earlier by publicly supporting marriage equality, the Cathedral continued its advocacy for the LGBTQ+ community by holding a special Eucharist in honor of Pride Month. Partridge's participation was one of the Eucharist's signature moments. The sermon was noted in mainstream as well as alternative media across the country, from the *New York Times* to GLAAD to the Christian Broadcasting Network.[1] In nearly every case, the reports highlighted the "historic" nature of the event. Many of the press releases also referred to Gene Robinson, who presided over the ceremony. Robinson had been at the center of controversy in 2003 when he became the Episcopal Church's first openly gay bishop. His ascension to that position resulted in opposition from hundreds of Episcopal parishes whose members, many of whom would later leave the church, believed the Episcopal faith had become too liberal. Allegations of impropriety on Robinson's part were made.[2] A schism was threatened.[3] Death threats were issued.[4] Nevertheless, the church pushed forward, and Robinson was elected and consecrated by a sizable majority. That he should preside over the Eucharist and the Partridge sermon eleven years later is evidence of the progress the LGBTQ+ community was making among Episcopalians.

Robinson referenced this progress as part of the Pride Month Eucharist: "What you have seen over the past decade in this beloved church of ours risking its life for those of us who are gay, lesbian, bisexual, transgender . . . is an astounding thing, and we should all give thanks to see this movement of God in our midst."[5] Not only, then, was the event highlighted as a "first," but it became imbued with divine will, as though the hand of God were moving history in this direction. Robinson also came out of retirement to deliver the keynote sermon at the interment of Matthew Shepard, the young gay man who had been savagely killed in Wyoming two decades earlier.

The relative lack of controversy surrounding Robinson's leadership, Partridge's presence at the cathedral pulpit in 2014, and the interment of Matthew Shepard in 2018 points to the rhetorical success of the LGBTQ+ movement nationally. The United States was in the midst of a sea change in public opinion regarding nonconforming identities of gender and sexual orientation. Beginning around 2008, state judiciaries began overturning bans on same-sex marriage. In late 2009, the Matthew Shepard and James Byrd Jr. Hate Crimes Bill was passed by Congress and signed into law by President Obama. By early 2015, thirty-six states had declared same-sex marriage or civil union to be legal. Then, in June of that year, same-sex marriage was made legal across the United States by federal judicial mandate.[6] People were interested in the politics and civil rights of queer populations, and state and federal governments were taking notice.

The Episcopal Church's trajectory on these matters somewhat paralleled that of the American legal system. I note above the controversy surrounding Gene Robinson's election as an openly gay and partnered bishop, but the matter of transgender clergy remained unsettled. In the mid-2000s, Episcopal clergy began coming out as transgender. Then, in 2012, during its General Convention, the Episcopal Church passed with overwhelming support resolutions that prohibited discrimination based on gender identity and expression in clerical ordination.[7] The Massachusetts diocese, Partridge's home diocese, demonstrated leadership for transgender issues.[8] It seemed the Episcopal Church was participating in the touchstone civil rights movement of the twenty-first century, and people like Partridge and Robinson were uniquely positioned to declaim on its behalf.

The Pride Month Eucharist

The prepared program of the Eucharist on June 22, 2014, emphasized the event's civil and political aspects. The service included readings and prayers by members of the LGBTQ+ community. A cathedral press release highlighted Partridge's role "as an advocate both within the Church and wider community" whose presence would "send a symbolic message in support of greater equality for the transgender community, which suffers from acts of violence, discrimination, unemployment, homelessness, and financial inequality."[9] In other words, the cathedral used its platform to highlight the way Partridge would help to advance key goals related to LGBTQ+ rights. Largely unnoticed, however, was that the political and civic character of the service rested on a rich theological fulcrum.

It was Partridge himself who would complicate the political emphasis by suggesting his appearance as a trans clergyman was about more than trans civil rights. "I don't think the intersection of trans people and religion has received a whole lot of conversation yet," he commented in one interview.[10] In another, he gently pushed against the media's tendency to use him as a lens into trans identity, and suggested instead that his trans identity might be used as a lens into questions of identity more universally. "In one sense," he commented, "my being trans doesn't matter. In another way, I'm able to have certain conversations about the complexities of human identity with [people] who are figuring out their own identities."[11] Chris Paige, a transgender activist with an interest in matters of faith and spirituality, was asked to comment on Partridge's appearance at the cathedral. Like Partridge, Paige wanted to resist the urge to silo the event as a commentary on the transgender experience, or even the queer experience. "There is such an intersection between being trans and religious," he said. "Some of the fundamental religious questions—'Who am I? How do I fit into the world?'—those are very familiar questions that people ask on a journey of gender exploration."[12] Perspectives like these suggest that people interested in the Partridge sermon might overlook what his address says about his community's—and the human community's—*spiritual* birthright. They were suggesting not that queer identities ought not to be mentioned, but only that they ought to be framed as lenses into deeper, more complex, and more explicitly spiritual questions about the human condition writ large.

So, although the cathedral's open affirmation of a transgender priest is significant, it is not the focus of this chapter. My aim is not to overlook notions of gender identity and how they inform the sermon but to look beneath their surface. I argue that the sermon's social significance stems from a recondite philosophical orientation that, once unearthed, reveals a theology of the American Civil Religion that might provide a starting point for the nation, if it ever intends to fill in the civil religious gaps left by centuries of exposure. To explicate this theology, I perform a close reading of Partridge's personal narrative and exegesis of the scriptures. My meta-analysis puts Partridge's ideas in conversation with John Durham Peters's radical theory of communication as "broadcast" and embodied "caress," a theory that rejects the old communication model of "shared minds" and argues instead that communication "entails bearing oneself in such a way that one is open to hearing the other's otherness. . . . Communication is about the constitution of relationships, the revelation of otherness, or the breaking of the shells that encase the self, not about the sharing of private mental property."[13] In Peters's view, communication is a form of revelation of the self and the other. As I hope the following analysis shows, this "constitution of relationships" and "revelation of otherness" may provide one step further toward a lasting American Civil Religion.

This distinction between a theological framework and a call for social justice is subtle but important. Partridge implies that Christian devotion is not primarily about ministering to the temporal needs of the less fortunate, though doing so is an essential consequence of that devotion. For Partridge, devotion is engagement with the hidden world. It is about finding the people who languish in darkness and lifting the veil that bars them from the immanent space shared by the rest of the community. In the same way, I propose to look beneath the observable progress (e.g., legal recognition) of a marginalized community in order to pursue the civil-religious theology of which that progress is but one evidence. What this civil-religious theology reveals is something akin to Peters's notion of communication as broadcast and caress. The disciple, which is to say, the devotee of this theology, creates spaces wherein those who were invisible become broadly visible. The whole project of discipleship devolves upon this ability to *see* and recognize one another. A civil religion that entails civil rights, therefore, must begin with what I am calling civil seership.

For civil seership to work effectively it must occur in a place and time set apart for the purpose. An observer is not likely to see, let alone offer recognition to, an other if they pass them on a quotidian sidewalk; but if the observer occupies sacred ground in common with the other—that is, if the two people inhabit the same kairos, recognition becomes virtually unavoidable. The project of seership calls for the creation of such spaces. This view assumes that social advocacy starts much further back than a call to legal or political action; it begins in a *somewhere* that merits careful analysis. How do we find, build, and access spaces where "the least of these, my brethren," become seen and recognized?[14] Doing this sort of work has increasingly become the project of Washington National Cathedral.

Partridge's Path to the Priesthood

Having grown up in an Episcopal household, Partridge long maintained a background interest in religion. Even as a teen, he nursed a quiet ambition to become a priest. He, then identified as a woman, attended Bryn Mawr College, where he came out as both a lesbian and an aspiring priest. It was also at Bryn Mawr that he met his future wife. From there it was on to Harvard Divinity School, where he earned master of divinity and doctor of theology degrees, and thence to the priesthood, thanks to the sponsorship of a progressive Episcopal church in Boston.[15] His queerness notwithstanding, Partridge's path to the Episcopal priesthood seems conventional: a young mind given to philosophical and religious questions, educated at prestigious universities, imbued with a sense of calling. But during the ordination process in 2001, Partridge revealed he was transitioning, a development that ensured his path would not be so standard.

For one thing, Partridge's bishop, M. Thomas Shaw, admitted discomfort with the notion of his transitioning; and although Shaw would soon throw his support behind Partridge, he feared there would always be public tension surrounding Partridge's identity. Questions of doctrine aside, he would always have to answer for his gender. It was a well-founded concern. Partridge was asked to speak for his gender identity on a near regular basis as he progressed toward ordination and well beyond. In all of his interviews, the topic centered on him, and while he accepted the responsibility to discuss it, he also pushed for a broader view of his role as a clergyman and a human being.[16] It became clear early in his career that he would never be able to conceal his queerness from the public eye again. Nevertheless, in 2008, eight years after his coming out, Partridge achieved his goal of being ordained to the priesthood. After three years of serving in various positions in local congregations, he was appointed by Shaw as chaplain at Boston University, a high-profile post that lent visibility to transgenderism within the Episcopal Church leadership. By the time Partridge delivered his sermon at Washington National Cathedral, he was one of seven openly transgender clergy in the church.[17]

Partridge's Ecumenical Sermon

When Partridge stepped to the cathedral pulpit, it was to be expected that this tension between theology and social advocacy would present itself. Throughout the address, he works hard to embody both identities in harmony and to ground his occasional calls for social justice in an expansive and developed discussion of biblical ideas. He sees it as his task to embrace the ambiguity and tension of his priestly role and to translate it into something parishioners will find worth hearing. For him, this embrace of ambiguity defines his faith. As he noted in an interview with the Religion News Service, "[M]ost of all I appreciate what's called 'Anglican comprehensiveness,' which often calls us to embody ambiguity. Sometimes that causes us discomfort, even conflict, but it's at the heart of who we are as Anglicans."[18] Partridge's view of Anglicanism coincides remarkably well with the way I have framed the cathedral throughout this book, as a place fraught with unsettling tensions that would seem to belie any claim to harmony. On one hand, these tensions may be read as a symptom of some underlying flaw. On the other, they may be the natural and perhaps intended consequence of a history in which traditional, high church culture meets the messy enterprise of activist politics. Without this pairing, it is difficult to imagine that Partridge could have found his way to the clergy, let alone to the Canterbury Pulpit.

On its face, the sermon appears to be another call for tolerance and acceptance—a safe proclamation to a friendly audience that the gender binary discriminates against certain citizens. The language is largely accessible. The tone is conversational. Partridge makes generous use of scripture to promote a familiar progressive creed designed to take on the "oppression, isolation, and despair" of marginalized communities. He also relies heavily on personal narrative. In short, it is in many ways a standard homily based on well-worn liberationist themes.

Driving the sermon's ideas, however, is Partridge's sophisticated play with the notion of space as well as his interrogation of the word "revelation." Specifically, Partridge radicalizes the concept of revelation by returning to the term's spatial roots: revelation as an uncovering, an *apocalypse* in the original sense. As with the King, Bush Sr., and Bush Jr. speeches, I am interested in the sermon's spatial and temporal dynamics, particularly as they relate to notions of uncovering. Partridge's version of justice is advanced through a process of kairotic immanence, not a forensic argument or a deliberation over policy, or even an ideological contest between progressives and conservatives; nor is justice a matter of social protest and demand making—at least, not yet. For Partridge, justice begins in the ellipses of space and time where the world's casualties get passed over. True disciples must descend into these ellipses.

My reading of the sermon draws out two central metaphors, *the Circle of Oppression* and *the well*, both of which are spatial. By examining these metaphors, I seek to reveal that Partridge's civil-religious theology is shaped according to the kind of kairos I have outlined throughout the book. He recognizes the basic need and function of immanent spaces wherein people encounter and are revealed to one another. I am reminded of King's own play with notions of space when, in his Sunday sermon, he pointed his audience to the hidden spaces where people languish, the ghettoes where the poor are isolated, the gaps and holes where vermin hide. Bush Jr. made a similar move in his National Day of Prayer and Mourning address when he pointed his audience to the oft-overlooked spaces, such as desks and stairwells, that were transformed into sites of divine justice. Like King and Bush, Partridge calls his listeners to uncover and enter into these spaces, to transform them and be transformed by them. This act of encounter, I argue, is the first step in Partridge's civil-theological project. Following my reading of the metaphors, I turn to a discussion of Partridge's notion of revelation, or uncovering, as *apocalypse*, which I regard as the second step.

The Circle of Oppression

Partridge begins the sermon with a temporal-spatial orientation. He tells his listeners of an event at an Episcopal retreat "about thirteen years ago" where he experienced a profound moment of change.[19] Right at the outset of the sermon, then, Partridge suspends his audience. They are directed to a place in historical time—literally, a "retreat" from the quotidian world. Partridge then explains one of the exercises he completed as part of the retreat. Called "Circle of Oppression," the exercise asked participants to stand in the form of a circle. As the facilitator identified marginalized groups to which participants might belong, those participants who qualified were invited to step into, then back out of, the circle. "As I contemplated the categories that might move me into the circle," Partridge recalls, "I began to panic. At this point I was known as an openly gay partnered woman, and I was just beginning to come to terms with being trans. I was still discerning how I might be called to embody that identity. . . . And so I stood there thinking if I hear 'step into the circle if you're trans,' I'll pass out." By describing his experience of the circle, Partridge begins to build a textbook kairos. He describes a suspended, though temporary, space and time wherein people are revealed and encountered and from which new possibilities emerge. The whole act is one of showing. The participants in the Circle of Oppression are not expected to say anything or to dialogue with each other. No arguments, appeals, or proclamations are made. The simple movement is more or less an uncovering, but it is pregnant with implication. Unsure if he is ready to broadcast himself, Partridge frets.

The retreat leader continued: " '[I]f you are gay, lesbian, bisexual or transgender, step into the circle.' " Partridge breathed a sigh of relief, knowing that these four identities grouped into a single category would allow him to be "both seen and not seen." Then, the leader declared, "If you're a woman, step into the circle." At that moment, Partridge froze "for what felt like an eternity." The kairos had struck. Faced with a defining moment, he felt time stop. For Partridge, the circle was so charged with possibility, he was not ready to confront it. So he "slid my foot halfway in and hoped no one would notice." Such was the simultaneous allure and terror of the kairotic circle. It had the power to change everything in an instant. What he had planned to pursue in a methodical, linear fashion over the course of months or years had taken on a sudden immanence. The Circle of Oppression had behaved as a kind of personal apocalypse. Partridge's effort to mitigate the risk by sliding a foot part of the way into the circle did not exactly solve matters. But during a break shortly afterward, an anonymous woman made her way over to Partridge and offered words of recognition: " 'I saw what you did in the circle, and I don't know how you identify, but my partner identifies as trans.' " For Partridge, the moment was more than a civil encounter with an ally. It carried the weight of something religious.

Partridge does not allow the audience to hear yet how the situation was resolved. He leaves his listener there, poised on a narrative cliff, whereupon he introduces a scripture from the gospel of Matthew: "Nothing is covered up that will not be uncovered, and nothing secret that will not become known. What I say to you in the dark, tell in the light; and what you hear whispered, proclaim from the housetops."[20] Although Partridge does not draw attention to the circle as a metaphor or even a type of sacred space, the image calls for unpacking. For Partridge, and perhaps for anyone, the circle seems a space not of shelter but of exposure; a space not of comfort but of stupefying fear. There is a popular notion of sacred spaces as protected spaces, and they are, but protected does not mean *protective*. Revelations disrupt things. Such spaces can portend painful exposures.

One may note several examples from the scriptures. Moses's experience at Sinai portrays a sanctified space, the mountain, as anything but comforting and peaceful. It is a place of vulnerability, of fire and smoke, quaking and trembling.[21] Zacharias is troubled and struck with fear when he encounters an angel in the temple.[22] Jesus's experience at Golgotha is filled with storms, violence, mob ridicule, and even death, but it portends his resurrection. In other words, Partridge's experience of the circle resembles scriptural archetypes of revelatory experience. A sacred space may be unexpected, filled with the anxiety of transition from the profane to the sacred. Here is where Partridge's sermon begins to take noticeable shape as a meditation on revelation.

The Well

For inspiration in taking on the task, Partridge says, disciples could look to the Old Testament story of Hagar, "an Egyptian slave woman, forced into surrogacy for Sarah and Abraham. In our portion of the story her son Ishmael is pushed aside for Sarah's son Isaac. Ishmael and Hagar are banished to the wilderness with bread and a skin of water that soon run out, leaving them close to death. In the midst of her despair, God shows Hagar a well and they survive." Partridge's exposition of the story of Hagar is constrained by time. I offer a reading here that I believe is consistent with the spirit of his own. The image of the well is a useful parallel to the Circle of Oppression Partridge used to open the discourse. As a slave, Hagar had spent her life hidden from the world, even though she was "gifted by the complexities of vision." Only after she was cast from that world into the wilderness did she hear the voice of God. Hagar was actually exiled twice. In the first instance, she was pregnant with Ishmael and fled the house of Abram because of contention with Abram's wife Sarai, but as she reached a well, an angel interrupted her escape and directed her back to the house, but not before prophesying that she would have many descendants through her unborn son and that this son would be "a wild man; his hand will be against every man, and every man's hand against him."[23]

In the second instance, Hagar is banished with Ishmael, who is by this time "a lad." They are on the verge of dying in the wilderness of Beersheba when Hagar appears to give up. Seeing that Ishmael is about to die, she places him under a bush, while she, unable to watch her son perish, removes herself "about a bowshot" away. Resigned, she and Ishmael lift up their voices in weeping. God hears their cries and responds: "What ails thee, Hagar? Fear not. . . . Arise, lift up the lad, and hold him in thine hand; for I will make of him a great nation. And God opened her eyes, and she saw a well of water."[24] I suspect it is no coincidence that God finds Hagar at the edge of a fountain, a symbol of fertility. For in that moment God repeats his promise of a great posterity, in the second case a whole nation. With this knowledge, Hagar pulls her dying son, Ishmael, from beneath the bush where she had hidden him. She holds him aloft so he can receive the promised blessing from God.

A few implications are of special note thus far. First, God's promise of help comes only after Hagar has been purged from obscurity and forced into the open, twice. This open space renders her exposed, vulnerable, even at risk of perishing, but it is a condition of her deliverance. Second, while her exposure is necessary, it is not in itself sufficient to merit the promised blessing. In each case, help is offered at the lip of a well, a kairotic opening filled with the germ of new life. On her son Ishmael is bestowed the blessing only after he is thrown from the custody of Abraham's household and, later, only after he is pulled from the shadows and raised up to where God can, in effect, see him and reach him. In the first instance, Hagar refers to the angel as "Thou God [who] seest me," and she names the place of the well Beer-lahai-roi, which means "the well of him who liveth and seeth me."[25] Third, although Ishmael and his mother are already slaves and already refugees, the prophecy ensures that Ishmael will remain an outcast, beset with the hostility of "every man," even amid his own greatness. Ishmael becomes a symbol of apartness: forgotten while hidden, persecuted while in view.

Ultimately, Partridge's aim is to glorify "the God of seeing." As he nears his conclusion, he makes the parallels more explicit: "So often, the worlds we live in have either failed to see us, have stared at us, or have sought to erase us. In the midst of this wilderness, we have needed to seek out and see each other . . . engaging this work of sight. One to one, people have reached out to one another to say I see you, I care about you, I join with you in creating spaces for you to be and become who you are." Partridge's references to sight and seeing culminate in a mandate to "create spaces" of new life. These spaces, like wells of water, become openings outside the death blows of time. In the wilderness of "interlocking oppressions," those who suffer wander alone and invisible, but in the place of seeing, they become "revelations to one another." Such, in Partridge's view, was the call of the original disciples, not only to nurse but above all to see and be seen.

Partridge concludes by coming full circle (if I may be so intentional with a pun). He returns to the Circle of Oppression and the stranger-friend who introduced herself. "That is the kind of revelation my friend and colleague offered to me thirteen years ago. What she did in a spacious and unassuming way was to see me, to walk across that circle of difference and to share what she saw." For Partridge, this gesture of creating a space of contact is the great act of discipleship. Note the relationship Partridge constructs between the space of contact and the experience of revelation. The stranger-friend, playing the role of Christian disciple, behaves "spaciously" by seeing Partridge and his hidden struggle. By virtue of their shared presence within the circle, she is able to discern him, and her recognition prompts a new vision for Partridge of himself. In other words, shared occupation of a kairotic space enables the revelation of the other.

John Durham Peters writes: "Touch and time, the two nonreproducible things we can share, are our only guarantees of sincerity . . . presence becomes the closest thing there is to a guarantee of a bridge across the chasm."[26] What Partridge constructs through the sermon is a theory of revelation that relies on the collapse of space and time into powerful new possibilities—a cosmic sense of opportunity that becomes viable only when and where people can truly see each other. That is where the empathy is found, in the mutual, simultaneous acceptance and contemplation of the other. To anchor such recognition, spaces of seeing must be prepared and preserved. Like wells of living water, these spaces are where we escape the wilderness of a profane world and achieve the longed-for encounter with God in the form of each other.

The Salvation of Matthew Shepard

In October 2018, Washington National Cathedral embodied Partridge's message of revelation when it became the final resting place of Matthew Shepard, the twenty-one-year-old gay man who was beaten to death in Laramie, Wyoming, almost exactly twenty years earlier. Two men who were the same age as Shepard lured him away from a bar, robbed him, beat him savagely with a gun, tied him to a fence outside town, set him on fire, and left him to die. Though likely unconscious, he remained alive throughout the freezing night. The location of the crime is a mile or so outside Laramie, and it is every bit as austere as the wilderness of Beersheba. It is a dry, treeless prairie of rock, sagebrush, and tufts of yellow grass. Hovering at a breathtaking seven thousand feet, it looks and feels like the roof of the world. The attack happened on a typical fall night, with the air thin and quiet, the sky starry and black, the temperature around thirty degrees. Eighteen hours after it happened, Shepard was discovered by a bicyclist who initially mistook him for a scarecrow.[27] He was taken to a hospital where he remained on life support for almost six days, before his body finally succumbed to the trauma.

The tragedy became a global scandal. Candlelight vigils flared up across the nation and elsewhere, politicians and celebrities spoke out indignantly, and hate crimes reform got the momentum it needed. To this day, productions and organizations such as the Laramie Project and the Matthew Shepard Foundation draw on Shepard's legacy to perform local, regional, and national outreach on behalf of the LGBTQ+ community, particularly the youth who identify as part of that community. In the years since his death, Shepard has become not only a symbol of the long road the LGBTQ+ community still faces but also a sort of religious icon. His death has the biblical quality of a martyr-dom or crucifixion, and his memory has the ring of ascension. At the funeral, which was held in St. Mark's Episcopal Church in Casper, Wyoming, where Shepard had been baptized as a boy, Shepard's godfather spoke: "There is an image seared upon my mind when I reflect upon Matt on that wooden cross-rail fence. However, I have found a different image to replace that with and this is the image of another man, almost 2,000 years ago."[28] Since then, the fence where Shepard was tied and tortured has become a place of pilgrimage, and the motif of Shepard as a Christ figure, or at the very least a martyr to the cause of social justice, has taken strong hold in the LGBTQ+ movement.

A painting by Carl Grauer titled "The Ascension of Matthew Shepard" depicts Shepard floating amidst night stars over the infamous fence; his skin is blood red; tears of gold stream down his face; but his hands are free from their lashes; his wounds are healed; his body is in repose but very much alive; and a host of obeisant angels bear him up while slackening the ropes strung around his waist. Grauer depicts each angel with the face of St. Sebastian, "the patron saint of those who conceal their identities to avoid persecution."[29] The tableau is striking for the way it removes Shepard from concealment. He is framed at the center of an oval created by the edges of the angels' wingtips. His head with its open, weeping eyes is thrown into relief by a golden halo. But for the ropes, his body is naked. The angels look intently upon him as he looks directly upon us.

This image of Shepard rising over the wilderness also recalls, perhaps not intentionally, the image of Ishmael born aloft by his mother in view of God and angels, so that the boy, barely a teenager, might receive the blessing of multitudes and nations. Shepard's mother recalls conversations she had with her son about the challenges he had faced throughout his life, includ-ing being ostracized and bullied because of his small stature; even as an adult, he was often mistaken for a young teenager. "Do you think I'll be famous?" she recalls him asking on more than one occasion. "Absolutely," she would respond. "God would not put you through all this and not let you be famous."[30]

Doc O'Connor, a friend of Shepard's, commented after the funeral, "Matthew Shepard—that's a pretty spiritual name. Who do you know who is as big today—who reached out and touched as many people as Matthew Shepard of Laramie, Wyoming, population 27K?"[31] The Matthew Shepard story has become part of the canon of the social justice movement. His sojourn in the wilderness, his abuse at the hands of persecutors, and his ascension into public view evoke the journey of the movement as a whole. His death has been called "the murder that changed America."[32]

For twenty years, however, between Shepard's death and his interment in the cathedral, even as his memory inspired change and his ethos became that of a saint, elements of the attack became challenged or shrouded in mystery. Especially in recent years, questions regarding the motivations of Shepard's murderers have plagued LGBTQ+ advocates. Reports emerged that his attackers were not homophobic strangers who robbed, tortured, and murdered their victim out of hate, but fellow drug dealers and meth users who were motivated by greed and addiction. Shepard was troubled and mentally ill; he was involved in drug using and dealing and even prostitution; and, the reports contend, the attackers were ensconced in the same crowd. Stephen Jimenez spent thirteen years investigating the "hidden truths" of the Shepard tragedy and found that the narrative of a noble gay martyr was much more complicated than people presumed.[33] Jimenez went so far as to argue that Shepard was involved not only in drug use, drug dealing, and prostitution but also sexually with one of his attackers, suggesting that the crime had less to do with anti-gay hate than with personal and business vendettas.

Jimenez's book stirred up a backlash among queer rights activists who wanted to maintain the purity of Shepard's iconic status.[34] Mainstream and activist voices have begun to acknowledge the persuasiveness of Jimenez's work. JoAnn Wypijewski, a senior editor at *The Nation* at the time of the murder, had been suggesting almost from the beginning that there was more going on than "a very simple story . . . with angels and demons."[35] John Stoltenberg, a gay rights activist, agreed with Jimenez, who is also gay, and argued that the true story of Shepard's demise was not one of redneck homophobia but one of young men "who are sold for sex, ravaged by drugs, and generally exploited," men who "remain invisible and lost."[36] The tragedy of Shepard is that he suffered in the darkness and wilderness, that in the midst of so much tribulation he remained unseen, not for a single night on the prairie but for much of his life.

There is no doubt that Shepard's queerness was endemic to his suffering, but Partridge's broader theology of seership applies beautifully to both versions of the Shepard story. It may also apply even more powerfully to the messier version. Hagar was not perfect, nor I suspect was Ishmael. Even if they had been perfect, it would not have been their perfection that made their story immanent. It was their obscurity, struggle, and exploitation, and it was the transformation that was wrought when they cried out to God. Partridge defines the term "revelation" according to a Greek word, *apokalypsis*, which means "an uncovering or unveiling of that which is hidden." In popular consciousness, revelation comes from the heavens, as if the clouds part and God and angels show themselves. Partridge's view of revelation points in the opposite direction. One must pull revelation from the recesses, the elliptical places where suffering so often sets up camp. The narrative of Shepard as a martyr unspotted by the world misses the whole point. His infirmities were all along the truths that needed to be recognized. They, even more than the scars inflicted by his attackers, called for the care and attention of his community.

Gene Robinson's Prophetic Embrace

The resurgence of attention to Shepard's death and the questioning of the narrative that had dominated the story for so long probably played a role in unsettling Shepard's parents. Judy and Dennis Shepard had grown anxious about his legacy. They had kept his ashes at home, partly out of fear that a memorial in public view would be vandalized and their son's memory desecrated. They reached out to Gene Robinson, the former bishop of Washington and a fellow Episcopalian. Together, they arranged to have Shepard's ashes interred in Washington National Cathedral, where he would be permanently and safely home. "It is so important that we now have a home for Matt," Dennis Shepard remarked. "A home that others can visit, a home that is safe from haters."[37] On October 26, 2018, Shepard's ashes were interred in the cathedral's crypt, where lie the remains of roughly two hundred other Americans, including many luminaries. The service was, like Grauer's painting, a tableau of Shepard's salvation.

Robinson opens the sermon by invoking the prophetic mantle: "Lord, take my lips and speak through them. Take our minds and think with them. Take our hearts and set them on fire with love for you." This was a sermon, after all. There would be no deliberation or argument, only sacred truth. Then, he announces to the one thousand congregants: "A week from now we will be celebrating All Saints Day. And in many parts of Latin America, on All Saints

Fig. 8.1. Rev. Gene Robinson delivers remarks at the interment of Matthew Shepard, October 26, 2018. Reuters / Alamy Stock Photo

Day there is a custom where people in the congregation are invited to say the names of those who have departed this life but somehow are still present. If you close your eyes and open your hearts, Matt is right here. What the congregation says when the name is called out is *presente*—present, here. And so I invite you. 'Matthew Shepard: *presente*.'" Many worshipers then deliver the command in unison with Robinson. As if by spell, the congregation appears to feel the advent of Shepard's presence in the cathedral. Such is the power of kairos. It collapses all moments into an eternal present. Christopher Rowe's insight, quoted in chapter 5, seems to apply here: "When a pilgrim in a Gothic cathedral gazes upon an image of Moses delivering the tablets of the Law they are not merely evoking the event through 'memory' . . . but are, in kairos, actually participating in the event itself."[38] Such is the power of sacred space and sacred rhetoric. The charge of Shepard's life is sustained.

For most of the sermon, Robinson tells stories of Shepard's life and ties them to principles of the gospel. About two-thirds through the sermon, Robinson's voice shifts from that of a teller of truths to that of an exhorter. "If you are here just to pay your respects and to remember Matthew, it's not enough," he says thrusting his hand into the air. "If you're not here to be transformed, you've come for the wrong reason." His voice has taken on a hint of umbrage. After a pause, he transitions into didactic voice. He refers to the Greek word *anamnesis*, which literalized means against forgetting or, more directly, re-membering, "but in a very special way. It is the word we use to talk about the Communion service in the Christian faith, and it's what happens when you go to a Sadr meal in a Jewish home. It's to recall a past event so dramatically that you bring it into the present moment, and it becomes *your* event. Not just stuck in the past. That's the kind of remembering I pray for today. Transfor-mative remembering." Like Partridge, Robinson calls for more than recogni-tion; he calls for transformation. It is not sufficient to "pay respects." One must share the space and time of the other. Otherwise, one is merely spectat-ing the other as forces "erase them from America. . . . They need us to stand with them. That's the kind of transformation today makes possible." Sharing space with the other, he concludes, is how we remember. He adds: "[T]hen vote and go to work."

In his sermon, Partridge speaks of transformation in which the worshiper does the work not only of seeing but also of uncovering and proclaiming: "When Jesus tells his disciples to speak in the light, to uncover the hidden, to proclaim from the heights, . . . [h]e is calling them to see, uncover, and pro-claim God's work in the world, knowing that in doing so they will participate in the transformation of that world." Likewise, Robinson views the work of seeing as the first step in something bigger. For him, bringing Matthew Shep-ard into the kairotic light of the cathedral must be followed by transformative, embodied action. "To view communication as the marriage of true minds," Peters observes, "underestimates the holiness of the body. Being there still matters. . . . The paradox of love is that a neighbor in need exerts a stronger claim on your help than all the hungry orphans in the world."[39] In other words, what we see matters more than what we do not see, even if what we do not see may be demonstrably more urgent. Shepard had been lost to the world first by way of bigotry, addiction, abuse. Then, after his death, his mem-ory was lost to the world by controversy. The cathedral offered him a place to be recognized in perpetuity.

Still in Search of a Great Church

Both Partridge and Robinson construct a theology that relies on the sharing of space and time before the true work of justice can be accomplished. Like Peters, they suggest that spiritual transformation requires proximity. An appeal for help for children in Africa might be answered remotely, but it will only satisfy temporal needs; it will not leaven the soul. In Partridge's terms, it is not *discipleship*. Likewise, an illness may be removed by a surgeon, but the act does not constitute neighborliness. Humans can see each other standing in line at the grocery store or walking down a school hallway, but this is not the nature of the proximity for which Peters, Partridge, and Robinson call. Proximity matters, but it must be infused with a sense of calling. Without a space that enforces both bodily proximity and sacred calling, such discipleship becomes impossible. There must be a *theology* of shared space.

I argue throughout this book that the notion of "a great church for national purposes" was meant to be such a space. Following Partridge's sermon, Gene Robinson referenced Washington National Cathedral explicitly: "The cathedral's voice is being heard in a new and powerful way. . . . [It] has come out to the world in new and bold ways."[40] For Robinson, as for Partridge, the cathedral has become the place of seeing, where, like Hagar and Matthew, those who were oppressed, isolated, and despairing are hailed into the open to receive long-promised blessings. Like the well in the wilderness, the cathedral becomes not only a refuge of healing water but also a platform upon which the obscure is made visible to God.

And yet, while Washington National Cathedral can open its doors to everyone, it can never be what L'Enfant imagined. Neither Partridge nor Robinson is shy about quoting Christian scripture, and why should they be? They are Christian clerics, speaking in their capacity as priests from the floor of a Christian cathedral. It would be odd if they were not to preach in the way they are called by their faith to preach. I hope my discussion of Partridge has made clear his mastery of the Christian scriptures. Robinson, perhaps because his sermon is directed to a more public and more diverse audience, is more circumspect in his references to Jesus and scripture, but he is clear enough. He tells in detail the story of the prodigal son. He speaks of Jesus's miraculous love. He is careful to complete his appeals with references to "God" rather than to "Christ," and he takes pains to embrace non-Christians, but he also invokes his role as a bishop in the Episcopal Church. His own Christian faith is, after all, the very thing that drives his embrace of everyone. His sermon is a master class on inclusion, but it is unapologetically and justifiably still a Christian sermon.

There is a moment early in Shepard's interment service when Robinson—unwittingly, I believe—reveals the whole problem and wonder of Washington National Cathedral: "This cathedral is actually serious about being a place of prayer for all people. So, if you are a person of faith, but not Christian, please know that you are our special guest—be you Jew or Muslim, Hindu or Sikh or Buddhist, or whatever, you are welcome here. And even if you're not a person of faith, if you identify with no religious community, please know how welcome you are."

Our special guest. Robinson acknowledges that these other groups are, in some sense, transients. It is the cathedral's mission to welcome them, but this place is not their home. When I watched Robinson make this statement, it was a moment of clarity. I did not feel critical. There was no *gotcha* factor. In fact, to me there was something noble in the statement. At its best, Washington National Cathedral owns its identity as a place of Christian worship, while volunteering, in the name of its Christian mission, to do what the nation has not done. It is a private church that recognizes a gap in the civil-religious bedrock of the country and has decided to open its doors to everyone, to welcome the nation's spiritual refugees and castaways. The Jew, the Muslim, and the atheist are welcome here, but, to be clear, they are only passing through. Never could they find their civic birthright under the crucifix, under the gaze of Peter and Paul, within the nave of a medieval, Gothic cathedral.

Nevertheless, the sermons of Partridge and Robinson, and the theory of communication outlined by Peters, provide useful ways to think about what a true civil-religious space might mean for Americans. If the United States of America is to build a civil religion that meets the spiritual needs of its citizens qua citizens, it will have to embrace a theology of shared space and time. It will have to recognize the kairotic immanence of the other. It will have to build a platform from which each person, community, and tradition can be seen and recognized in counterpoise with each other, a place where all identities can contemplate and be contemplated in their solitude. Americans do not, as Peters's notion of "broadcast" makes clear, have to be subsumed by one another; they do not even have to know the experiences of one another, so long as they recognize the sacred ground they share in common. This kairotic space creates a point of seeing and contact between peculiar souls rather than a vortex into which our differences and identities disappear.

Conclusion

[S]o, out of the series of the preceding social and political universes,
now arise these States. We see that while many were supposing things
established and complete, really the grandest things always remain; and
discover that the work of the New World is not ended, but only fairly
begun.

Walt Whitman, *Democratic Vistas* (1871)

In June 1931, Arthur Rudd, canon of Washington National Cathedral, wrote to James Freeman, bishop of Washington: "I once heard you say that you would like a memorial to Robert E. Lee in the Cathedral." He then indicated that the Texas chapter of the United Daughters of the Confederacy (UDC) would like to raise money to place just such a memorial in the Cathedral. In October of that year, it was reported that the Cathedral's Committee on Monuments and Memorials had resolved to accept an offer from the UDC. Bishop Freeman remarked, "I feel about any memorial to General Lee, that it should be as beautiful in character as was his notable life." In the coming years, as a memorial to Lee was debated, the only question of any concern was whether there was a location in the Cathedral of sufficient prominence for a figure of Lee's character and significance. It should be noted that Lee was, by any measure, a talented leader. Not only was he arguably the most effective military leader of the Civil War, but his views on the morality of slavery were on par with many of his Northern counterparts. He found slavery to be a moral evil, even though he owned enslaved people himself and believed fatalistically that "the painful discipline they are undergoing, is necessary for their instruction as a race."[1] And while he helped liberate slaves in Liberia and upon his death freed his own slaves, he also saw no way of eliminating slavery by government mandate. His ambiguous views with respect to Black slavery and the effectiveness of his leadership made Lee someone the North could respect, despite his enemy status. The North's respect combined with the South's veneration made Lee a fitting choice for memorialization in the Cathedral.

When the UDC got word that the Cathedral was in favor of a monument to Lee, they reacted with two emotions. First, they were elated with the opportunity to immortalize the memory of Lee in a place of such sacredness and prominence in the nation's capital. Second, they were suspicious. When they received word that Cathedral officials had found the perfect spot for the memorial, they began to wonder about how the Cathedral would interpret the memorial. For instance, the Cathedral offered half of a prominent bay in the nave, which would include stained-glass windows depicting the general. Who, the UDC openly wondered, would occupy the other half? During the 1948 UDC convention, some members protested the memorial idea, presuming that the Cathedral would wish to place Lee next to some northerner. A Mrs. Coleman theorized, "It would be most probably that people who are more emotional than intelligent would suggest that because we are a reunited country, Lincoln or Grant should be memorialized side by side with Lee." Coleman's concern was apparently shared by others despite the Cathedral officials' many assurances that they were enthusiastic about honoring Lee in his own right.[2] The same convention voted down the proposal to fund the memorial.

A year later, Cathedral officials were able to pass the sincerity test. After more assurances that Lee would be memorialized on the UDC's terms, the United Daughters of the Confederacy voted in favor of funding. Sometime after 1951, the Cathedral backed up its claims when it agreed that Stonewall Jackson, one of Lee's celebrated lieutenants, would be memorialized in the bay's adjoining half. The UDC was flush with satisfaction:

> Now that we have accepted the unusual, the magnificent opportunity extended to us to honor [Lee's] spiritual pilgrimage on earth in the very same city which—in the 1860s—scourged our Southland and belabored our heroes, we have the privilege of memorializing him in the blessed sanctuary and, in so doing, we memorialize our entire South and its titanic struggle of the past. . . . The South needs no stronger proof of the justice of Her cause, than the fact that Robert E. Lee led Her forces and went down in physical defeat, only to rise the hero of an immortal moral victory and become the uncrowned king of free men.[3]

A generous reading of the UDC's sentiments might conclude that the idea of a window honoring General Lee and Stonewall Jackson is consistent with the Cathedral's mission to unite the country, especially to heal long-standing fractures such as those left by the Civil War; and, further, that to do so meant seeing the other, in this case, the South, from the perspective *of* the South. The language of the UDC as quoted above, however, suggests the South did not see the matter in the same spirit of empathy. To them, the Northern capital had been the scourge of the Southland and the abuser of its heroes. Lee's memory was proof not of the nation's unity but of the South's moral superiority. Indeed, it is Lee, not any Northern tyrant, who is the true "king of free men." For the UDC, unity with the North was to come by way of the South's magnanimity in sharing Lee with the Cathedral, which southerners agreed was a sacred national shrine. "America's immortal Lee . . . will bring an added glory to those enshrined in that sacred Val Halla, not one of whom is greater than he."[4]

The Cathedral leaders remained sanguine about the partnership. The March 1952 press release announcing the memorials to Lee and Jackson read in part:

> Memorials to Robert E. Lee and Stonewall Jackson will be constructed in Washington Cathedral, in a move that could help obliterate the Mason-Dixon line. Members of the [UDC], with the help of an anonymous "dam yankee," have raised money for small chapels honoring the two Confederate Generals in the Cathedral. . . . [The UDC selected the Cathedral as a] natural site as a "House of Prayer for All People." The memorials will honor the two Civil War generals not as soldiers, but as Christian gentlemen. Biographies of both men allow that they placed faith in God always in the foreground of their military lives.

The language is careful. The Cathedral wished to honor not the generals' fighting careers but their faith, and it wished to do so in the spirit of blurring the lines between North and South. The bay and windows were dedicated on November 10, 1953, with Dean Sayre, of all people, officiating. I do a brief reading of the windows in chapter 5. Lee and Jackson's accoutrements of war are interpreted as the armor of God. Their body language is as much that of pious priests and scholars as that of military generals. Each soldier is given four panels. In the top right panel in each case, the subject is depicted as what I can only describe as a resurrected Christ figure, with arms outstretched in triumphal glory.

The windows were doomed, as we now know and perhaps should have known all along. Installed just a few years before the civil rights movement took off, their presence in the Cathedral portended controversy. Kelly Brown Douglas, the Cathedral's canon theologian in 2016, speculated that the windows got into the Cathedral just in time. A year later and they might not have passed the test of social acceptability. Over the years, the leadership of the Cathedral has struggled to reconcile this bay and these windows with the Cathedral's larger mission. They have interpreted the windows in evolving ways, first as honorifics, then as invitations to national conversation and reflection, and finally as problems that must be dealt with. In 2015, following the Charleston, South Carolina, church massacre, which left nine people dead, the Cathedral's dean, Gary Hall, called for the windows to be removed. His call triggered a two-year process of public deliberation on the part of Cathedral officials regarding the fate of the windows. In 2016, the Confederate flag images on the windows were removed. Finally, on September 6, 2017, Cathedral officials announced that the windows would be removed entirely.[5]

Over the following two years, the Cathedral made public its reflection on the question of removal. In one discussion, Dr. Douglas articulated the tension the Cathedral faced between its sectarian commitments and its civil-religious identity.

> We have to ask the question, who are we? Are we more driven by the nation's civil religion and its sense of itself, or are we more compelled by who we are as a church, and the theology of a church whose God liberated the slaves . . . whose God was made manifest in Jesus and set the captives free. . . . What does it mean for us to be Washington National Cathedral? Does it mean that we . . . are a social institution that happens to be religious, and so we serve as the civil religion of the nation? Or are we indeed a church, called to show forth a glimpse of God in the world?[6]

Douglas goes on to argue that the windows represent not only civil religion as a principle but also the South's civil religion in particular. She points out that the windows portray Lee and Jackson not simply as heroes of the Confederacy but as saints. Her thoughts point to several tensions worth noting. First, she acknowledges the confusion about the Cathedral's mission. What are this institution's commitments, and in which order? Is it the civil-religious sanctuary it has always claimed to be, or is it something more sectarian? For Douglas, the presence of the windows is evidence of the Cathedral's civil-religious commitments; ergo, to remove them would be to demonstrate that this institution is not ultimately the civil-religious temple we presume it to be—an argument I make throughout this book.

Her comments also reveal, however, the tensions within the notion of an American Civil Religion itself, which is that there is not *an* American Civil Religion but competing American civil religions. The UDC's interpretation of the windows was never based on the same underlying principles that Cathedral officials used in interpreting the windows. The Cathedral viewed the windows as an act of reconciliation with a subdued foe. For the UDC, there was nothing subdued about the installation. The windows were a reassertion of the justice of the Southern cause, a moral stand against the Northern mono-lith, and a declaration that their leader, though uncrowned, remained the true "king of free men." The whole affair belies yet again the claim that the United States has a strong civil-religious identity. We are a people of diverging civil-religious souls trying to inhabit the same civic body. On September 7, 2017, the Lee and Jackson windows were officially deconsecrated by Bishop Mariann Budde and removed. They now reside out of public view in the Cathedral's storage bowels.

A similar, if more spectacular, drama played out on January 6, 2021, when a mob of Confederate flag–waving insurrectionists, feeling like the true he-roes of the country, stormed the Capitol of the United States to claim it for their own. As the UDC viewed the Cathedral, so these insurrectionists viewed the sacredness of the building they entered. They did not want to destroy it, or to share it. They wanted to claim it for the true "free men" of the republic, and for their wrongfully vanquished hero, Donald Trump. And, like the Lee and Jackson windows, the insurrectionists were ultimately purged from the building, but the ghost of their resentment still haunts its halls. The symbols displayed during the storming of the Capitol were explicitly reli-gious. Banners declaring "Jesus Saves" and flags bearing the Stars and Bars, not to mention anti-Semitic symbols, a hangman's noose, and other violent nationalist images, flooded the site L'Enfant designated two and half centu-ries ago for Congress to perform its sacred obligations. The religious violence of the moment is only now being processed. Among other projects, "Uncivil Religion: A Collaborative Effort to Understand January 6, 2021," has begun to examine how that day opened the nation's chronic civil-religious wounds.[7]

It may be that Americans will never find the sacred common ground re-quired for a unified civil religion. Like all religions, the American Civil Reli-gion must do the dirty work of boundary maintenance. It must draw lines of order, and it will always be the object of contempt, sometimes violent con-tempt, from the fundamentalists or the apostates of its creeds. Perhaps the Cathedral should never have embraced the Lee and Jackson windows. Cer-tainly, President Trump should never have incited a deadly insurrection at the Capitol. These incursions highlight the fraught nature of our national soul, but they also reveal a will to realize a whole and coherent civil religion. That the windows were removed and the insurrectionists were expelled (and are now facing court trials and jail time) should remind US Americans that a civil religion of real weight may be within reach, a birthright still waiting to be claimed.

In a way, the civil religious breakdown of January 6 is evidence of a civil-religious yearning. As Shadi Hamid has argued in *The Atlantic*, the decline in the sectarian religious commitments of Americans is correlated with the increase in political zeal and violence. "What was once *religious* belief has now been channeled into *political* belief," he writes. "Political debates over what America is supposed to mean have taken on the character of theological disputations. This is what religion without religion looks like."[8] Contrary to the Christian nationalists of our day, I do not believe Americans need to find God, but I do think we ought to find religion, and I echo Oge Maduike's call for a "Third Founding Moment," though I would suggest we are still awaiting the first founding of our civil religion.[9] But how does one "found" a civil religion? I do not know exactly, but I am convinced L'Enfant was on to something when he thought of his church.

There is so much evidence that Americans want a civil religion and so little evidence that they actually have one of any coherence. Kairos, in its simplest meaning, means the opportunity, or right time, to learn or perform something wholly new. As difficult as it may be to imagine a *new* civil religion, and as imperfectly as I have tried to give shape to such a project, now seems the opportune moment. Americans are filled to overflowing with passion over the soul of their country, but many of us are more likely to quote a pundit than a founder or philosopher or one of our founding texts. This fact is alarming, because Americans need a civil religion more than do citizens of other countries. In the same piece in *The Atlantic*, Hamid points out that Americans seem to have a need to discuss the meaning of America, or Americanness. These discussions have "a fervor that would be unimaginable in debates over, say, Belgian-ness or the 'meaning' of Sweden." To call someone "un-American" is to charge apostasy.[10] The lack of a robust articulation of civil religion that might protect our republic from collapse, combined with our willingness to discuss how such a lack might be filled, suggests a unique opportunity. Once and for all we ought to build a resilient National Faith.

Lessons from the Past

In the months and years following Pierre L'Enfant's dismissal as planner of the federal city and George Washington's death at Mount Vernon, Thomas Jefferson and his cohort faced little opposition in their push to keep the federal government as decentralized and desacralized as possible. "Within a few years of Jefferson's election in 1800," Nathan O. Hatch observes, "it became anachronistic to speak of dissent in America—as if there were still a commonly recognized center against which new or emerging groups defined themselves." Having vanquished the civil religion L'Enfant and Washington had envisioned, Jefferson sat by to let liberty do its work. Hatch continues: "There was little to restrain a variety of new groups from vying to establish their identity as a counterestablishment. . . . Churches and religious movements after 1800 operated in a climate of withering ecclesiastical establishments. The federal government, a 'midget institution in a giant land,' had almost no internal functions."[11] In other words, without a strong center of political or religious gravity, competition between outsider religious groups to define the spiritual identity of the nation became fierce. There was no controlling narrative to ground the nation's moral life in some sort of shared identity.

There were, of course, benefits to the freedoms these religious groups enjoyed. Where the institutions of power were limited, outsiders could flourish. Although Hatch points out that this development in the early nineteenth century was a great victory for freedom, he acknowledges some of the unintended consequences. Religious demagogues flourished; more radical religious groups, having supplanted the old traditions, turned their attentions to one another and, in many cases, drove people further asunder.[12] Simple disagreements turned into rivalries, then rivalries into schisms; thoughts and theories morphed into conspiracies, then conspiracies into widely accepted "facts." The National Bank became a symbol of secret tyranny. Masonry became a cult of deviancy and intrigue. Both in politics and religion, charismatic leaders invented bogeymen and cabals, harangued their followers into hysterics over imagined threats, and used issues like slavery to drive wedges deeper between the states as well as the sects.[13] All of which is to say that the great freedoms of the era cut both ways. Individual movements could innovate and flourish, but the American body politic got mangled in the process.

If each private faith or ideology becomes the guide for its acolytes' citizenly duties, what hope is there of a shared civil religion? As Ronald Beiner puts it in his study of Hobbes, a nonreligious political order cannot tolerate the "subordination of political concerns to religious imperatives. . . . [It must] preclude a usurpation of political authority on the part of authentically religious claimants."[14] As I argue in chapter 5, one of nativism's rhetorical tropes was to impugn Roman Catholicism for this very reason. It was supposed that the pope's authority would undermine the state's. Ironically, the Roman Catholics of America have shown little interest in theocratic regimes, whereas the more nativist elements of Protestantism have seemed, at times at least, quite comfortable with the idea of a Christian state. That idea's appeal is just one result of the nation's divided convictions and allegiances.

This is not what Jefferson had in mind. Jefferson and his fellow anti-Federalists understood that the vastness of the nation would create challenges for governance. But, rather than administer the nation's affairs with strong centralized institutions, which they believed would not be up to the task, they put their trust in the people to pursue varying interests in a way that would smooth off the edges of fundamentalism and bring the nation's frenzies into some sort of balance. R. Laurence Moore writes: "Thomas Jefferson did not sponsor religious freedom with the expectation . . . that religious Americans would long continue their religious squabbles or find pretexts to start new ones. . . . Jefferson believed that legal tolerance would move his countrymen toward a sensible and nondividing religious center."[15] In short, Jefferson did not undermine Washington, L'Enfant, and the Federalists for the sake of watching a free-for-all of religious enthusiasm. Quite the opposite. He believed the surest path to a cohesive and sober public was *more* freedom. "When the result proved to be different," Moore continues, "those who followed in Jefferson's ideological tracks argued that Americans simply had not matured enough to discover their common religious outlook. The possibility that American religious energy would necessarily expend itself with everlasting centrifugal force was one they tried to ignore."[16] By the time of Jefferson's election to the presidency in 1800, the nation was awash in sectarianism, revivalism, spiritualism, folk magic, and utopian experiments. The Second Great Awakening shifted the way Americans viewed themselves and the mission of the country, and it lacked the philosophic dignity Jefferson had imagined for the frontier.

Despite its messiness, this period is not to be regretted. The Second Great Awakening not only set the stage for the coming abolitionist and suffragist reforms but, perhaps at its most fundamental level, reminded Americans that regular people can do significant things, that they do not need the indulgence of faraway institutions and elite clerics. By the time of Andrew Jackson's presidency, barely two decades after Jefferson's, the United States was a populist dreamland. Anti-establishment ideals were the rule rather than the exception. Even groups that remained oppressed or marginalized at least had the rhetorical resources to argue for their place in society.[17] Again, though, that the early-nineteenth-century democratic surge had so many benefits does not mean it did not also entail serious costs—most notably, a secession crisis in the name of noble rebellion on one hand and, on the other, a grotesque zealotry for slavery in the name of republican rights.

A Civil Religious Wilderness

The stark fact of the American Civil War is enough to prove that the nation lacked spiritual cohesion, but what took place after the war only reaffirms this absence. When slavery was abolished and the Civil War finally ended, the best the federal government could do was to make a short-lived effort at reconstruction and agree to a kind of civil-religious détente in which the South was left to cultivate its own myths about what made the nation special. Populism's success at exalting the rights of the individual while failing to build a strong national identity created a landscape strewn with the raw materials of civil religion but with no way to compose those materials into a common faith. The military and the economy grew, and so, at long last, did the power of the federal government, but a national morality remained elusive. Reflecting on this situation near the end of his life, Walt Whitman lamented: "Though I think the essential elements of the moral nature exist latent in the good average people of the United States of to-day, and sometimes break out strongly, it is certain that any mark'd or dominating National Morality, (if I may use the phrase) has not only not yet been develop'd, but that—at any rate when the point of view is turn'd on business, politics, competition, practical life, and in character and manners in our New World—there seems to be a hideous depletion, almost absence, of such moral nature."[18] Whitman extends the nation's moral incoherence to the whole of the nation's social and political fabric. Without a "National Morality," all of society, from business and politics to practical life and personal character, is marked by a "hideous depletion." Today, as then, evidence for such depletion is found in the battle cries of *This is a Christian nation* and even *This is a white republic*.[19] Whitman died not long after he wrote the quoted words. One year after his death, Washington National Cathedral was chartered, almost as if it was an answer to Whitman's plea, though it is not likely the answer he wanted. Our nation's soul must be created from the shared soil of the American experiment, not grafted from some independent branch.

The absence of a national moral core is captured by Kirk Savage in his gripping *Monument Wars*, which includes an examination of the National Mall and its environs. Savage examines the history of how the Mall and its monuments were conceived, arranged, and interpreted over time. What this history reveals is the same sort of incoherence I point to elsewhere in this book. For example, when writing of the Lincoln Memorial, Savage comments that it "carried an impossible collective burden: to demonstrate that a unified national community could reemerge from a deadly Civil War and a lapsed Reconstruction." Notice the language Savage chooses: a *re*emergent unity, as though there had been a unity in some mythical past. "In actuality," Savage clarifies, "the memorial reopened the very issue that had divided the nation and confounded its identity in the first place."[20] Savage's work reveals that the nation's monumental core, though intended to create a sense of national unification, in many ways reinforced a spiritual unintelligibility.

Over the years, the Mall's empty grassy space took on different purposes. Dating all the way back to L'Enfant himself, it was meant to be a garden of calm, order, and reflection, "with a smattering of well-behaved visitors strolling on prescribed paths."[21] Over time, however, it became a tabula rasa upon which various groups imposed their own dogmas. Starting with Coxey's Army in 1894, which marched for workers' benefits, and continuing with the Bonus Army in 1932, which had a similar purpose, the Mall evolved into a space of activism. In 1939, acclaimed contralto Marian Anderson was invited by Howard University to give a concert on the Mall, which attracted a staggering 75,000 people of various races. Although the concert "had concrete political goals, on the Mall they staked out a different and more ambitious rhetorical territory, engaging in a quasi-religious campaign to return the nation to its true moral bearings."[22] To be sure, America has been a place of moral ideals, but these were never made fast like bearings. This fact was famously articulated in 1963, during the March on Washington for Jobs and Freedom, which broke all records by attracting between 200,000 and 250,000 people. It was there, overlooking the Mall, that Martin Luther King Jr. delivered his soaring "I Have a Dream" oration and reminded the nation that although promises were made, they were never kept. As a consequence, the nation's ideals have too often been tranquilizing abstractions. King was not celebrating the dream of equality so much as he was calling for the dream to end and the ideals to be made real.

The notion that the soul of the United States is what we make of it has an inspiring ring. The Mall, the capital, the nation, they belong to *me* as much as to *you. You* have as much right to shout your truth upon these grounds as *I* do. We could console ourselves by believing that these spaces stand in a kind of holy silence, awaiting the next voice to breathe life into them, but this view masks an uncertainty about the meaning of citizenship in the United States.

If *my* group and *your* group are merely passing through the void at different times shouting our convictions into the dead air, what might this suggest about the ground on which we stand? Does it not reveal that the ground is dead, since it has no voice but what my group or yours gives it? Does this fact not also suggest that our voices will never meet? Or, if they do happen to encounter each other, are they not likely to meet in opposition to each other, such as when the civil rights activists of the 1960s were met with American Nazis or Christian nationalists in a clash of moral consciences on the Mall?[23] In this light, the holy silence of the National Mall and the broader landscape of Washington, DC, seems more like a mute ambivalence. It becomes the same wilderness L'Enfant had hoped to transform into a glorious city. Savage remarks, "[N]o space of conscience was ever visible here."[24]

A Civil Religious Orphanage

With L'Enfant's dream of a sacred American capital having effectively vanished by the turn of the nineteenth century, and with the promise of Reconstruction blocked well before the end of that century, it seemed as if whatever civil religion the United States was trying to raise up had been caught in arrested development. With no spiritual home, the nation's soul went wandering across the frontier. It found great adventures, but it also committed terrible sins. In a generous sense, the Cathedral Church of Saint Peter and Saint Paul saw the orphaned child and offered sanctuary, a place to learn and reflect and pray, to be seen and recognized, and, one hoped, to mature. This interpretation seems consistent with Bishop Gene Robinson's words, quoted in chapter 8, welcoming people of all faiths and no faith to the Cathedral as "guests." Like a shelter for spiritual refugees, the Cathedral opened its doors to all people not despite its own Christian mission but because of it.

Of course, this generous view is belied by the dogmatism of the Cathedral's early years when Bishop Henry Satterlee set out to consolidate all Christendom beneath the banner of his church. It has been a long time since that view was held by the Cathedral or its leaders, but like Satterlee's leadership, that of subsequent Cathedral officials, including Sayre, Walker, Robinson, Schori, Budde, and many others, "came from a place of deep Christian faith." Their leadership was and is "a proclamation of [their] religion."[25] More to the point, they have enacted that leadership because they believe "Americans needed a sacred space to call our own."[26] These leaders presumed— rightly, in my view—that Americans had never truly built a spiritual home for themselves; that the federal city never became the sacred center it was meant to be; that, as Whitman observed, there never was a national morality to speak of; and that Americans were therefore lost in a spiritual fog. They also presumed—wrongly, in my view—that this English Gothic Episcopal Cathedral could be the fulfillment of that need.

The distinctiveness of the Cathedral's voice has always been embedded in its Christian mission. Even today, when someone as eloquent as Bishop Katharine Jefferts Schori speaks about flocks and unity from the Cathedral pulpit, she speaks dutifully as an Episcopalian: "We are sheep of one fold, and we are the keepers of our sister and brother sheep, whether white or brown or spotted, the ones with horns and the bald ones, the pregnant and the elders, the lambs and the rams."[27] It is a powerful message; but a distinctly Christian voice will never have the Olympian reach that an American Civil Religion will need if the United States wishes to build a spiritual home of its own. For more than a century now, Washington National Cathedral has done what other Christian churches have done so well over the centuries. It has served as a kind of orphanage, doing the Christian work of providing asylum. It has devoted itself to this task in behalf of all Americans. For that much, Americans should be grateful, but not satisfied. Having passed through adolescence, it is time Americans think about moving beyond their spiritual puerility and building a permanent home.

A Civil Religious Home

To this point, I have argued that the United States of America has never actually created the civil religion it needs, let alone built the church the planners once envisioned. I agree with Peter Gardella, who writes that the American Civil Religion may be "the strongest and most elaborate" civil religion in the world.[28] It must be even stronger, though, if it is to address the exigencies of a nation teeming with so many cultures and ideologies. I submit that we ought to build the church L'Enfant proposed. As I hope I make clear in this book's first chapter, the "church for national purposes" was always meant to be more than just a static monument. It was meant to be part of the spiritual infrastructure that the nation and the desolate capital city lacked. Perhaps it would not have served this purpose the way L'Enfant hoped. Perhaps it would have failed to bring added unity to Americans, and perhaps it would fail still, but as Americans split and careen into the furthest corners of the ideological map, it may be worth a try.

The reader may recall that L'Enfant's church was described as a shrine intended for such things as "public prayer and meditation, thanksgiving, funeral orations, and assigned to the special use of no particular sect or denomination, but equally open to all."[29] It was to be a place in which our national dogmas are enshrined and taught, in which our heroes and heroines are eulogized and memorialized as "decreed by the voice of a grateful nation." If, as I have argued, L'Enfant's notion of a national church was patterned after the Pantheon of Paris, it would also be an institution of learning, ritual, celebration, and remembrance, something wholly original to the project that is the United States. Washington National Cathedral has done a noble work, but perhaps it is time to reimagine and finally build the temple that was meant to reside in the federal city all along.

One could argue that the US Capitol Building fills this need. Like Washington National Cathedral, the Capitol Building merits awe for the beauty and ambition of its vision, but as a civil-religious shrine, it falls short as well. It has become a symbol of our house divided, rife with intrigue, corruption, and the mundane business of politicking. For all its civil-religious iconography, it does not serve as a permanent place of rest for our illustrious dead or a sanctuary for our mourning and thanksgiving—temporary lie-in-state ceremonies being a minor exception. Our most sacred rituals, from National Days of Prayer, to presidential swearing-in ceremonies, to memorials for our fallen heroes are carried out in various places that are devoid of any sacred meaning. Today's government buildings and the monuments and other memorials that grace the National Mall can only do so much. They can inspire, console, enrage, and shape our memory and identity, but they remain limited in their ability to serve as sites for a formal, coordinated program of civic rites, education, celebration, and mourning. I am reminded of the image of a great stone as a symbol of wholeness, the realization of the complete Self, the culmination of what Jung calls "individuation."[30]

I imagine a shrine in which presidents swear their oaths, citizens of distinction are given their medals, and our heroes are entombed and, yes, revered—apologies to Jefferson whose remains would be rolling eternally in such a place. President Washington famously requested to be buried at Mt. Vernon in his last will, but as I point out in chapter 1, he originally supported the idea of being laid to rest in L'Enfant's church or, failing that, the Capitol or a public shrine dedicated to his memory. His wife, Martha, also agreed to let her husband be interred in the Capitol. We also know that Washington's remains were very nearly moved on several occasions. In 1800, 1816, 1824, 1829, and 1830, efforts were made to move the first president's body to a location of greater public significance.[31] I applaud such efforts and regret their lack of success, largely because that lack seems to symbolize an even broader failing. Americans would rather retreat to their tribal homes than to converge in the public square.

None of this is to say that Americans are supposed to achieve some sort of shared essence. A healthy civil religion is not tantamount to nationalism, and a healthy *American* Civil Religion is not tantamount to "Americanization." In his book *The Broken Covenant*, Robert Bellah complicates his own theory of the American Civil Religion by telling the story of a festival sponsored by Henry Ford in the early 1920s. "A giant pot was built outside the gates of his factory into which danced groups of gaily dressed immigrants singing their native songs. From the other side of the pot emerged a single stream of Americans dressed alike in contemporary standard dress and singing the national anthem."[32] The celebrated "melting pot" metaphor implied a blending so consummate that everyone merged into the same essence. Bellah notes that efforts to Americanize immigrants were successful in many respects. Immigrants became socialized in the ideals and pieties of US citizenship, and they developed healthy convictions about their new home, but too often this process resulted in a spiritual displacement. Immigrants were not asked simply to honor and reverence their adopted country; they were expected to sheer away their own ethnic backgrounds. The most vocal proponents of Americanization were often representatives of the WASP establishment who felt themselves qualified to define a universal American essence.[33]

My reading of the shrine that L'Enfant had in mind, repurposed for a twenty-first-century United States, is an ideal of common ground on which each American's distinctiveness is recognized and honored. Common ground does not mean common minds or common hearts, let alone common dress and appearance. For this reason, I have chosen kairos as the guiding framework for my study. I have defined kairos as a shared space and time in which ideas and other beings become immanent, such that new opportunities for action and connection are revealed. If we, as unlike beings, share that immanent space, we can remain unlike even as we finally *see* each other in the kairotic light. Kairos does not presume to create shared minds or even a consensus of ideas. It circumvents the whole notion of same essences and transfers attention to something external. Some Americans will always believe themselves to have something inborn that makes them superior, but such people fail to realize that their Americanness is not inborn; it is a *space* and *moment* they inhabit. When they enter into it, they take upon themselves certain covenant relationships. When they violate those relationships, they not only violate the object of their disdain but also profane sacred ground.

A physical structure in which this principle is somehow concretized will not be easy to imagine, let alone to build. L'Enfant himself barely got past a few cursory notes in his proposal of it. We must infer the significance he assigned to the building by noting its place on his map, considering the size of the lot and its spatial relationship to the houses of government. All we know of its physical design is the elegant oval he drew on the grid, suggesting something monumental and classical in style. We also know that, as churches go, it would not just be a space for rote rituals and moldering bones. As I read L'Enfant's notes as well as his life, I imagine his church as a place of ritual and memorial, yes, but also a great center of civic education where students and citizens come to study, debate, and celebrate the rights, responsibilities, and implications of their citizenship, including the responsibility to atone for past sins. To this end, such a church might also host schools and libraries, symposia and debates, artists and scholars in residence, and of course great speeches and civil-religious sermons. I hope such a place would not be too proud to take its cue from Washington National Cathedral, which has striven to create exactly these sorts of opportunities. Especially in its more recent years, Washington National Cathedral has given us a blueprint for pursuing with fearless wonder just what it means to be American, and what it ought to mean. Such a church must always be a place of *seeing*, not covering up, even when seeing makes us uncomfortable.

American Incoherence

Civil religion, that system of shared beliefs, values, symbols, rituals, and hopes that Bellah spoke of a half-century ago, remains a powerful idea for Americans, even if they are not familiar with the term. The current scholarship in rhetorical studies characterizes the American Civil Religion as "the tie that binds all Americans, regardless of their demographic background."[34] I believe this statement to be true, but scholars could say more about whether the fibers of this tie are sufficiently strong. In his recent book *American Covenant: A History of Civil Religion from the Puritans to the Present*, Philip Gorski argues that the American Civil Religion needs "to be more clearly roped off" from fringe interests on the far right and far left, what he calls "American religious nationalism" and "radical secularism."[35] What I intend to add to this sentiment is an appreciation that roping off the civil religion from unsavory elements will not be a matter of making adjustments. It will require (1) an acknowledgement that we have never had a coherent civil religion to rope off, and (2) a wholesale reexamination of what kind of civil religion we should therefore build and *then* rope off.

The great hope of Reconstruction after the Civil War, like the hope of an illustrious capital after the Revolution, was left on the cutting-room floor. The ratification of the Constitution and of the Bill of Rights did not end the fractures between Federalists and Anti-Federalists. The Civil War and Reconstruction did not end the divide between North and South. The Union, including the Supreme Court in *Plessy v. Ferguson*, gave in to white supremacy in the form of "separate but equal" segregation. Jim Crow was born, and the nation succumbed to a monstrous incongruity. Southern generals were immortalized in equestrian statues; the Confederacy's battle flag was left to endure as an American emblem.[36] White supremacist paramilitary groups intimidated or otherwise disrupted democratic processes. Whether extending the olive branch of segregation to the South was a gesture of magnanimity or pragmatism is beside the point. The indulgence did not work, and it uncovered the same sort of fractures that left the capital city in limbo a hundred years earlier. What has been called "America's Second Founding" fell short for roughly the same reasons as the first.[37]

Many American Christians tend to believe that the answer to these failures lies in the gospel of Jesus Christ and that the United States can once and for all achieve its moral destiny by embracing a Judeo-Christian—and presumably Protestant—moral order. Wrongly claiming that the United States was founded as a Christian nation, these Christians often sacralize the country but not for the country's sake. For them, the nation's wealth, power, and prestige are means to realize an eschatological vision of the Second Coming of Christ.[38] But where they would have the voice of God be the voice of the people, the Founders had it the other way around. Drawing on the more radical texts of English Whigs in the early eighteenth century, the American Founders embraced the principle of *vox populi vox Dei*. The voice of the people is the voice of God. As one famous Whig pamphlet from 1710 reasoned: "There being no natural or divine Law for any Form of Government, or that one Person rather than another should have the sovereign Administration of Affairs, or have Power over many thousand different Families, who are by Nature all equal . . . ; therefore Mankind is at liberty to choose what Form of Government they like best."[39] The American revolutionaries added their own inflection to this argument in declaring that equality and liberty are, in fact, providential principles, but the political order that enforces these principles should be determined by the voice of the people, not by a canon of ancient doctrines and scriptures. Where do the people have space in which to identify, interpret, and debate these sacred principles? Certainly not in the Capitol, and not in a Christian cathedral.

In Christian nationalism, one sees again the tell-tale signs of the civil-religious vacuum that has always stifled the country. From Billy Graham to Pat Robertson to Jerry Falwell to Ralph Reed, evangelical leaders have insisted the country lacks a coherent morality, and they have presumed to fill that lack with "a Protestant-based moral order."[40] It is an old story of bifurcations: Anti-Federalist and Federalist, South and North, Christian and non-Christian, white and Black, conservative and liberal. In other words, the vacuum has always doubled as a wedge. This sort of division was the whole point of Jim Crow: to remove shared space, literally, and to create two separate American cosmos—one profane and the other special, and ne'er the twain shall meet. For this reason, there has long been precedent for faithful Christians to look upon non-Christians as less American or even as un-American.

I would not compare Billy Graham Protestants to the likes of Jim Crow southerners. My point is not to suggest that the ennobling values of today's Washington National Cathedral or the many patriotic preachers who call the country to its better angels are somehow tantamount to the supremacists and segregationists of our past. Christianity has always played a role in pushing the country closer to its ideals. To say that civil-religious saints like Abraham Lincoln were not motivated by a Christian impulse would be absurd. The work of scholars such as Michael Novak and Jacques Maritain provides clear evidence that Christian reason and morality informed the philosophy of natural rights that undergirds American life to this day.[41] But the presence of a Christian ethic or ideal does not imply Christian privilege. When we point to examples like Lincoln, MLK, the Grimke sisters, or even Jane Addams, we see civil religious leaders who draw on their faith to perfect their country, not cryptotheocrats who would exploit the country to enthrone their faith.

If we are to begin the process of imagining an American Civil Religion that is riveted to the hearts of all Americans, we must begin with the premise that the United States is sacred on its own terms. And I argue we must build a space, explicitly sacred and fearlessly unique to us, that makes this point clear. L'Enfant was right to imagine his church as the central node of the nation's spiritual life. There would be no limit on the autonomy and practice of sectarian faiths. Indeed, such faiths would be encouraged and embraced, even granted their own plots of land in the capital district where they could build shrines and do the important work of ministering according to the dictates of their own creeds and consciences, but they would not claim the role of religious primus inter pares. If they wanted to play a role in the nation's life, that role would have to be an auxiliary one. The flag did not exist to support the cross or any other symbol of an external religious order. For L'Enfant, it had to be the other way around. The national church would serve as a civil-religious clearinghouse where the ideals of the nation are made articulate.

It Must Be New

I have titled this book *The* New *Civil Religion*, because by "new" I mean *novel* or *original*, not a different version of a former thing. Although I look to the past, I do so only to locate the raw materials of a great civil religion, one that Americans are yet to build. Rifling through our history to find the one "right" way to move forward will only reinscribe the tensions we are trying to move beyond. I echo Bruno Macaes's sentiment in *History Has Begun*. Macaes, a Portuguese diplomat and a student of US culture and history, argues that the notion of an America in decline may just as likely point to an America poised for transformation and for another century or more of cultural leadership. To put Macaes's view into my own words, he sees the potential for an American *kairos*. "We want to know," he writes, "whether the dynamism of the United States in the twentieth century might not prefigure something new and whether the current turmoil could in fact be better interpreted as the birth pangs of a new culture instead of . . . the death throes of an aged civilization."[42] Macaes sees an America that is not in the thrall of some imagined history as a European heir or a Christian scion. He sees a future in which the United States of America blazes a path wholly original.

Macaes's point that America is *not* endemically European (and not, by extension, endemically Christian) is especially important. He argues that the United States has asserted itself *against* Europe more often than it has asserted itself in league with Europe. "America was always conscious that it descended from many different nations or civilizations, the new country was always a crossing of many strains of culture and history." In addition to America's European, Native American, and African genes, he adds, "there was the final polyglot mass of migrants: Russians, Jews, Mexicans, Latin Americans and the Chinese, Japanese, Filipinos. For contemporary Americans, recognition of this multiple heritage has become a moral duty."[43] It is true that, at its founding, the United States claimed European ideals. And, where doing so made sense, it claimed these ideals with fervency, but the United States has also always been pragmatic. Two centuries ago, European ideals and Western civilization ruled the globe. Today, too many other cultural influences play leading roles.

The United States would do well to imagine itself at the helm of something unique, something that draws on the lived experience of Americans *as* Americans, something like what Whitman imagined, something shaped from the vast and mixed soil of the landscape. We might begin the project by throwing out all notions that we are a nation with a distinct religious or ethnic past. From there, we will find that we remain as rich as ever in the raw materials of civil-religious potential: great texts, timeless ideals, noble debates, worthy protests, and a pantheon of heroes and heroines who merit our study and reverence. Today, these materials seem more scattered and chaotic than ever. Blame it on a lack of civic education, leadership, conscience, or what have you. The plain fact is that our government institutions have failed to provide spiritual leadership commensurate with the needs and potential of the people. I hope to have shown that one reason for this institutional failure is that one of the key, founding institutions was never established in the first place. Just as America's civil religion waits to be shaped and articulated, so the great church for national purposes waits to be designed and built.

NOTES

Preface

1. Thomas Mole, "The Secret Life of Books," invited lecture at Brigham Young University, September 6, 2018.

2. See Jill Lepore, *These Truths: A History of the United States* (New York: W. W. Norton, 2018), 786. Bruno Macaes does an excellent job of capturing these sentiments in chapter 1 of his book *History Has Begun: The Birth of a New America* (New York: Oxford University Press, 2020), 1–24.

3. See Lepore, *These Truths*, 311. See also Rogers M. Smith, *Civil Ideals: Conflicting Visions of Citizenship in U.S.* History (New Haven, CT: Yale University Press, 1997).

Introduction

1. "To George Washington from Pierre-Charles L'Enfant, 22 June 1791," *Founders Online*, National Archives, https://founders.archives.gov/documents/Washington/05 -08-02-0199, originally published in *The Papers of George Washington*, Presidential Series 8, 22 March 1791–22 September 1791, ed. Mark A. Mastromarino (Charlottesville: University of Virginia Press, 1999), 287–93.

2. Peter Charles L'Enfant, "Plan of the city intended for the permanent seat of the government of t(he) United States: projected agreeable to the direction of the President of the United States, in pursuance of an act of Congress passed the sixteenth day of July, MDCCXC, 'establishing the permanent seat on the bank of the Potowmac,'" facsimile of the 1791 L'Enfant plan (Washington, DC: United States Coast and Geodetic Survey, 1887), LCCN 88694201, Library of Congress Geography and Map Division, Washington, DC.

3. "To George Washington," 287–93.

4. Adam Goodheart, "Back to the Future: One of Washington's Most Exuberant Monuments—the Old Patent Office Building—Gets the Renovation It Deserves," *Smithsonian Magazine* (July 2006), par. 9.

5. The site continues to be called the Old Patent Office Building, but this building now also houses the Smithsonian's National Portrait Gallery and American Art Museum.

6. Richard Hewlett, *The Foundation Stone: Henry Yates Satterlee and the Creation of Washington National Cathedral* (Rockville, MD: Montrose Press, 2007), 39, 47–49.

7. William Reed Huntington to Douglas, July 15, 1890, George William Douglas

Papers, St. John's Church, Washington, DC (hereafter cited as Douglas Papers). See also Lesley A. Norther, "William Reed Huntington: First Presbyter of the Late Nineteenth Century," *Anglican and Episcopal History* 62 (June 1993): 193–213.

8. Sigourney Fay, "Protestant Episcopal Church in the United States of America," in *The Catholic Encyclopedia* (New York: Robert Appleton Company, 1911), online at *New Advent*, accessed July 31, 2019, http://www.newadvent.org/cathen/12493a.htm.

9. Richard Benjamin Crosby, "Civil Religion, Nativist Rhetoric, and the Washington National Cathedral," *Journal of Communication and Religion* 39, no. 4 (2016): 62–63.

10. "The Chicago-Lambeth Quadrilateral" (1886), *Anglicans Online*, accessed July 31, 2019, http://anglicansonline.org/basics/Chicago_Lambeth.html.

11. "Chicago-Lambeth Quadrilateral."

12. William Reed Huntington, *The Church-Idea: An Essay towards Unity* (New York: E. P. Dutton, 1870), 9–11.

13. Hewlett, *Foundation Stone*, 40.

14. Henry Yates Satterlee to George Frederick Bodley, undated, Satterlee Correspondence Files, 162, Washington National Cathedral Archives (hereafter cited as WNCA).

15. "1898: The Birth of a Superpower," Office of the Historian, Department of State, United States of America, accessed July 31, 2019, https://history.state.gov/department history/short-history/superpower.

16. Richard Hewlett, *Washington Cathedral and Its National Purpose: The Emergence of an Ideal, 1867–1990* (Washington, DC: Washington National Cathedral, 1992), 3.

17. Henry Yates Satterlee, "Address to the Annual Convention," in *Journal of the 11th Annual Convention of the Protestant Episcopal Church* (Washington, DC: The Convention, 1906).

18. "Washington Cathedral and the Cause of Religion: Report of the Cathedral Council as Approved and Adopted by the Bishop and Chapter" (May 28, 1936), 18, WNCA, file 102-2-5.

19. The cathedral's various names have a complicated history. Its first and most official name remains the Cathedral Church of St. Peter and St. Paul. Other names, such as Washington Cathedral, have emerged in unofficial or quasi-official ways. Today, the cathedral is variously called Washington Cathedral, Washington National Cathedral, or the National Cathedral in popular correspondence.

20. See the cathedral's website for the history of some of the cathedral's most prominent services of national mourning and celebration. "National Services," Cathedral.org, accessed July 31, 2019, https://cathedral.org/history/prominent-services/national -services/.

21. George H. W. Bush, "Remarks at the Washington National Cathedral Dedication Ceremony," September 29, 1990, *American Presidency Project*, accessed June 11, 2022, https://www.presidency.ucsb.edu/documents/remarks-the-washington-national -cathedral-dedication-ceremony.

22. Bethel is where the Old Testament patriarch Jacob (later known as Israel) erected stones and anointed them with oil to claim the land as a divine inheritance where his people would be able to worship their God.

23. Meghan McCain, "Meghan McCain Pays Tribute to Her Father, John McCain" (Washington, DC, September 1, 2018), CNN.com, accessed July 31, 2019, https://www

.cnn.com/2018/09/01/politics/meghan-mccain-full-remarks-john-mccain-funeral
/index.html.

24. Peter Baker, "In Funeral of Pomp and Pageantry, Nation Bids Farewell to George
Bush," *New York Times*, December 5, 2018.

25. John Meacham, "Transcript: Jon Meacham's Eulogy for Former President
George H. W. Bush" (Washington, DC, December 6, 2018), CBSnews.com, accessed
July 31, 2019, https://www.cbsnews.com/news/transcript-jon-meachams-eulogy-for
-former-president-george-hw-bush-funeral.

26. Werner Jaeger, *Paideia: The Ideals of Greek Culture*, vol. 1, 2nd ed., trans. Gilber
Highet (New York: Oxford University Press, 1965), 286–87.

27. Jaeger, 286–87.

28. That presidents serve as "national priests" is a well-established notion among
scholars from a variety of disciplines, particularly among scholars of presidential
rhetoric. See, for example, Richard Benjamin Crosby, "Toward a Practical Civic Piety:
Mitt Romney, Barack Obama, and the Race for National Priest," *Rhetoric and Public
Affairs* 18, no. 2 (2015): 301–30; and Karlyn Cohrs Campbell and Kathleen Hall Jamieson, *Presidents Creating the Presidency: Deeds Done in Words* (Chicago: University of
Chicago Press, 2008), 101. Brian T. Kaylor argues that, rather than priest, "pastor"
might a better conceptual vehicle, because it invokes a "democratic congregational
model in which religious leaders are selected based on their ability to communicate
persuasively with a faithful audience." Kaylor, *Presidential Campaign Rhetoric in an
Age of Confessional Politics* (Lanham, MD: Lexington Books, 2011), 196–97.

29. See the cathedral's official timeline, "History," Washington National Cathedral,
accessed June 11, 2022, https://cathedral.org/history/timeline.

30. Robert N. Bellah, "Civil Religion in America," *Daedalus: Religion in America* 96,
no. 1 (Winter 1967): 1–21.

31. Frederick Quinn, *A House of Prayer for All People: A History of Washington
National Cathedral* (New York: Morehouse, 2014).

32. Ronald Bier, *Civil Religion: A Dialogue in the History of Political Philosophy* (New
York: Cambridge University Press, 2011), 2.

33. Jason A. Edwards and Joseph M. Valenzano III, eds., *The Rhetoric of American
Civil Religion: Symbols, Sinners, and Saints* (Lanham, MD: Lexington Books, 2016), xii.

34. Yuval Noah Harari, *Sapiens: A Brief History of Mankind* (New York: Harper
Perennial, 2015), 210.

35. Jean-Jacques Rousseau, *The Social Contract* (New York: Cosimo Classics, 2008).

36. Peter Gardella, *American Civil Religion: What Americans Hold Sacred* (New
York: Oxford University Press, 2014), 1.

37. John A. Coleman, "Civil Religion," *Sociological Analysis* 31, no. 2 (Summer 1970):
74, https://doi.org/10.2307/3710057.

38. Robert Bellah, *The Broken Covenant: American Civil Religion in a Time of Trial*
(Chicago: University of Chicago Press, 1975), 96–97.

39. Alexis de Tocqueville, *Democracy in America* (New York: Bantam, 2000), 346.

40. Tocqueville, *Democracy in America*, 353–54.

41. Raymond T. Bond, *The Man Who Was Chesterton* (Garden City, NJ: Image Books,
1960), 125.

238   *Notes to Pages 14–18*

42. Will Herberg, *Protestant, Catholic, Jew* (Garden City, NJ: Doubleday, 1955), 78.

43. Matthew Wills, "James Truslow Adams: Dreaming Up the American Dream," *JSTOR Daily*, May 18, 2015, https://daily.jstor.org/james-truslow-adams-dreaming -american-dream/.

44. Bellah, *Broken Covenant*, 12.

45. Gardella, *American Civil Religion*, 6.

46. Gardella, 6.

47. Gardella, 4.

48. Most historians acknowledge that the Greco-Roman model formed the balance of the nation's legal and philosophical bedrock at the time of the founding. See, for example, Caroline Winterer, *The Culture of Classicism: Ancient Greece and Rome in American Intellectual Life, 1780–1910* (Baltimore: Johns Hopkins University Press, 2004); Carl J. Richard, *The Founders and the Classics: Greece, Rome, and the American Enlightenment* (Cambridge, MA: Harvard University Press, 1994); Eric Nelson, *The Greek Tradition in Republican Thought: Ideas in Context* (New York: Cambridge University Press, 2004); Eran Shalev, *Rome Reborn on Western Shores: Historical Imagination and the Creation of the American Republic* (Charlottesville: University of Virginia Press, 2009); and Howard John Smith, *The First Great Awakening: Redefining Religion in British America, 1725–1775* (Madison, NJ: Fairleigh Dickinson University Press, 2015), 2. The founding documents not only are devoid of any official Christian commitments but also reflect distinctly classical notions of natural law, citizenship, and an open and enlightened citizenry. See Paul Conkin, *Self-Evident Truths* (Bloomington: Indiana University Press, 1974), 77; and Vincent Martin Bonventure, "A Classical Constitution: Ancient Roots of Our National Charter," *New York Bar Journal*, December 1, 1987, https://papers.ssrn.com/sol3/papers.cfm?abstract_id=1154706.

49. For a thorough study of the democratic flavor of American Christianity at this point in history, see Nathan O. Hatch, *The Democratization of American Christianity* (New Haven, CT: Yale University Press, 1989). For further reading in this area, see E. Brooks Holifield, *Theology in America* (New Haven, CT: Yale University Press, 2003); Edwin S. Gustaud and Mark A. Noll, *A Documentary History of Religion in America to 1877*, 3rd ed. (Grand Rapids, MI: William B. Eerdmans, 2003); Sidney E. Ahlstrom, *A Religious History of the American People* (New Haven, CT: Yale University Press, 1972); Peter Manseau, *One Nation, Under Gods: A New American History* (New York: Little Brown and Company, 2015).

50. J. D. B. De Bow, "Editorial and Literary Department," *De Bow's Review* 11 (December 1851): 681.

51. For a photographic history of antebellum architecture that reflects Greek Revival and romantic styles, see Lane Mills and Van Jones Martin, *Architecture of the Old South: Greek Revival and Romantic* (Savannah: Beehive Press, 1996).

52. Douglass speaks in particular of the book's portrayal of arguments between a master and a former slave. See Frederick Douglass, *Narrative on the Life of Frederick Douglass: An American Slave* (London: H. G. Collins, 1851), 40.

53. Frederick Douglass, *Great Speeches by Frederick Douglass* (Mineola, NY: Dover, 2013), 33.

54. James Darsey, *The Prophetic Tradition and Radical Rhetoric in America* (New York: New York University Press, 1997), 6.

55. Matthew Arnold, *Culture and Anarchy*, ed. L. Dover Wilson (Cambridge: Cambridge University Press, 1960), 131.

56. Abraham Lincoln, "Address at Cooper Institute, New York City," in *Lincoln Speeches* (New York: Penguin, 2012), 98.

57. Abraham Lincoln, "Address Delivered at the Dedication of the Cemetery at Gettysburg," in *Lincoln Speeches*, 149–50.

58. Ulysses S. Grant, *The Best Writings of Ulysses S. Grant*, ed. John F. Marzalek (Carbondale: Southern Illinois University Press, 2015), 142.

59. For an overview of Grant's unprecedented record on civil rights, see "The Racial Views of Ulysses S. Grant," *Journal of Blacks in Higher Education*, no. 66 (Winter 2009–10): 26–27, http://www.jstor.org/stable/20722155.

60. Niebuhr was a famous opponent of racial segregation, which he regarded as a national sin. For more on how his views relate to questions of civil religion, see Philip Gorski, *American Covenant: A History of Civil Religion from the Puritans to the Present* (Princeton, NJ: Princeton University Press, 2017), 126.

61. George W. Bush, "Remarks at the National Day of Prayer & Remembrance Service" (September 14, 2001), American Rhetoric, accessed July 31, 2019, https://www.americanrhetoric.com/speeches/gwbush911prayer&memorialaddress.htm.

62. See Richard Benjamin Crosby, "Kairos as God's Time in Martin Luther King's Last Sunday Sermon," *Rhetoric Society Quarterly* 39, no. 3 (July 2009): 262.

63. James S. Baumlin and Tita French Baumlin, "Chronos, Kairos, Aion: Failures of Decorum, Right Timing, and Revenge in Shakespeare's *Hamlet*," in *Rhetoric and Kairos: Essays in History, Theory, and Praxis*, ed. Philip Sipiora and James S. Baumlin (Albany: State University of New York Press, 2002), 178.

64. Debra Hawhee, *Bodily Arts: Rhetoric and Athletics in Ancient Greece* (Austin: University of Texas Press, 2004), 66.

65. Dale Sullivan, "Kairos and the Rhetoric of Belief," *Quarterly Journal of Speech* 78, no. 3 (1992): 319.

66. Scott Consigny, *Gorgias: Sophist and Artist* (Columbia: University of South Carolina Press, 2001), 154.

67. James L. Kinneavy, "Kairos Revisited: An Interview with James S. Kinneavy," *Rhetoric Review* 19, no. 1–2 (2000): 77–78.

68. Diane Ney, "To Excel All Others: How the Cathedral Came to Be Gothic," in *Living Stones: Washington National Cathedral at 100* (Washington, DC: Washington National Cathedral, 2007), 37.

69. Robert Wuthnow, "Divided We Fall: America's Two Civil Religions," *Christian Century*, April 20, 1988, 395–96.

70. David C. Innes, "Civil Religion as Political Technology in Bacon's *New Atlantis*," in *Civil Religion in Political Thought: Its Perennial Questions and Enduring Relevance in North America*, ed. Ronald Weed and John von Heyking (Washington, DC: Catholic University of America Press, 2010), 121.

71. For overviews, see Beiner, *Civil Religion: A Dialogue in the History of Political Philosophy* (New York: Cambridge University Press, 2011); Weed and von Heyking, *Civil Religion in Political Thought*; Thomas Frohlich, "Civil Religion on a Confucian Basis," in *Tang Junyi: Confucian Philosophy and the Challenge of Modernity* (New York: Brill, 2017); John A. Coleman, "Civil Religion," 70–71.

Chapter 1 • Pierre L'Enfant's Great Church for National Purposes

1. Prior to H. Paul Caemmerer's work, it was assumed that L'Enfant spent these years in military training and that he was a lieutenant in the French army. In fact, he had no military training, and he spent these years studying painting and sculpture under his father. See Caemmerer, *The Life of Pierre Charles L'Enfant* (New York: De Capo Press, 1970), 9.

2. "How Much Did It Cost to Build Versailles?" *History Extra* (February 26, 2016), https://www.historyextra.com/period/stuart/how-much-cost-build-versailles-money/.

3. This language comes not from Louis XIV himself but from a 1649 pamphlet describing him as a youth. The king embraced the symbol unreservedly. Louis XIV quoted in T. C. W. Blanning, *The Culture of Power and the Power of Culture: Old Regime Europe, 1660–1789* (Oxford: Oxford University Press, 2002), 34.

4. This language is Louis XIV's own, quoted in Blanning, *Culture of Power*, 34.

5. Scott W. Berg, *Grand Avenues: The Story of Pierre Charles L'Enfant* (New York: Vintage, 2007), 31.

6. Quoted in Caemmerer, *Life of Pierre Charles L'Enfant*, 41.

7. "To George Washington from Major General Lafayette, 1 September 1778," *Founders Online* (National Archives), https://founders.archives.gov/documents/Washington/03-16-02-0503, originally published in *The Papers of George Washington*, Revolutionary War Series 16, 1 July–14 September 1778, ed. David R. Hoth (Charlottesville: University of Virginia Press, 2006), 461–64. It seems Lafayette had arranged the meeting between Washington and L'Enfant to get a likeness of Washington until something more permanent could be had, something by, say, the famous American painter Charles Willson Peale, whom Lafayette had been hounding for almost a year.

8. Quoted in Caemmerer, *Life of Pierre Charles L'Enfant*, 66.

9. Quoted in Berg, *Grand Avenues*, 240–45; Caemmerer, *Life of Pierre Charles L'Enfant*, 3.

10. Friedrich Wilhelm Ludolf Gerhard Augustin, Baron von Steuben, comp., *Regulations for the Order and Discipline of the Troops of the United States, Part 1*, illustrated by Pierre Charles L'Enfant (Philadelphia: Styner and Cist, 1779), American Imprint Collection and John Davis Batchelder Collection, Library of Congress, accessed June 12, 2022, https://www.loc.gov/item/05030726/.

11. Harris, "Washington's Gamble, L'Enfant's Dream: Politics, Design, and the Founding of the National Capital," *William and Mary Quarterly* 56, no. 3 (July 1999): 538; "To Alexander Hamilton from Pierre Charles L'Enfant, 8 April 1791," *Founders Online*, National Archives, https://founders.archives.gov/documents/Hamilton/01-08-02-0196, originally published in *The Papers of Alexander Hamilton*, vol. 8: *February 1791–July 1791*, ed. Harold C. Syrett (New York: Columbia University Press, 1965), 253–56.

12. Caemmerer, *Life of Pierre Charles L'Enfant*, 66–67.

13. Quoted in William Tindall, *Standard History of the City of Washington from a Study of the Original Sources* (Knoxville: H. W. Crew & Co., 1914), 60.

14. "Memorandum by Pierre-Charles L'Enfant, 26 March 1791," in *Founders Online*, National Archives, https://founders.archives.gov/documents/Washington/05-08-02-0005, originally published in *Papers of George Washington*, Presidential Series 8, 5–9.

15. Jefferson was incensed by L'Enfant's profligate spending during his assigned

trip to Paris to prepare the engravings of the Society of the Cincinnati and to establish a branch of the society there. The debts took years to resolve and remained a source of embarrassment for Jefferson on behalf of the government.

16. See Harris, "Washington's Gamble, L'Enfant's Dream," 530.

17. "George Washington to David Stuart, 20 November 1791," in *Founders Online*, National Archives, https://founders.archives.gov/documents/Washington/05-09-02 -0118, originally published in *Papers of George Washington*, Presidential Series 9, 209–14.

18. For Washington's views on the dangers of disunion to the nation, see "Washington's Farewell Address, 1796," originally published in David Claypole's *American Daily Advertiser*, September 19, 1796, under the title "The Address of General Washington to The People of The United States on his declining of the Presidency of the United States." For a full transcript see George Washington's Mount Vernon, https://www.mountvernon .org/education/primary-sources-2/article/washington-s-farewell-address-1796/. For a comment on his much lesser known role as city planner, see Harris, "Washington's Gamble, L'Enfant's Dream," 529, 534.

19. "Thomas Jefferson to Pierre Charles L'Enfant, [2] March 1791," in *Founders Online*, National Archives, https://founders.archives.gov/documents/Jefferson/01-19 -02-0093, originally published in *The Papers of Thomas Jefferson*, vol. 19: *24 January–31 March 1791*, ed. Julian P. Boyd (Princeton, NJ: Princeton University Press, 1974), 355–56.

20. Saul K. Padover, ed., *The Washington Papers: Basic Selections from the Public and Private Writings of George Washington* (New York: Grosset and Dunlap, 1955), 56.

21. Kirk Savage, *Monument Wars: Washington, D.C., the National Mall, and the Transformation of the Memorial Landscape* (Berkeley: University of California Press, 2011), 26.

22. Pierre Charles L'Enfant to Thomas Jefferson, 11 March 1791, in *Founders Online*, National Archives, https://founders.archives.gov/documents/Jefferson/01-20-02 -0001-0004, originally published in *The Papers of Thomas Jefferson*, vol. 20: *1 April–4 August 1791*, ed. Julian P. Boyd (Princeton, NJ: Princeton University Press, 1982), 76–78.

23. Quoted in Kenneth R. Bowling, *Peter Charles L'Enfant: Vision, Honor, and Male Friendship in the Early American Republic* (Washington, DC: Friends of GW Libraries, 2002), 223.

24. "Pierre-Charles L'Enfant to George Washington, 19 August 1791," in *Founders Online*, National Archives, https://founders.archives.gov/documents/Washington/05 -08-02-0307. originally published in *The Papers of George Washington*, Presidential Series 8, 439–48.

25. See letters to George Washington from Pierre Charles L'Enfant: September 11, 1789, *Founders Online*, National Archives, https://founders.archives.gov/documents /Washington/05-04-02-0010, originally published in *The Papers of George Washington*, Presidential Series 4, *8 September 1789–15 January 1790*, ed. Dorothy Twohig (Charlottesville: University Press of Virginia, 1993), 15–19; June 22, 1791, *Founders Online*, National Archives, https://founders.archives.gov/documents/Washington/05-08-02 -0199, originally published in *The Papers of George Washington*, Presidential Series 8, *22 March 1791–22 September 1791*, ed. Mark A. Mastromarino (Charlottesville: University Press of Virginia, 1999), 287–93.; August 19, 1791, *Founders Online*, National Archives, https://founders.archives.gov/documents/Washington/05-08-02-0307, originally

published in *The Papers of George Washington*, Presidential Series 8, *22 March 1791–22 September 1791*, ed. Mark A. Mastromarino (Charlottesville: University Press of Virginia, 1999), 439–48.

26. "Pierre Charles L'Enfant to Thomas Jefferson, 4 April 1791," in *Founders Online*, National Archives, https://founders.archives.gov/documents/Jefferson/01-20-02-0001 -0012, originally published in *Papers of Thomas Jefferson*, 20:83–84.

27. "Thomas Jefferson to Pierre Charles L'Enfant, 10 April 1791," in *Founders Online*, National Archives, https://founders.archives.gov/documents/Jefferson/01-20-02-0001 -0015, originally published in *The Papers of Thomas Jefferson*, 20:86–87.

28. "Thomas Jefferson to Pierre Charles L'Enfant, 18 August 1791," in *Founders Online*, National Archives, https://founders.archives.gov/documents/Jefferson/01-22 -02-0047; originally published in *The Papers of Thomas Jefferson*, vol. 22: *6 August 1791–31 December 1791*, ed. Charles T. Cullen (Princeton, NJ: Princeton University Press, 1986), 47–48.

29. "Thomas Jefferson to Pierre Charles L'Enfant, 18 August 1791." See also Les Standiford, *Washington Burning: How a Frenchman's Vision for Our Nation's Capital Survived Congress, the Founding Fathers, and the Invading British Army* (New York: Crown, 2008), 67.

30. Harris, "Washington's Gamble, L'Enfant's Dream," 535.

31. Savage, *Monument Wars*, 25.

32. Harris, "Washington's Gamble, L'Enfant's Dream," 536–37, 541. See also Donald Jackson and Dorothy Twohig, eds., *The Diaries of George Washington* (Charlottesville: University of Virginia Press, 1978), 164–66; *The Papers of Thomas Jefferson*, vol. 23: *1 January–31 May 1792*, ed. Charles T. Cullen (Princeton, NJ: Princeton University Press, 1990), 23:322–23.

33. Nicholas Mann, *The Sacred Geometry of Washington, DC: The Integrity and Power of the Original Design* (Glastonbury, UK: Green Magic Press, 2006), 157.

34. Peter Charles L'Enfant, "Library of Congress: Plan of the city intended for the permanent seat of the government of t(he) United States;" facsimile of manuscript of L'Enfant plan (Washington, DC: United States Coast and Geodetic Survey, 1887).

35. L'Enfant, "Library of Congress."

36. Bowling, *Peter Charles L'Enfant*, 223.

37. Savage, *Monument Wars*, 34.

38. Savage, *Monument Wars*, 31; see also Mann, *Sacred Geometry*, 174.

39. This "Memoire to Washington" is archived in the Records of the Columbia Historical Society, 2: 26–47, and is reproduced in Elizabeth Sarah Kite, ed., *L'Enfant and Washington, 1791–1792: Published and Unpublished Documents* (Baltimore: Johns Hopkins University Press, 1929), 68–69.

40. "Pierre-Charles L'Enfant to George Washington, 19 August 1791."

41. "Memorandum by Pierre-Charles L'Enfant, 26 March 1791."

42. Jennifer Llewellyn and Steve Thompson, "The Civil Constitution of the Clergy," Alpha History, September 22, 2020, https://alphahistory.com/frenchrevolution/civil -constitution-of-the-clergy/.

43. Alexia Lebeurre, *The Pantheon: Temple of the Nation* (Paris: Ed. du patrimoine, 2000), 17.

44. The changes to the frieze did not take place until the nineteenth century; however, they represent the powerful momentum established with the Revolution.

45. L'Enfant, "Library of Congress."

46. L'Enfant's handwritten manuscript notes, James Dudley Morgan (1862–1919) collection, Digges-L'Enfant-Morgan papers, 1674–1923 (bulk 1778–1828), Local shelving no.: MMC-3131 Oversize 4:3 Microfilm 18,780-2N-2P, Library of Congress, https://lccn.loc.gov/mm82018481.

47. Herbert M. Morais, "Deism in Revolutionary America (1763–89)," *International Journal of Ethics* 42, no. 4 (1932): 434–53, esp. 434–35, http://www.jstor.org/stable/2378041.

48. Kite, *L'Enfant and Washington*, 19.

49. Savage, *Monument Wars*, 31.

50. Harris, "Washington's Gamble, L'Enfant's Dream," 544.

51. Harris, 544.

52. "George Washington to David Stuart, 8 March 1792," in *Founders Online*, National Archives, https://founders.archives.gov/documents/Washington/05-10-02-0036, originally published in *The Papers of George Washington*, Presidential Series 10, *1 March 1792–15 August 1792*, ed. Robert F. Haggard and Mark A. Mastromarino (Charlottesville: University of Virginia Press, 2002), 62–67. See also Harris, "Washington's Gamble, L'Enfant's Dream," 552.

53. "To George Washington from Pierre-Charles L'Enfant, 19 August 1791," *Founders Online*, National Archives, https://founders.archives.gov/documents/Washington/05-08-02-0307, originally published in *The Papers of George Washington*, Presidential Series 8, *22 March 1791– 22 September 1791*, ed. Mark A. Mastromarino (Charlottesville: University Press of Virginia, 1999), 439–448).

54. "From George Washington to Pierre L'Enfant, 2 December 1791," *Founders Online*, National Archives, https://founders.archives.gov/documents/Washington/05-09-02-0146, originally published in *Papers of George Washington*, Presidential Series 9, 244–45.

55. "Pierre L'Enfant to George Washington, 7 December 1791," in *Founders Online*, National Archives, https://founders.archives.gov/documents/Washington/05-09-02-0157, originally published in *Papers of George Washington*, Presidential Series 9, 263–66.

56. For the various letters exchanged in this tense period between L'Enfant, Roberdeau, Washington, Jefferson, and the commissioners, see Kite, *L'Enfant and Washington*, 77–133.

57. An example of Washington's more gentle correction can be found in his letter to L'Enfant following the unauthorized demolition of the home of Mr. Carroll of Duddington. "George Washington to Pierre L'Enfant, 2 December 1791."

58. Standiford, *Washington Burning*, 118; see also Kite, *L'Enfant and Washington*, 145–50.

59. Standiford, *Washington Burning*, 118. See also Washington's sentiments regarding L'Enfant's "repugnance" and dismissal in "George Washington to David Stuart, 8 March 1792."

60. "Thomas Jefferson to Pierre Charles L'Enfant, 27 February 1792," in *Founders Online*, National Archives, https://founders.archives.gov/documents/Hamilton/01-11-02-0061, originally published in *The Papers of Alexander Hamilton*, vol. 11: *February*

1792 – June 1792, ed. Harold C. Syrett (New York: Columbia University Press, 1966), 50–51.

61. "Thomas Jefferson to George Walker, 1 March 1792, with Copy," reel 015, Series 1: General Correspondence, 1651 to 1827, Thomas Jefferson Papers, Manuscript Division, Library of Congress, https://www.loc.gov/item/mtjbib005943/.

62. Adam Goodheart, "Back to the Future: One of Washington's Most Exuberant Monuments—The Old Patent Office Building—Gets the Renovation It Deserves," *Smithsonian Magazine* (July 2006), para. 12.

63. Quoted in Jean Jules Jusserand, *With Americans of Past and Present Days* (New York: Charles Scribner, 1916), 191. See also Charles Dickens's descriptions of the city upon his visit in the mid-nineteenth century, in *American Notes for General Circulation* (Paris: Baudry's European Library, 1842), 146.

64. Savage, *Monument Wars*, 40.

65. Fergus M. Bordewich, "A Capital Vision from a Self-Taught Architect," *Smithsonian Magazine* (December 2008).

66. Charles M. Harris, "William Thornton (1759–1828)," Library of Congress, Prints and Photographs Reading Room, last modified October 2015, https://www.loc.gov/rr/print/adecenter/essays/B-Thornton.html; see paras. 13–14.

67. Harris, "William Thornton," 13–14.

68. See Harris, "Washington's Gamble, L'Enfant's Dream," 553. For primary sources on Thornton's plan, see "William Thornton to Thomas Jefferson, ca. 12 July 1793," in *Founders Online*, National Archives, https://founders.archives.gov/documents/Jefferson/01-26-02-0436, originally published in *The Papers of Thomas Jefferson*, Vol. 26: *11 May–31 August 1793*, ed. John Catanzariti (Princeton, NJ: Princeton University Press, 1995), 489–95. For a substantial statement from George Washington on his civil-religious views, see his farewell address, or "Circular," to the nation, "George Washington to The States, 8 June 1783."

69. The fascinating history of Washington's oblique consent to the capitol crypt and Jefferson's oblique rejection of it is captured in Savage, *Monument Wars*, 37–39.

70. Harris, "Washington's Gamble, L'Enfant's Dream," 559–60.

71. Harris, "Washington's Gamble, L'Enfant's Dream," 561.

72. Alexander Hamilton passionately outlines the Federalist lines of argument, including those concerning the mausoleum and the federal city, in "An Address to the Electors of the State of New-York, 21 March 1801," in *Founders Online*, National Archives, https://founders.archives.gov/documents/Hamilton/01-25-02-0197, originally published in *The Papers of Alexander Hamilton*, vol. 25: *July 1800 – April 1802*, ed. Harold C. Syrett (New York: Columbia University Press, 1977), 349–71.

73. Jusserand, *With Americans of Past and Present Days*, 188.

74. See Kite, *L'Enfant and Washington*, 24. L'Enfant ran afoul of his employers for the rigidity of his point of view and the grandiosity of his designs.

75. Jusserand, *With Americans of Past and Present Days*, 190.

76. Savage, *Monument Wars*, 4.

77. This phrase is from Charles Dickens's underwhelming description of Washington, DC, during a nineteenth-century visit. Keith Melder has written a book by this title: *City of Magnificent Intentions: A History of Washington, District of Columbia*, 2nd ed. (Washington, DC: Intac, 1997).

78. "Relics of Maj. L'Enfant: Meeting of the Club Which Will Perpetuate His Memory," *Washington Post* (1877–1922), August 21, 1892, https://library.access.arlingtonva.us/login?url=https://search-proquest.

79. Quoted in Kite, *L'Enfant and Washington*, 28. See also "The L'Enfant & McMillan Plans," Washington, DC: A National Register of Historic Places Travel Inventory, preserved at Internet Archive Wayback Machine, accessed June 13, 2022, https://web.archive.org/web/20071105022149/http:/www.nps.gov/history/nr/travel/wash/lenfant.htm. See also US Congress, Senate, Committee on the District of Columbia, *The Improvement of the Park System of the District of Columbia. I.—Report of the Senate Committee on the District of Columbia. II.—Report of the Park Commission*, ed. Charles Washington Moore (Washington, DC: Government Print Office, 1902), https://lccn.loc.gov/02026044.

80. The reinterment of L'Enfant's body was a long and complex process. For years, offers had been made to move and host his remains in more fitting places, including Washington National Cathedral itself and the Catholic University of America campus. See "Offers Grave for L'Enfant: Bishop Satterlee Tenders Site in Grounds of Cathedral," *Washington Post* (1877–1922), October 14, 1904: "Will Move L'Enfant's Body: District to Have It Reinterred in Catholic University Campus," *Washington Post* (1877–1922), July 18, 1908. The announcement that L'Enfant qualified as a former military officer to be buried at Arlington came in December 1908. See "To Move L'Enfant's Body: Will Be Taken from Digges Farm to Arlington," *Washington Evening Star*, December 4, 1908; "Honor to L'Enfant Tardy but Sincere." *Washington Evening Star*, April 28, 1909; "L'Enfant Disinterred," *Washington Post* (1877–1922), April 23, 1909; "Honor to L'Enfant: Memorial to City's Designer Unveiled at Arlington," *Washington Post* (1877–1922), May 23, 1911.

81. "Pierre L'Enfant," Arlington National Cemetery, accessed June 13, 2022, https://www.arlingtoncemetery.mil/Explore/Notable-Graves/Science-Technology-Engineering/Pierre-Charles-LEnfant.

Chapter 2 • *Henry Yates Satterlee's Westminster Abbey*

1. "Mission and Vision," Washington National Cathedral, accessed March 30, 2022, https://cathedral.org/about-the-cathedral/mission-and-vision.

2. L'Enfant's planning notes specify a church "intended for national purposes," and his subsequent explanatory letter to George Washington refers to this church as the "grand church." Use of the word "great" appears to be the choice of later generations, perhaps the cathedral organizers themselves. See Peter Charles L'Enfant, "Plan of the city intended for the permanent seat of the government of t(he) United States: projected agreeable to the direction of the President of the United States, in pursuance of an act of Congress passed the sixteenth day of July, MDCCXC, 'establishing the permanent seat on the bank of the Potowmac,'" facsimile of the 1791 L'Enfant plan (Washington, DC: United States Coast and Geodetic Survey, 1887), LCCN 88694201, Library of Congress Geography and Map Division, Washington, DC; and "To George Washington from Pierre-Charles L'Enfant, 19 August 1791," *Founders Online,* National Archives, https://founders.archives.gov/documents/Washington/05-08-02-0307, originally published in *The Papers of George Washington,* Presidential Series 8, *22 March 1791–22 September 1791*, ed. Mark A. Mastromarino (Charlottesville: University Press of Virginia, 1999), 439–48.

3. Satterlee used the same phrasing, "a great church for national purposes," in describing one of the cathedral's three missions. See Hewlett, *Washington Cathedral and Its National Purpose*, 3.

4. Henry Yates Satterlee, "History of the Cathedral of St. Peter and St. Paul: Private Record of Henry Y. Satterlee," WNCA, 2-12-15 (hereafter cited as Satterlee, "Private Record." See also Hewlett, *Foundation Stone*, 3.

5. L'Enfant's minimal description clarified that the church be "assigned to the special use of no particular denomination or sect." L'Enfant, "Plan of the city."

6. Henry Yates Satterlee, "Address by the Rt. Rev. Henry Y. Satterlee, D.D., LL. D., Bishop of Washington," in *Appendix: Journal of the Eighth Annual Convention of the Protestant Episcopal Church of the Diocese of Washington* (Washington, DC: Published by the Convention, May 6 and 7, 1903), 41.

7. Satterlee, "Address," 42.

8. Washington National Cathedral Strategic Planning Committee, *A New Century, a New Calling* (Washington, DC: Washington National Cathedral, 2007), 5.

9. Fay, "Protestant Episcopal Church in the United States of America."

10. Brooks quoted in David L. Holmes, *A Brief History of the Episcopal Church* (Harrisburg, PA: Trinity Press International, 1993), 69.

11. The Episcopal Church's tensions with other religious groups at the time, mainly Roman Catholicism, are discussed in detail in chapter 3.

12. D. W. Rowlands, "How the D.C. Area's Population Density Has Changed since 1970," D.C. Policy Center, July 24, 2019, https://www.dcpolicycenter.org/publications /regional-population-density-since-1970/.

13. Hewlett, *Foundation Stone*, 47.

14. Douglas and McKim to William Paret, Bishop of Washington, October 27, 1890, WNCA, 117-1-2.

15. Kite, *L'Enfant and Washington*, 28. See also "The L'Enfant & McMillan Plans."

16. W. R. Huntington to Douglas, July 15, 1890, Douglas Papers. See also Hewlett's commentary in Richard Greening Hewlett, "The Creation of the Diocese of Washington and Washington National Cathedral," *Anglican and Episcopal History* 71, no. 3 (September 2002): 362.

17. "History," Saint John's Church, accessed June 18, 2002, https://stjohns-dc.org /welcome-to-saint-johns-church/history/.

18. "History," Saint John's Church.

19. George William Douglas, *Sermons Preached in St. John's Church, Washington, D.C.* (New York: Anson D. F. Randolph and Company, 1893), 17.

20. Randolph Harrison McKim, *A Soldier's Recollections: Leaves from the Diary of a Young Confederate, with an Oration on the Motives and Aims of the Soldiers of the South* (New York: Longman's Green, and Co., 1910), 1–4.

21. Aaron Sheehan-Dean, "Virginia Soldiers (Confederate) during the Civil War," in *Encyclopedia Virginia*, accessed June 18, 2022, https://www.encyclopediavirginia.org /entries/virginia_soldiers_confederate_during_the_civil_war.

22. Sheehan-Dean, 30–31.

23. Randolph Harrison McKim, *Problem of the Pentateuch: An Examination of the Higher Criticism* (New York: Longmans, Green, 1906); McKim, *The Numerical Strength*

of the Confederate Army: An Examination of the Argument of the Hon. Charles Francis Adams and Others (New York: Neale Publishing Company, 1912).

24. William Paret, *Reminiscences* (Philadelphia: George W. Jacobs & Co., 1911), 107–8.

25. Paret, 107–8.

26. Paret to Douglas and McKim, October 28, 1890, WNCA, 117-1-4.

27. Paret's involvement in the cathedral was complicated from the outset. Beginning with his letter of October 28, his tone was guarded even when he wanted to signal support, and he always kept a hard line when it came to matters of carving up the existing diocese. In addition to his initial letter response to Douglas and McKim, several sources referenced here and in subsequent notes reveal that Paret's attitude toward the project could be interpreted either as reticent or supportive, depending on the details. Hewlett's work indicates that Paret harbored strong reservations about cathedral building, including, initially, in DC. Henry Yates Satterlee's own history of the building of the cathedral, however, shows that Paret "had always seen the need of a cathedral in the capital." See Henry Yates Satterlee, *The Building of a Cathedral* (New York: Edwin S. Gorham, 1901; reprinted, Washington, DC: Cloud Light, 2020), 205–6. In addition, whereas people like Douglas and, later, Satterlee himself complained of Paret's uncertain approach, others viewed Paret as a man of "bold statements, tackling problems, [and] facing criticism" when it came to matters of principle. See "From the Archives: William Paret," *Maryland Episcopalian*, July 22, 2020, https://marylandepiscopalian.org/2020/07/22/from-the-archives-william-paret/; "New Diocese of Washington: Its Establishment in Large Measure Due to Bishop Paret," *New York Times*, March 22, 1896, in Satterlee Box, WNCA.

28. Hewlett, *Washington Cathedral and Its National Purpose*, 3.

29. Nelson Falls to Paret, October 21, 1891; Douglas to Paret, October 26, 1891, both WNCA, 117-1-4.

30. See Hewlett, "Creation of the Diocese of Washington," 370.

31. Richard Greening Hewlett, "Washington Cathedral and Its National Purpose: The Emergence of an Ideal, 1867–1990" (unpublished study, 1992), 50, WNCA, 163-4-5.

32. Mary Elizabeth Mann to Paret, September 26, 1892, both WNCA, 117-1-6.

33. Mann to Paret, September 26, 1892 (emphasis in original).

34. Douglas to Paret, October 14, 1892, WNCA, 117-1-6.

35. See Hewlett, "Creation of the Diocese of Washington," 369–71. Note that a congressional charter does not indicate a state or national affiliation, only that Congress has granted federal permission for the cathedral to be built. A charter from the city or district would have granted similar legal permission, but a congressional charter conferred prestige on the project as an institution with national significance.

36. Hewlett, *Foundation Stone*, 54–58; Britton to Douglas, April 30, 1895, WNCA, 117-3-4; Paret to Britton, May 21, 1895, WNCA, 134-7-5, and reply, June 3, 1895, both WNCA, 134-7-1.

37. Arthur Powell to Satterlee, December 9, 1895, Satterlee Box, Correspondence, WNCA.

38. In 1887, Satterlee was elected assistant bishop of Ohio, a role he declined. In 1889, he was elected bishop of Michigan; again, he declined. See Richard Hewlett's

"Chronology" of Satterlee's life and career in Hewlett Box, WNCA. In the Episcopal Church, one may be elected to such positions without seeking them or announcing a candidacy for them. Candidates may not even be aware that they are being considered. If elected, they may consent or decline.

39. "Consecration Services of the Rev. Dr. Henry Y. Satterlee," *New York Times*, March 22, 1896; "Satterlee NY Times," Hewlett Box, WNCA.

40. "Dr. H. Y. Satterlee Honored," *Washington Examiner*, December 26, 1895, Satterlee Box, WNCA.

41. Washington National Cathedral Strategic Planning Committee, *A New Century, a New Calling*, 5.

42. Charles Henry Brent, *A Master Builder: Being the Life and Letters of Henry Yates Satterlee, First Bishop of Washington* (New York: Longmans, Green, and Co., 1916), 7.

43. Brent, 7.

44. Brent, 3.

45. Hewlett, "Washington Cathedral and Its National Purpose," 4.

46. Hewlett, 4–5.

47. Quoted in Brent, *Master Builder,* 10–11.

48. Quoted in Brent, 10–11.

49. Brent, 13, 25–26.

50. "Enlistment Age Distribution, All Years: Union Army," American Civil War Research Database, accessed June 18, 2022, www.civilwardata.com/ca_demo2.html.

51. "Obituary: Edward Satterlee," *New York Times,* May 1, 1878, https://timesmachine.nytimes.com/timesmachine/1878/05/01/80375518.pdf.

52. Brent, *Master Builder,* 24.

53. Brent, *Master Builder*, 14–15.

54. Hewlett, *Foundation Stone,* 7.

55. Satterlee, "Private Record." See also Hewlett, *Foundation Stone*, 149.

56. Brent, *Master Builder,* 31.

57. Edwin G. Burrows and Mike Wallace, *Gotham: A History of New York City to 1898* (New York: Oxford University Press, 2000), 1186–87.

58. Hewlett, *Foundation Stone*, 35.

59. Henry Yates Satterlee, *A Creedless Gospel and the Gospel Creed* (New York: Scribner's, 1895), 26.

60. Brent, *Master Builder*, 49.

61. Burrows and Wallace, *Gotham*, 116–17.

62. Ten years after Satterlee assumed the rector position in New York, the parish had grown by more than three times as measured by Christmas communicants; parish buildings were expanded and refurbished; staff increased; and temporary initiatives were so successful they became permanent. See Brent, *Master Builder*, 50. See also "Consecration Services of the Rev. Dr. Henry Y. Satterlee," *New York Times*, March 22, 1896, Satterlee NY Times, Hewlett Box, WNCA.

63. Satterlee, "Private Record." See also Hewlett, *Foundation Stone*, 89.

64. McKim, one of the two rectors who had proposed the cathedral project in the first place, was passionately in favor of the Gothic style. He went so far as to take his objections public, publishing a local missive that the *Washington Post* later called

"recriminative and almost personal in tone." It didn't matter. The board had already reaffirmed, by a vote of 12–3, the committee's overwhelming preference for a Renaissance cathedral. See "Imposing Marble . . . ," *Washington Post*, January 5, 1896, archived at Via Lucis, accessed June 18, 2022, https://vialucispress.files.wordpress.com/2012/02/article-on-flagg-design001.jpg.

65. A tympanum is a decorative sculpture on a wall surface over a building entrance. It is used in both classical and medieval architecture. In classical, or neoclassical and Renaissance, architecture, it often decorates the wall face of a pediment, which is a triangular cap above an entrance, often resting on columns.

66. Flagg, memorandum submitted with the Cathedral Plan, n.d., WNCA, 117-3-12.

67. "Imposing Marble. . . ."

68. McKim to Hearst, May 14, 1895, WNCA, 134-7-5, and reply, June 3, 1895, both WNCA, 134-7-1.

69. Phoebe Hearst was finally pacified, due in large part to the fact that the Cathedral School for Girls, which was her chief interest, was built in the Renaissance style.

70. Hewlett, *Foundation Stone*, 71.

71. Satterlee, "Private Record," 147.

72. Satterlee, "Private Record," 150–53.

73. Hewlett, *Foundation Stone*, 74. Henry Yates Satterlee to the Trustees, December 28, 1905, WNCA, 162-18-6.

74. Hewlett, *Foundation Stone*, 75.

75. Brent, *Master Builder*, 39.

76. Daniel H. Burnham to Henry Yates Satterlee, June 25, 1906, WNCA, 162-18-12.

77. Satterlee, "Private Record." See also Hewlett, *Foundation Stone*, 92.

78. Satterlee, "Private Record." See also Hewlett, *Foundation Stone*, 151.

79. Satterlee, *Building of a Cathedral*, 220.

80. Satterlee, *Building of a Cathedral*, 220.

81. Satterlee, "Private Record." See also Hewlett, *Foundation Stone*, 90–91.

82. Hewlett, *Foundation Stone*, 64.

83. Satterlee, "Private Record." See also Hewlett, *Foundation Stone*, 93.

84. Satterlee, "Private Record." See also Hewlett, *Foundation Stone*, 94.

85. Satterlee, "Private Record." See also Hewlett, *Foundation Stone*, 95.

86. Satterlee, "Private Record." See also Hewlett, *Foundation Stone*, 95.

87. Douglas's painstakingly crafted charter for the cathedral envisioned two, independent sets of leadership, one to pursue the cathedral's diocesan mission and the other to pursue its more national vision as a mother church.

88. Hewlett, *Washington Cathedral and Its National Purpose*, 3.

89. Hewlett, *Foundation Stone*, 40.

90. Henry Yates Satterlee, "Address to the Annual Convention," in *Journal of the Eleventh Annual Convention of the Protestant Episcopal Church*, St. Paul's Church (Washington, DC: Published by The Convention, 1906).

91. Right Rev. Francis Patrick Kenrick, "Letter on Christian Union, Addressed to the Bishops of the Protestant Episcopal Church," 1841, Project Canterbury, accessed June 18, 2022, http://anglicanhistory.org/rc/kenrick1841.html.

92. William T. Manning, S.T.D., "The Protestant Episcopal Church and Christian Unity," reprinted by permission, from *Constructive Quarterly* (December 1915), Project

Canterbury, accessed June 18, 2022, http://anglicanhistory.org/usa/wtmanning/unity 1915.html.

93. Among the most notable of these Anglican thinkers was John Henry Newman.

94. Henry Yates Satterlee, "The National Episcopal Cathedral at the Capital of the United States" (pamphlet), 1898, WNCA, 129-4-3.

95. See Hewlett, *Washington Cathedral and Its National Purpose*, 168–69.

96. In the 1920s and 1930s, Bishop Freeman promoted the cathedral using this nickname in a broad publicity campaign. See Hewlett, *Washington Cathedral and Its National Purpose*, 169.

97. Washington Cathedral Executive Committee, *Eminent Opinion regarding the Cathedral at Washington: Representative Americans State Their Views* (Washington, DC, 1929), 4.

98. Washington Cathedral Executive Committee, 20.

99. Washington Cathedral Executive Committee, 18.

100. Washington Cathedral Executive Committee, 42, 10, 68.

101. Theodore Roosevelt, for example, highlighted the cathedral's symbolic importance when he noted in effect that the cathedral's political mission enables it to transcend denomination. Washington Cathedral Executive Committee, 42–43.

102. Satterlee to Bodley, January 11, 1907, WNCA 162-7-2.

103. Satterlee to Bodley, undated, WNCA, 162-7-2.

104. Hewlett, *Foundation Stone*, 65.

105. Satterlee, "Private Record." See also Hewlett, *Foundation Stone*, 99–100.

106. Satterlee, "Private Record." See also Hewlett, *Foundation Stone*, 100.

107. Satterlee, "Private Record." See also Hewlett, *Foundation Stone*, 100.

108. Satterlee, "Private Record." See also Hewlett, *Foundation Stone*, 102.

109. Washington Cathedral Executive Committee, *Eminent Opinion*, 29.

110. Satterlee, "Private Record." See also Hewlett, *Foundation Stone*, 103.

111. One exception to this observation is that in 1904, several years after the Peace Cross event, the *Washington Post* reported that Satterlee and the cathedral had offered to provide a resting place for L'Enfant's remains, which were to be moved from their location at the Digges Farm. The report indicates that the remains could be transferred to the cathedral "grounds," not to its crypt or nave. That the cathedral did not become the permanent resting place of L'Enfant's remains has to do, some speculated, with the tension between the cathedral's Protestant identity and L'Enfant's Roman Catholic faith. See "Offers Grave for L'Enfant."

112. This statement by Roosevelt is quoted in Satterlee's "Private Record," but it has been quoted dozens of times since by prominent civic leaders, including President George H. W. Bush in his remarks at the cathedral's dedication in 1990. See "Remarks at the Washington National Cathedral Dedication Ceremony."

113. Hewlett, *Foundation Stone*, 159.

114. Bush, "Remarks at the Washington National Cathedral Dedication Ceremony."

115. See, for example, Tony Pettinato, "On This Day: Dedication Ceremony for the Washington National Cathedral," *GenealogyBank*, September 29, 2020, https://blog.genealogybank.com/on-this-day-dedication-ceremony-for-the-washington-national-cathedral.html; Standiford, *Washington Burning*, 105; Bush, "Remarks at the Washington National Cathedral Dedication Ceremony."

116. Satterlee, *Creedless Gospel*, 6.

117. Hewlett, *Foundation Stone*, 63.

Chapter 3 • The National Church in an Age of Nativism

1. Between the nation's founding and the middle of the nineteenth century, the Roman Catholic population in the United States shot up by 500 percent, and its rate of growth continued to increase from that point. See Julie Byrne, "Roman Catholics and Immigration in Nineteenth-Century America," National Humanities Center, June 1, 2016, http://nationalhumanitiescenter.org/tserve/nineteen/nkeyinfo/nromcath.htm.

2. One reason the Puritans saw such hope in North America was that it was largely free of Roman Catholic influence and some Protestant forces were already established there. For further documentation of Roman Catholic growth during the period in question, see Charles H. Lippy and Peter W. Williams, "Roman Catholicism: Catholics in the New World and Early Republic," in *Encyclopedia of Religion in America*, ed. Charles H. Lippy and Peter W. Williams (Thousand Oaks, CA: Sage, 2010).

3. Michael Schwartz, *The Persistent Prejudice: Anti-Catholicism in America* (Huntington, IN: Our Sunday Visitor, 1984), 25.

4. Schwartz, 25.

5. In 1642, the Colony of Virginia and the Massachusetts Bay Colony enacted laws restricting Roman Catholic settlement. In 1692, Maryland, formerly a Catholic stronghold, fell to Protestant pressure and repealed laws of religious toleration, then imposed double taxes on Catholics for the purpose of promoting Anglicanism. Rhode Island passed similar laws in 1792. Numerous sources document the history of colonial anti-Catholic laws. See, for example, John M. Scheb II, "Catholicism and Anti-Catholicism," in *Encyclopedia of American Civil Rights and Liberties*, rev. ed., ed. Kara E. Stooksbury, John M. Scheb II, Otis H. Stephens Jr. (Santa Barbara, AC: ABC-Clio, 2017), 1:131–32.

6. Byrne, "Roman Catholics and Immigration."

7. "From George Washington to Roman Catholics in America, c. 15 March 1790," *Founders Online*, National Archives, accessed August 14, 2022, https://founders.archives.gov/documents/Washington/05-05-02-0193, originally published in *The Papers of George Washington*, Presidential Series 5, *16 January 1790–30 June 1790*, ed. Dorothy Twohig, Mark A. Mastromarino, and Jack D. Warren (Charlottesville: University Press of Virginia, 1996), 299–301.

8. A number of sources have documented the decline of Puritanism. A good place to start is David D. Hall, "New England, 1660–1730," in *Cambridge Companion to Puritanism*, ed. John Coffey and Paul C. H. Lim (New York: Cambridge University Press, 2008), 143–58. Hall discusses the emergent tensions that divided Puritanism and its contending leaders as the nation matured around the turn of the century.

9. Ahlstrom, *Religious History of the American People*, 555.

10. Boardman quoted in Mark S. Massa, S.J., *Anti-Catholicism in America: The Last Acceptable Prejudice* (New York: Crossroad, 2003), iv.

11. Boardman quoted in Massa, *Anti-Catholicism in America*, 8.

12. R. Laurence Moore, *Religious Outsiders and the Making of Americans* (New York: Oxford University Press, 1986), 61.

13. Moore, *Religious Outsiders*, 58.

14. Ryan K. Smith, *Gothic Arches, Latin Crosses: Anti-Catholicism and American*

Church Designs and the Nineteenth Century (Chapel Hill: University of North Carolina Press, 2006), 5.

15. Smith, *Gothic Arches, Latin Crosses*, 5.

16. Quoted in Smith, *Gothic Arches, Latin Crosses*, 18.

17. Smith, *Gothic Arches, Latin Crosses*, 20.

18. Allen C. Guelzo, "Ritual, Romanism, and Rebellion: The Disappearance of the Evangelical Episcopalians, 1853–1873," *Anglican Episcopal History* 62, no. 4 (December 1993): 553–58.

19. Smith, *Gothic Arches, Latin Crosses*, 12.

20. See Schwartz, *Persistent Prejudice*, 23. See also Edward Vallance, "Loyal or Rebellious: Protestant Associations in England, 1584–1696," *Seventeenth Century* 17, no. 1 (2002): 17.

21. See, for example, Jon Gjerde, *Catholicism and the Shaping of Nineteenth-Century America*, ed. S. Deborah Kang (New York: Cambridge University Press, 2011), 19.

22. Schwartz, *Persistent Prejudice*, 19.

23. Considerable scholarship has engaged the question of how Protestantism framed itself as the natural conscience of America's democratic, rational ethos. Consider Charles Taylor, *A Secular Age* (Cambridge, MA: Harvard University Press, 2007), specifically his discussion of the "buffered self." Also consider Max Weber's "Reenchantment via Disenchantment" hypothesis, described in Sung Ho Kim, "Max Weber," in *The Stanford Encyclopedia of Philosophy* (Summer 2021 edition), ed. Edward N. Zalta, https://plato.stanford.edu/archives/sum2021/entries/weber/; Thomas Lessl, "The Innate Religiosity of Public Life: An A Fortiori Argument," *Journal of Communication and Religion* 32, no. 2 (2014): 319–46.

24. John H. Hopkins, *Anti-Catholicism in America, 1841–1851: Three Sermons* (New York: Arno, 1977), 4.

25. Hopkins, *Anti-Catholicism in America*, 5.

26. Throughout its materials, including its website, the present-day Washington National Cathedral highlights its role "at the intersection of civic and sacred life." In its strategic plan for 2019–23, it states, "In a country that has no national church, the cathedral's founders envisioned a church for national purposes." See "Strategic Plan, 2019–2023," Washington National Cathedral, November 2018, https://cathedral.org/wp-content/uploads/2019/03/strategic-made-book-smaller.pdf.

27. Brent, *Master Builder*, 94, 29.

28. Quoted in Brent, *Master Builder*, 59.

29. His Holiness Pope Leo XIII, "Apostolicae Curae: On the Nullity of Anglican Orders," New Advent, September 15, 1896, https://www.newadvent.org/library/docs_le13ac.htm.

30. In a private letter to another researcher, named John, Hewlett makes this point clear and identifies the pope's encyclical as a cause of the broken relationship. WNCA, 2-12-10.

31. George F. Edmunds to Henry Yates Satterlee, 25 January 1898, WNCA, 2-15-2.

32. "Find a Church," The Episcopal Church, accessed June 1, 2016, http://www.episcopalchurch.org/browse/cathedral/gmap.

33. Douglas to Paret, December 7, 1893; Paret to Douglas, December 28, 1893, both WNCA, 117-1-8.

34. S. M. Haskins to Bishop Satterlee, December 13, 1895, WNCA.

35. J. H. Gantt to Satterlee, December 11, 1895, WNCA.

36. *Cathedral Age* 2, no. 4 (1927): 37, WNCA.

37. Anson Phelps Stokes, D.D., LL. D, Canon of Washington Cathedral, "Why a Cathedral at the Nation's Capital?" marketing materials reprinted from *Cathedral Age* (1926), WNCA, 152-5-6.

38. Mark Chapman, *Anglicanism: A Very Short Introduction* (Oxford: Oxford University Press, 2006), 2.

39. Stokes, "Why a Cathedral?"

40. Henry Yates Satterlee, "Being a Portion of an Address Recently Delivered in New York by the Rt. Rev. Dr. Satterlee, Bishop of Washington," Hewlett Box, WNCA.

41. Satterlee, "Being a Portion of an Address."

42. Satterlee.

43. Henry Yates Satterlee, "Address to Annual Convention, St. Paul's Church, Washington, D.C.," *Journal of the Second Annual Convention of the Protestant Episcopal Church* (Washington, DC: Published by The Convention, 1897).

44. Satterlee, "Address to Annual Convention" (1897).

45. Satterlee, "Address to Annual Convention" (1897).

46. Summary of Correspondence re Satterlee's Consecration, 6, WNCA, 2-15-4.

47. Satterlee, *Building of a Cathedral*, 25.

48. Quoted in *New York Times*, January 29, 1900.

49. "Washington Letter," *Church Standard* 20, no. 1 (November 2, 1901): 67.

50. Richard Lewis Howell to Henry Y. Satterlee, undated (but a note by the cathedral historiographer indicates it was written in the fall of 1901), Satterlee Papers, Hewlett Box, WNCA.

51. Satterlee to Howell, November 15, 1901, Satterlee Papers, WNCA, 2-13-2.

52. Richard Hooker did not actually use the term *via media*, and the implications of his philosophy have been complicated by recent scholarship, but many still consider his articulation of Anglicanism's role and structure in *Law of Ecclesiastical Polity* to be a quintessential expression of the via media philosophy. See Lee W. Gibbs, "Richard Hooker's Via Media Doctrine of Scripture and Tradition," *Harvard Theological Review* 95, no. 2 (2002): 227–35, http://www.jstor.org/stable/4150721.

53. Richard Hewlett, "Henry Yates Satterlee and 'The House of Prayer for All People,' " November 7, 1990, Hewlett Box, WNCA, 2-9-9.

54. Around the turn of the century, there was much discussion between Episcopalians and other Protestant denominations regarding how to build Protestant unity and even, in some cases, whether actual mergers might be accomplished. See, for example, "Encyclical Letter from the Bishops with the Resolutions and Reports," Conference of Bishops of the Anglican Communion, Lambeth Palace, July 1897, WNCA 2-9-9; and Hewlett, "Henry Yates Satterlee and 'The House of Prayer for All People' ". Reed Huntington, whose ideas formed the basis for the Chicago Quadrilateral, played a key role in these discussions. See Stuart H. Hoke, "Broken Fragments: William Reed Huntington's Personal Quest for Unity," *Anglican and Episcopal History* 69, no. 2 (2000).

55. Personal correspondence between George W. King and Henry Yates Satterlee, WNCA, 2-12-10.

56. See Rev. R. Douglas, M.A., "A British-Ephraim Catechism: Biblical and Histori-cal," WNCA, 2-9-9.

57. Douglas, "British-Ephraim Catechism."

Chapter 4 • Francis B. Sayre the Prophet and
Mariann Edgar Budde the Pastor

1. Richard Hewlett, *Step by Step and Stone by Stone: The History of Washington National Cathedral—A Chronology* (Washington, DC: Communications Office of Washington National Cathedral), 15.

2. "History," Washington National Cathedral, https://cathedral.org/history/timeline/.

3. See Hewlett, *Step by Step*, 3–4.

4. "Washington Cathedral and the Cause of Religion," Report of the Cathedral Council as Approved and Adopted by the Bishop and Chapter, May 28, 1936, prefatory note, WNCA, 102-2-5.

5. "Washington Cathedral and the Cause of Religion," 11–12.

6. "Washington Cathedral and the Cause of Religion," 13–14.

7. "Washington Cathedral and the Cause of Religion," 18.

8. "Washington Cathedral and the Cause of Religion," 18.

9. "Architecture and History," Washington National Cathedral, accessed June 24, 2022, https://cathedral.org/architecture-history/.

10. "Washington Cathedral and the Cause of Religion," 26. Here the authors are quoting President Taft.

11. Dean Francis B. Sayre, interview by Robert Becker, November 10, 2000, 60, WNCA, 163-5-5.

12. Sayre interview, 19.

13. Sayre interview, 24.

14. Plenty of scholarship on these terms is available. For work on leaders who have embodied both personas, see Andrew S. Finstuen, *Original Sin and Everyday Protestants: The Theology of Reinhold Niebuhr, Billy Graham, and Paul Tillich in an Age of Anxiety* (Chapel Hill: University of North Carolina Press, 2009). See, in particular, the chapter "Reinhold Niebuhr, America's Prophet-Pastor," 93–122.

15. Sayre interview, 17–18.

16. Richard E. Mooney, "13 Protestant Leaders Rap Anti-Catholicism," *New York Times*, May 3, 1960.

17. See Hewlett, *Step by Step*, 21–27.

18. Dennis Hevesi, "Francis Sayre Jr., National Cathedral Dean, Dies at 93," *New York Times*, October 11, 2008, A33.

19. Sayre interview, 42–43.

20. Sayre interview, 44.

21. Sayre interview, 3.

22. Sayre interview, 3–4.

23. Quoted in Hevesi, "Francis Sayre Jr."

24. Francis B. Sayre Jr., "Statement on the Inauguration of the American President for Use in Australia," Francis B. Sayre Jr. Papers, WNCA (hereafter Sayre Papers).

25. Dorothy Parker, "In Recognition of the United Church," *Cathedral Age* (Spring 1958), WNCA.

26. Francis B. Sayre Jr., "Introduction," in *A Guide to Washington National Cathedral* (Washington DC: National Cathedral Association, 1953), 2.

27. Francis B. Sayre, Jr., "Marvel Not," June 6, 1971, sermon, Sayre Papers.

28. George Wharton Pepper, quoted on front cover, *Guide to Washington Cathedral*.

29. "Episcopalians Differ on Church's Activism and Mixing Faith and Politics," Episcopal News Service, March 9, 2017, https://www.episcopalnewsservice.org/2017/03/09/episcopalians-differ-on-churchs-activism-and-mixing-faith-and-politics/.

30. *Journal of the General Convention of the Protestant Episcopal Church in the United States of America*, item no. 33, report no. 13 (W. P. Conkey Co., 1958), 318.

31. David Hein and Gardiner H. Shattuck Jr., *The Episcopalians* (New York: Church Publishing, 2004), 135.

32. Hein and Shattuck, *Episcopalians*, 136.

33. "Ordination of Women," in *An Episcopal Dictionary of the Church*, ed. Don S. Armentrout and Robert Boak Slocum, Episcopal Church, accessed August 3, 2022, https://www.episcopalchurch.org/glossary/ordination-of-women/.

34. Since Satterlee's death, the cathedral has been the headquarters for both the bishop of Washington and the dean of the cathedral, two distinct positions. At times, the bishop has served *as* the cathedral dean, but usually each position is held by a distinct person. Depending on the personality and agenda of a given bishop or dean, the cathedral has assumed various levels of activism. For instance, the current dean as of this writing, Randolph Hollerith, has focused primarily on practical needs related to growth and fund-raising, while Bishop Budde ministers more publicly with respect to the social and theological needs of the diocese and nation. Hollerith's predecessor, Gary Hall, on the other hand, took high-profile stances on social justice issues to the neglect, his critics would claim, of the cathedral's finances. See Michelle Boorstein, "Exclusive: Gary Hall, Dean of Washington National Cathedral, to Step Down," *Washington Post*, August 18, 2015, https://www.washingtonpost.com/news/acts-of-faith/wp/2015/08/18/exclusive-gary-hall-dean-of-washington-national-cathedral-to-step-down/.

35. Preston Hannibal, priest and head of pastoral care, Washington National Cathedral, personal communication with author, May 13, 2016.

36. "Political Polarization in the American Public," Pew Research Center, June 12, 2014, https://www.pewresearch.org/politics/2014/06/12/political-polarization-in-the-american-public/.

37. For example, Chane's most strident remarks in favor of LGBTQ+ rights came after a fellow Anglican leader, a bishop in Nigeria, came out in support of an extremely antigay law in his home country. Chane joined other Episcopal leaders in condemning the law and the bishop's support of it. Chane also blessed same-sex unions once they were legalized.

38. Mariann Edgar Budde, "Autobiographical Statement," Episcopal Elections, accessed June 24, 2022, http://episcopalelections.com/elections/minnesota/nominees/BuddeBio.pdf.

39. David Paulsen, "Q&A: Washington Bishop Mariann Budde Says Church Should 'Lead with Jesus' in Its Nonpartisan Advocacy," Episcopal News Service, February 4, 2021, https://www.episcopalnewsservice.org/2021/02/04/qa-washington-bishop-mariann-budde-says-churchs-nonpartisan-advocacy-should-lead-with-jesus/.

40. Mariann Edgar Budde, *Gathering Up the Fragments: Preaching as Spiritual Practice* (Lima, OH: CSS, 2009), foreword.

41. Mariann Edgar Budde, *Receiving Jesus: The Way of Love* (New York: Church Publishing), 2019.

42. Mariann Edgar Budde, interview by Diane Rehm, *Diane Rehm*, National Public Radio, December 21, 2011, https://dianerehm.org/shows/2011-12-21/bishop-mariann-edgar-budde.

43. "Trump Migrant Separation Policy: Children 'in Cages' in Texas," BBC.com, June 18, 2018, https://www.bbc.com/news/world-us-canada-44518942.

44. Phil Davis, "'Come on, man. What's that about?' U.S. Rep. Cummings Blasts Acting DHS Chief over Child Detainment Conditions," *Baltimore Sun*, July 18, 2019, https://www.baltimoresun.com/politics/bs-md-pol-cummings-ice-dhs-child-detainment-20190719-w666k6du6zayzoufpxao53d75q-story.html.

45. Quoted in Davis, "'Come on, man. What's that about?'"

46. Quoted in William Cummings, "Trump Tells Congresswomen to 'Go Back' to the 'Crime Infested Places from Which They Came,'" *USA Today*, July 14, 2019, https://www.usatoday.com/story/news/politics/arizona/2019/07/14/president-donald-trump-tells-democratic-congresswomen-go-back/1728525001/.

47. "Have We No Decency? A Response to President Trump," Washington National Cathedral, July 30, 2019, https://cathedral.org/press-room/decency/.

48. Michelle Boorstein and Sarah Pulliam Bailey, "Episcopal Bishop on President Trump: 'Everything He Has Said and Done Is to Inflame Violence,'" *Washington Post*, June 1, 2020, https://www.washingtonpost.com/religion/bishop-budde-trump-church/2020/06/01/20ca70f8-a466-11ea-b619-3f9133bbb482_story.html.

49. "Faith Leaders on Efforts to Unite a Divided Country," *Diane Rehm Show*, December 20, 2016, National Public Radio.

50. Jeffrey Walton, "DC Riots and Bishop Mariann Budde's Selective Episcopal Outrage," *Juicy Ecumenism: The Institute on Democracy and Religion's Blog*, June 2, 2020, https://juicyecumenism.com/2020/06/02/bishop-mariann-budde/.

51. Draft: The Planning Context 1990, WNCA, 106-2-17.

52. Hannibal, personal communication May 13, 2016.

Chapter 5 • *Philip Hubert Frohman's Fourth Dimension*

1. Philip Hubert Frohman to Ogilby, June 26, 1933, WNCA.

2. Frohman to Ogilby, June 26, 1933.

3. Frohman, "The Fourth Dimension in Architecture" (manuscript for an unfinished and unpublished article, files of Cathedral Clerk of the Works, Canon Richard T. Feller, WNCA.

4. Frohman, "The Fourth Dimension in Architecture."

5. See Richard Benjamin Crosby, "Kairos as God's Time in Martin Luther King Jr.'s Last Sunday Sermon," *Rhetoric Society Quarterly* 39, no. 3 (2009): 260–80, DOI:10.1080/02773940902991411; "Cathedral of Kairos: Rhetoric and Revelation in the 'National House of Prayer,'" *Philosophy and Rhetoric* 46, no. 2 (2013): 132–55.

6. Victoria Dawson and Erik Vochinsky, eds., *Washington National Cathedral Guidebook* (Washington, DC: Washington National Cathedral, 2008), 25.

7. Quoted in Samuel T. Lloyd III, "A Cathedral for the 21st Century," in *Living Stones*, 3.

8. *Washington National Cathedral Strategic Plan, FY2015–2017* (Washington National Cathedral, 2014), 96; see also "Olmsted Woods and Amphitheater," All Hallows Guild, accessed June 26, 2022, https://allhallowsguild.org/the-grounds/olmsted-woods-amphitheater/.

9. Washington National Cathedral Strategic Planning Committee, *A New Century, a New Calling*, 5.

10. Mircea Eliade, *The Sacred and the Profane: The Nature of Religion*, trans. Willard Trask (New York: Houghton Mifflin Harcourt, 1968), 31.

11. Peter's biblical life is marked by spectacular fears. He sees Jesus fill his boat with fish to the point of sinking and begs for Jesus to depart, not because he fears drowning but because he fears his own sins in the face of death (Luke 5:8). Later, girding himself for a test of faith, he follows Jesus onto the water and manages to walk a few steps before fearing for his life and beginning to sink (Matthew 14). Finally, and perhaps most memorably, Peter is struck with great anxiety when he is challenged to disclaim Jesus; then he suffers bitter sadness at the realization that he has done so three consecutive times (Mark 14:66–72). The expression on the Peter statue's face, then, is not entirely surprising. The man himself was the tortured product of two always competing worlds, one of temporality and subsistence and one of eternity and faith. The statue shows Peter intolerably torn between these worlds, living in one while looking anxiously into the other. Peter's response to the fear entailed by the miracles he observed was ultimately to follow his God more devoutly, to enter the new space that the sacred presents.

12. Frederick Hart, Frederick Turner, and Michael Novak, *Frederick Hart: Changing Tides* (Manchester, VT: Hudson Hills Press, 2005), 24.

13. Dennis R. McNamara, *How to Read Churches: A Crash Course in Ecclesiastical Architecture* (New York: Rizzoli, 2011), 154.

14. Dawson and Vochinsky, *Washington National Cathedral Guidebook*, 57.

15. Satterlee to Bodley, January 11, 1907, Satterlee Correspondence Files, WNCA, 162-7-2.

16. Elody R. Crimi and Diane Ney, *Jewels of Light: The Stained Glass of Washington National Cathedral* (Washington, DC: Washington National Cathedral, 2004).

17. Typically, the multifoil of a stained-glass window is the image at the top, smaller than the others, framed by a multicurved edge. One might compare its outline to that of the face of a flower.

18. Crimi and Ney, *Jewels of Light*, 42.

19. Crimi and Ney, 43.

20. As a symbol, the Phoenix has its origins in Egyptian and Greek mythology; however, it was taken up in early Catholic Christianity as a symbol for Christ and the resurrection. Crimi and Ney, *Jewels of Light*, 61.

21. Crimi and Ney, 77.

22. Juliette MacDonald, "'Let Us Now Praise the Name of Famous Men': Myth and Meaning in the Stained Glass of the Scottish National War Memorial," *Journal of Design History* 14, no. 2 (2001): 117–28.

23. MacDonald, 121.

24. Known as "The Hand of God" speech, Wilson delivered these words to the Senate when he argued for the League of Nations and the Treaty of Versailles. *Address of the President of the United States to the Senate . . . July 10, 1919* (Washington, DC: Government Printing Office, 1919), reprinted as "An Address to the Senate (July 10, 1919)," in Arthur S. Link et al., eds., *The Papers of Woodrow Wilson*, Vol. 61: *June 19–July 25, 1919* (Princeton, NJ: Princeton University Press, 1989), 426–36.

25. Richard T. Feller and Marshall W. Fishwick, *For Thy Great Glory* (Ann Arbor: University of Michigan Press, 1965), 58.

26. Hewlett, *Step by Step*, 8.

27. Ney, "To Excel All Others," 37.

28. Lloyd, "A Cathedral for the 21st Century," 3.

29. Lloyd, 5.

30. Lloyd, 6.

31. Letter to a Mrs. Hallett, printed in unidentified, undated magazine article, Feller Files, WNCA.

32. Edwin Black, "Second Persona," *Quarterly Journal of Speech* 56, no. 2 (1970):109–19.

33. Hunt quoted in Christopher Dean Hamilton Rowe, "World Without End: Philip Hubert Frohman and the Washington National Cathedral" (PhD dissertation, Harvard University, 1999), 8, UMI Dissertation Services.

34. Rowe, 19.

35. Quoted in Rowe, 19.

36. Rowe, 20.

37. Washington National Cathedral Strategic Planning Committee, *A New Century, a New Calling*, 7.

38. "Proclaiming Peace," Washington National Cathedral, March 23, 2016, https://cathedral.org/cathedral-age/proclaiming-peace/.

39. In September 2021, the cathedral announced that the windows will be replaced with ones that will communicate the theme of racial justice. See Barbara Goldberg, "Washington Cathedral to Install Stained Glass with Racial Justice Theme," *Reuters*, September 23, 2021, https://www.reuters.com/world/us/washington-cathedral-install-stained-glass-with-racial-justice-theme-2021-09-23/.

Chapter 6 • *Martin Luther King Jr.'s Sacred Time*

1. Diane Ney, cathedral timeline on race, prepared for the author, May 12, 2013. The events cited here are taken from Ney's timeline.

2. Ney, cathedral timeline.

3. WNCA, 129-12-1.

4. Harbinson to Sayre, February 13, 1968, Washington National Cathedral, http://cathedral.org/wp-content/uploads/2018/01/1968-letter-protesting-King-invite.pdf.

5. Martin Luther King Jr., "Letter from Birmingham Jail," August 1963, International Education and Global Engagement, California State University, Chico, https://www.csuchico.edu/iege/_assets/documents/susi-letter-from-birmingham-jail.pdf. King makes a similar critique in this speech.

6. See Sayre's sermon delivered from the cathedral, "God and Race," October 25, 1953, Sayre Collection, WNCA.

7. Teresa Morales discusses the letters Sayre received in response to his views on race, including one rabidly racist one by a J. Dean, which Sayre appears to have singled out and saved. Morales, "The Last Stone Is Just the Beginning: A Rhetorical Biography of Washington National Cathedral" (PhD diss., Georgia State University, 2013), 175–76, Scholar Works, https://scholarworks.gsu.edu/communication_diss/42.

8. "Cathedral Jammed to Hear Dr. King," *Washington Post*, April 1, 1968, WNCA, 13-4-13.

9. A video recording of the sermon can be found on YouTube, "The Last Sunday Sermon of Rev. Dr. Martin Luther King Jr.," uploaded August 18, 2019, https://www.youtube.com/watch?v=uFmP3YA3i9g.

10. These parentheticals denote the page number and the paragraph number of the quotation as found on the archived copy of the address I cite (held in WNCA; quoted by permission of Joan Daves).

11. Rip Van Winkle is notorious because he "slept" through a revolution.

12. Michael Leff and Ebony A. Utley, "Instrumental and Constitutive Rhetoric in Martin Luther King Jr.'s 'Letter from Birmingham Jail,'" *Rhetoric and Public Affairs* 7, no.1 (2004): 43 (italics added).

13. Ephesians 1:22–23 (all biblical citations, KJV).

14. Ephesians 4:13; Colossians 1:19, 2:9.

15. Romans 15:29.

16. Emile Durkheim, *The Elementary Forms of Religious Life*, trans. Joseph Ward Swain (1915; reprinted, New York: New York Free Press, 1965), 24.

17. Richard McKeon, "Arts of Invention and Arts of Memory," *Critical Inquiry* 1, no. 4 (1975): 738.

Chapter 7 • *The Bush Presidents' Rock of Religious Faith*

1. George W. Bush, *Decision Points* (New York: Random House, 2010), 47–49.

2. "The Spirituality of George W. Bush," in "The Jesus Factor," *Frontline*, PBS.org, April 29, 2004, https://www.pbs.org/wgbh/pages/frontline/shows/jesus/president/spirituality.html. See also David Domke and Kevin Coe, *The God Strategy: How Religion Became a Political Weapon in America* (New York: Oxford University Press, 2010), 35–40.

3. George H. W. Bush, "Text of the Remarks by the President at the Final Stone Laying Ceremony at National Cathedral," Washington National Cathedral, September 29, 1990, WNCA, 106-4-11.

4. Matthew 16:18.

5. Chaim Perelman and Lucie Olbrechts-Tyteca, *The New Rhetoric: A Treatise on Argumentation*, trans. J. Wilkinson and P. Weaver (Notre Dame, IN: University of Notre Dame Press, 1969), 51.

6. George W. Bush, *A Charge to Keep* (New York: William and Morrow, 1999), 136.

7. Domke and Coe, *God Strategy*, 65–70.

8. Here Bush is quoting John Page's 1776 letter to Thomas Jefferson. See Joseph M. Valenzano III, "The Presidency That Almost Wasn't," In *The George W. Bush Presidency: A Rhetorical Perspective*, ed. Robert E. Denton Jr. (Lanham, MD: Lexington Books, 2012), 13.

9. George W. Bush, "Address to Joint Session of Congress," September 20, 2001, The White House: President George W. Bush, https://georgewbush-whitehouse.archives.gov/news/releases/2001/09/20010920-8.html.

10. Crosby, "Toward a Practical Civic Piety," 302. See also Campbell and Jamieson, *Presidents Creating the Presidency*, 12, 101.

11. George W. Bush, "President's Remarks at National Day of Prayer and Remembrance," Washington National Cathedral, September 14, 2001, White House: President George W. Bush, https://georgewbush-whitehouse.archives.gov/news/releases/2001/09/print/20010914-2.html.

12. Aristotle, *Physics*, trans. Robin Waterfield (New York: Oxford University Press, 1999), 105, IV.II, b27.

13. Lawrence Rosenfield, "The Practical Celebration of Epideictic," in *Rhetoric in Transition: Studies in the Nature and Uses of Rhetoric*, ed. E. E. White (University Park: Pennsylvania State University Press, 1980), 135; Sullivan, "Kairos and the Rhetoric of Belief."

14. Aristotle, *On Rhetoric: A Theory of Civic Discourse*, trans. George A. Kennedy (New York: Oxford University Press, 1991), 48.

15. Sullivan, "Kairos and the Rhetoric of Belief," 128.

16. Aristotle, *On Rhetoric*, 48; see also n79.

17. John Murphy, "Our Mission and Our Moment: George W. Bush and September 11," *Rhetoric and Public Affairs* 6, no. 4 (2003): 611.

18. Mark 14:1 (KJV). See also Matthew 26:4.

19. For example, Matthew 24:36; Revelation 3:3.

20. David Domke, *God Willing? Political Fundamentalism in the White House, the 'War on Terror,' and the Echoing Press* (London: Pluto Press, 2004).

21. John 16:33.

22. Quoted in Michael Hirsh, "Bush and the World," *Foreign Affairs* 81, no. 5 (September–October 2002): 19.

23. Domke, *God Willing?* 6.

24. Domke, 7.

25. Murphy, "Our Mission and Our Moment," 627.

26. "Bush: Join 'Coalition of the Willing,'" joint NATO news conference, CNN.com, November 20, 2002, http://edition.cnn.com/2002/WORLD/europe/11/20/prague.bush.nato/.

27. The United Kingdom, Australia, and Poland. Laura McClure, "Coalition of the Billing—Or Unwilling?" *Salon*, March 12, 2003, https://www.salon.com/2003/03/12/foreign_aid/.

28. "Presidential Approval Ratings—George W. Bush," *Gallup*, accessed July 2, 2022, https://news.gallup.com/poll/116500/presidential-approval-ratings-george-bush.aspx.

29. "U.S. Position in the World," *Gallup*, accessed July 2, 2022, https://news.gallup.com/poll/116350/position-world.aspx.

Chapter 8 • Civil Seership

1. "Transgender Priest Preaches at Washington National Cathedral," *New York Times*, June 23, 2014, video, https://www.nytimes.com/video/multimedia/100000002956629/transgender-priest-preaches-at-washingtons-national-cathedral.html; Jay Pulitano; "In Historic Moment, Transgender Priest Becomes First to Preach at National Cathedral," *GLAAD*, June 25, 2014, video, https://www.glaad.org/blog/video-historic-moment-transgender-priest-becomes-first-preach-national-cathedral; "Transgender

Priest Preaches at National Cathedral," *CBN News*, September 8, 2014, video, https://www1.cbn.com/cbnnews/us/2014/june/transgender-priest-preaches-at-national-cathedral.

2. Fred Barnes, "The Gay Bishop's Links," *Washington Examiner*, August 4, 2003, https://www.washingtonexaminer.com/weekly-standard/the-gay-bishops-links.

3. Peter J. Boyer, "A Church Asunder," *New Yorker*, April 9, 2006, https://www.newyorker.com/magazine/2006/04/17/a-church-asunder.

4. "Transgender Priest Preaches at Washington National Cathedral," *Reuters*, June 22, 2014, https://www.reuters.com/article/usa-washington-dc-cathedral/transgender-priest-preaches-at-washingtons-national-cathedral-idUSL2N0P307O20140622.

5. Jeffrey Walton, "National Cathedral 'Comes Out' with Transgender Preacher," *JuicyEcumenism: The Institute on Religion and Democracy's Blog*, June 25, 2014, https://juicyecumenism.com/2014/06/25/national-cathedral-comes-out-with-transgender-preacher.

6. "A Timeline of the Legalization of Same Sex Marriage in the United States," Georgetown Law Library, accessed September 13, 2019, https://guides.ll.georgetown.edu/c.php?g=592919&p=4182201.

7. The Acts of Convention, Archives of the Episcopal Church, accessed September 10, 2019, https://episcopalarchives.org/cgi-bin/acts/acts_resolution.pl?resolution=2012-A049.

8. Becky Garrison, "Crossing Boundaries: A Transgender Priest Becomes a University Chaplain," *Religion and Politics*, January 3, 2013, http://religionandpolitics.org/2013/01/03/crossing-boundaries-a-transgender-priest-becomes-a-university-chaplain.

9. "First Openly Transgender Priest to Preach at Washington National Cathedral," Washington National Cathedral, June 6, 2014, https://cathedral.org/press-room/first-openly-transgender-priest-preach-washington-national-cathedral/.

10. Justin Peligri, "A Milestone of Faith," *Washington Blade: America's LGBT News Source*, June 17, 2014, https://www.washingtonblade.com/2014/06/17/milestone-faith.

11. Yasmin Hafiz, "Reverend Cameron Partridge Will Be First Openly Transgender Priest to Preach at Washington National Cathedral," *Huffington Post*, June 23, 2014, https://www.huffpost.com/entry/transgender-priest-national-cathedral-pride_n_5459762.

12. Hafiz.

13. John Durham Peters, *Speaking into the Air: A History of the Idea of Communication* (Chicago: University of Chicago Press, 1999), 17.

14. Matthew 25:40.

15. Lauren Markoe, "Five Questions for Transgender Chaplain Cameron Partridge," *Washington Post*, July 19, 2013.

16. See, for instance, his comments in the interview with Rich Barlow of the Boston University newspaper *BU Today*. "New Episcopal Chaplain a Role Model," November 18, 2011, http://www.bu.edu/articles/2011/new-episcopal-chaplain-a-role-model/. See also his interview with *Religion and Politics*, Becky Garrison, "Crossing Boundaries: A Transgender Priest Becomes a University Chaplain," *Religion and Politics*, January 3, 2013, http://religionandpolitics.org/2013/01/03/crossing-boundaries-a-transgender-priest-becomes-a-university-chaplain/.

17. See Hafiz, "Reverend Cameron Partridge."

18. See Markoe, "Five Questions for Transgender Chaplain Cameron Partridge."

19. Cameron Partridge, guest sermon, LGBT Pride Month series, Washington National Cathedral, June 22, 2014.

20. Matthew 10:26–27 (KJV).

21. Exodus 19.

22. Luke 1:13.

23. Genesis 16:12.

24. Genesis 21: 14–19.

25. Genesis 16: 13–14; see footnote b.

26. Peters, *Speaking into the Air*, 270–71.

27. "Our Story," Mathew Shepard Foundation, accessed July 3, 2022, https://www.matthewshepard.org/about-us/our-story/.

28. Melanie Thernstrom, "The Crucifixion of Matthew Shepard," *Vanity Fair*, March 1999, https://www.vanityfair.com/news/1999/13/matthew-shepard-199903.

29. For image and commentary, see Katherine E. Standefer, "The Ascension of Matthew Shepard," *High Country News*, October 12, 2018, https://www.hcn.org/issues/50.18/art-the-ascension-of-matthew-shepard.

30. Thernstrom, "Crucifixion of Matthew Shepard."

31. Thernstrom, "Crucifixion of Matthew Shepard."

32. Jude Sheerin, "Matthew Shepard: The Murder That Changed America," BBC News, October 26, 2018, https://www.bbc.com/news/world-us-canada-45968606.

33. Stephen Jimenez, *The Book of Matt: Hidden Truths about the Murder of Matthew Shepard* (Hanover, NH: Steerforth Press, 2013).

34. See, for example, Alyssa Rosenberg, "The Book of Matt Doesn't Prove Anything, Other Than the Size of Stephen Jimemez's Ego," *Think Progress*, October 18, 2013, https://archive.thinkprogress.org/the-book-of-matt-doesn-t-prove-anything-other-than-the-size-of-stephen-jimenez-s-ego-c7ba5d0becee/.

35. JoAnn Wypijewski, "Laramie Revisited: The Myth of Matthew," *The Nation*, October 9, 2013, https://www.thenation.com/article/archive/laramie-revisited-myth-matthew/; Julie Bindel, "The Truth behind America's Most Famous Gay-Hate Murder," *The Guardian*, October 26, 2014, https://www.theguardian.com/world/2014/oct/26/the-truth-behind-americas-most-famous-gay-hate-murder-matthew-shepard.

36. Bindel.

37. Dennis Shepard's brief remarks begin at "Matthew Shepard Is Interred at Washington National Cathedral," *Washington Post*, YouTube, posted October 26, 2018, 31:00, https://www.youtube.com/watch?v=Sp8Ugqb4YuE.

38. Rowe, "World Without End."

39. Peters, *Speaking into the Air*, 270–71.

40. See Walton, "National Cathedral 'Comes Out.'"

Conclusion

1. Robert E. Lee to Mary Randolph Custis Lee, December 27, 1856, in *Encyclopedia Virginia*, https://encyclopediavirginia.org/entries/letter-from-robert-e-lee-to-mary-randolph-custis-lee-december-27-1856.

2. Quoted in Cary to Bashinsky, February 1948, in Diane Ney, "Chronology of the Lee-Jackson Bay and Windows," report prepared for James Shepherd, July 7, 2015, WNCA.

3. Report of the Robert E. Lee Memorial Committee, following the referendum to approve funding for the memorial by the UDC, undated (sometime after 1949), reprinted in Ney, "Chronology of the Lee-Jackson Bay and Windows."

4. Report of the Robert E. Lee Memorial Committee.

5. "Lee-Jackson Windows," Washington National Cathedral, accessed August 15, 2022, https://cathedral.org/lee-jackson-windows-task-force/.

6. Rev. Dr. Douglas's comments, in "March 29, 2017—Saints and Sinners: Robert E. Lee and Stonewall Jackson," in "Lee-Jackson Windows," Washington National Cathedral, https://cathedral.org/lee-jackson-windows-task-force/, beginning at 17:55.

7. "Uncivil Religion: January 6, 2021" (Columbian College of Arts & Sciences, George Washington University,), accessed August 14, 2022, https://uncivilreligion.org/home/index.

8. Shadi Hamid, "America without God," *The Atlantic* (April 2021), https://www.theatlantic.com/magazine/archive/2021/04/america-politics-religion/618072.

9. Oge Maduike, "America Needs a Third Founding Moment," *Georgetown Journal on Poverty Law and Policy*, February 25, 2021.

10. Hamid, "American without God."

11. Hatch, *Democratization of American Christianity*, 7–8.

12. Hatch, 16.

13. See, for example, Reinhard H. Luthin, "Some Demagogues in American History," *American Historical Review* 57, no. 1 (1951).

14. Beiner, *Civil Religion*, 62.

15. Moore, *Religious Outsiders*, viii.

16. Moore, viii.

17. Two edited volumes come to mind. Each examines the rhetorical and intellectual history of marginalized groups in nineteenth-century America. See Angela Ray and Paul Stob, eds., *Thinking Together: Lecturing, Learning, and Difference in the Long Nineteenth Century* (University Park: Pennsylvania State University Press, 2018); and Paul Stob, ed., *A Rhetorical History of the United States*, vol. 3 (Lansing: Michigan State University Press, forthcoming).

18. Walt Whitman, "Notes (Such as They Are) Founded on Elias Hicks," in *Prose Works* (Philadelphia: David McKay, 1892), 27.

19. Isaac Chotiner, "Learning from the Failure of Reconstruction," *New Yorker*, January 13, 2021, https://www.newyorker.com/news/q-and-a/learning-from-the-failure-of-reconstruction.

20. Savage, *Monument Wars*, 255.

21. Savage, 251.

22. Savage, 256.

23. The "clash" with Nazis during the March on Washington never materialized in the spectacular way George Lincoln Rockwell of the American Nazi Party had predicted, but the threat loomed over the plans for the march in the days leading up to it. Rockwell was arrested for making a speech without a permit during the event. See "Special

Collections: March on Washington," Open Vault (WGBH), accessed July 4, 2022, https://
openvault.wgbh.org/collections/march_on_washington/listening-guide.

24. Savage, *Monument Wars*, 261.

25. Preston Hannibal, Head of Pastoral Care, interview by the author, Washington
National Cathedral, May 13, 2016.

26. Hannibal, interview.

27. "Sermon: The Most Rev. Katharine Jefferts Schori, Washington National Cathedral April 29, 2012, https://cathedral.org/sermons/sermon-109.

28. Gardella, *American Civil Religion*, 6.

29. L'Enfant, "Library of Congress."

30. For commentary on Jung's theory of individuation, see Linda Forge Mellon, "An
Archetypal Analysis of Albert Camus's 'La Pierre qui pousse': The Quest as Process of
Individuation." *French Review* 64, no. 6 (May 1991): 941.

31. "The Resolution to Bury President George Washington at the U.S. Capitol, December 23, 1799," United States House of Representatives: History, Art, and Archives,
accessed April 4, 2019, https://history.house.gov/Historical-Highlights/1700s/The
-resolution-to-bury-President-George-Washington-at-the-U-S--Capitol/.

32. Bellah, *Broken Covenant*, 94–97.

33. Bellah, 94–97.

34. From publisher Rowman and Littlefield's promotional copy for Edwards and
Valenzano, *Rhetoric of American Civil Religion*,https://rowman.com/ISBN/9781498541480
/The-Rhetoric-of-American-Civil-Religion-Symbols-Sinners-and-Saints; see also
editors' introduction, xii.

35. Gorski, *American Covenant*, viii.

36. Jared Bowen, "Sonya Clark on the Confederate Truce Flag and the Collective
Work of Healing" (interview transcript), *PBS News Hour*, July 13, 2021, https://www
.pbs.org/newshour/show/sonya-clark-on-the-confederate-truce-flag-and-creating
-a-collective-work-of-healing. See also "Sonya Clark: Monumental Cloth, the Flag
We Should Know," Trustees, accessed July 4, 2022, https://thetrustees.org/exhibit
/monumental-cloth.

37. Oge Maduike, "America Needs a Third Founding Moment," *Georgetown Journal on Poverty Law and Policy*, February 25, 2021, https://www.law.georgetown.edu
/poverty-journal/blog/america-needs-a-third-founding-moment.

38. Wuthnow, "Divided We Fall," 395–96.

39. The quote comes from a famous 1710 Whig tract, probably written by Robert
Ferguson. See J. P. Kenyon, *Revolution Principles: Politics of Party, 1689–1720* (New
York: Cambridge University Press, 1990), 209.

40. Daniel K. Williams, *God's Own Party: The Making of the Christian Right* (New
York: Oxford University Press, 2010), 3.

41. Michael Novak, "The Faith of the Founding," *First Things* (April 2003), https://
www.firstthings.com/article/2003/04/the-faith-of-the-founding; Jacques Maritain,
Christianity and Democracy (San Francisco: Ignatius Press, 2011).

42. Macaes, *History Has Begun*, 16.

43. Macaes, 20.

* 9 7 8 1 4 2 1 4 4 6 4 2 4 *